Neoclassicism in Music
From the Genesis
of the Concept through the
Schoenberg/Stravinsky Polemic

Studies in Musicology, No. 101

George J. Buelow, Series Editor

Professor of Music
Indiana University

Other Titles in This Series

Neoclassicism in Music
From the Genesis
of the Concept through the
Schoenberg/Stravinsky Polemic

by
Scott Messing

UMI Research
Press

Ann Arbor / London

Permission to reprint excerpts from Debussy's *Pour le piano* has been granted by G. Schirmer.

Permission to reprint excerpts from the following works has been granted by G. Schirmer, sole U.S. representative for Editions Salabert: Satie, *Première sarabande* and *Trois valses distinguées du précieux dégoûté;* Chausson, *Concert en ré;* and Roussel, *Suite pour piano.*

Produced and distributed by
UMI Research Press
an imprint of
University Microfilms Inc.
Ann Arbor, Michigan 48106

Library of Congress Cataloging in Publication Data

Messing, Scott.
Neoclassicism in music.

(Studies in musicology ; no. 101)
Bibliography: p.
Includes index.
1. Neoclassicism (Music) I. Title. II. Series.
ML3877.M48 1988 780'.904 87-25534
ISBN 0-8357-1852-2 (alk paper)

British Library CIP data is available.

For my mother and father

Contents

Musical Examples

Preface

I arrived at the subject of this book from my interest as a graduate student in the music of the early 1900s. The specific topic I was studying at that time and which incited my attention was Ravel's changing use of sonata form before and after World War I. In consulting the body of research related to correlative issues which this subject suggested, I was struck by the invariable invocation of the term neoclassicism and the apparent absence of any historical account of the origins and development of the expression. In pursuing a usable definition of neoclassicism, I soon found two intriguing paradoxes: the presence of neoclassicism in studies of early twentieth-century music was so rife that almost every major figure composing during the first three decades of this century was tied, loosely or umbilically, to this term; yet a collation of usages produced such a variety of meaning that the expression seemed to possess no syntactical weight whatsoever. Too, for every cautionary statement warning against using the term because of its ambiguity, there were many times the appearance of the word without any context other than the apparent assumption that the reader would know the precise connotation the author intended for the term. The conflict between a frustrating lack of clarity in the meaning of neoclassicism and its general use in studies of twentieth-century music led me to the present topic of a historical survey of the origins and development of the term.

Why is it important that such an inquiry be undertaken at all? Any term, whether intended to signify specific compositional gestures in an artist's work or the general aesthetic tendencies of an era, is an approximate and unworked indication of the culture that produces it. An account of the nomenclature of an expression such as neoclassicism, though possessing semantic interest, cannot in itself serve to assess the evolution of an aesthetic or the musical style to which it applies. Yet such terms are continually invented by both the creators and observers of a given culture; their presence signifies a desire to give works of art a historical resonance by bestowing upon them signs which can stand for abstract concepts. I agree with René Wellek that terms such as "Renaissance, baroque, and realism crystallize ideas, formulate the problem of periodization and pervasive style, however uncertain and disputable may be the extension, valuation, and precise content of each term."[1] Musicologists have long recognized the value of such words. In addition to those borrowed from other disciplines, phrases specifically limited to music are often the first ways in which students are introduced to historical issues in the field; expressions such as *Ars nova*, *Ars antiqua*, *prima prattica*, and *seconda prattica*, as well as the documents which pertain to them, convey meanings that illuminate problems of period style.

The twentieth century is perhaps overstocked with such terms. This catalog of "isms" has become the foundation upon which musicologists balance otherwise disparate themes and images which collectively serve as a touchstone for judging the development of the idioms of contemporary music. In this context, the term neoclassicism appears to be unique. Other commonly employed "isms" enjoy both a narrowness and specificity of geographical and chronological focus and a pedigree drawn from literature and the visual arts.[2] By contrast neoclassicism has never found a home in literary criticism. In the fine arts, the late eighteenth century is the era dubbed neoclassic because its art objects often refer to an earlier age: the classicism of Greek and Roman antiquity. In music, the late eighteenth and early nineteenth centuries are commonly considered to be the period of classicism, and it acquired this authoritative seal through the agency of succeeding generations rather than during the late 1700s. Very little music from antiquity survived, however, and eighteenth-century music had almost nothing to do with the classicism discussed in the fine arts of that era.[3]

Current usage of the term neoclassicism in music has tended to two extremes. In surveys of music intended for the lay reader, including music appreciation texts, it invariably has one or both of two meanings. In a general cultural sense, neoclassicism is attended by a retinue of words such as clarity, simplicity, objectivity, purity, refinement, constructive logic, concision, sobriety, and so on. In a more specific stylistic sense, a work is said to be neoclassic if it employs musical means that borrow from, are modeled on, or allude to a work or composer from an earlier era, often from the eighteenth century, but equally from any composition regardless of period that has somehow entered into the canon of "great art." The combination of these two connotations obviously takes in a great deal of music, even when limited to the early twentieth century, and it is precisely this wholesale significance that has inspired several warnings against indiscriminate usage of the term neoclassicism.[4] This generalized meaning has surfaced in contrast to that in recent monographs of composers whose names elsewhere are often invoked in connection with the term, and whose authors show a wariness in employing it. When they articulate the concept of neoclassicism, these specialized and often highly technical studies invariably conclude that the term is woefully inappropriate or inadequate to their subject.[5]

Despite this circumspect attitude, the term neoclassicism has embedded itself securely in the parlance of studies of twentieth-century music and continues to incite ambivalence because of its ambiguous meaning. A historical survey and critical analysis of the origins and development of the term furnishes one means by which one can approach the problems of style and aesthetics which this term provokes. The absence of such a terminological scaffolding in any standard reference work obscures the fact that neoclassicism did not spring, Athena-like, from the mind of either critic or composer nor did it vault instantly into common parlance. Rather, the handful of initial appearances at the turn of the century remained at the time isolated, unrelated, and distinct from later, post-war usage, gaining currency only after a repertoire existed to which it could convincingly be grafted. Consideration of the nascent concept affords the criteria by which to evaluate the generally regarded view of neoclassicism as a post-war child of necessity. Such an explanation illuminates a stylistic change which proceeded more subtly than one based upon a conclusion suggested solely by external historical events.

The history of a term and the concepts that it is intended to convey at some point must address stylistic problems of specific composers and their works and at other times confront more general cultural issues. I have found one methodology to be inadequate to the task, and instead I have chosen to employ several approaches depending upon the nature of the material. In assessing the relationship between certain composers and their association with the term, I have selected an apparatus of music analysis, recognizing that such an approach might temporarily distract the general reader not acquainted with the terminology. Too, we shall discover that aesthetic issues underlay the dissemination of the term neoclassicism which carried beyond music. An investigation of this subject requires a comparative approach in which music is considered as one aspect of the culture in which it exists, and must be evaluated within a broader context than the score itself. Because we lack any individual document which first introduced the term and could thus isolate and embody the problem, we must patiently and thoroughly furnish the background from which the first appearances of the expression grew.

The term neoclassicism could not have appeared until there was a commonly understood meaning of classicism. As a concept that connotes works that are exemplary, authoritative, and paradigmatic, classicism is traceable at least to the second century. As a term that signifies these traits within specific styles or eras—the sense in which it is normally used in the arts—classicism appears to be an invention of the 1800s. Historians of the nineteenth century were preoccupied with defining a collective, public past of European high culture, and with characterizing for each country the art that should serve as models of perfection and greatness.[6] The notion that the work of Greek and Roman antiquity defined this classicism in the visual arts or lurked in the background as exemplars for literature of the seventeenth and eighteenth centuries was conceived as a cultural verity by nineteenth-century historicism. Music came late to a definition of classicism partly because barely any compositions from antiquity survived and because observers recognized that music was subject to whims of taste and fashion that did not affect literature and the fine arts.[7] Scarcely one hundred years ago, classicism in music, while signifying a body of work that was superior and excellent, referred to compositions as early as those of Palestrina and as late as those of Schubert, depending on which country's classicism was under discussion.[8] The current common usage of classicism in music as referring specifically to the works of Haydn, Mozart, and Beethoven was only secured early in this century.

The more objects of the past became authoritative icons during the nineteenth century, the more pressing seemed the responsibility for living artists to confront them. By the end of the century, the traits of classicism for each art form had become clearly established cultural norms, and its monuments cast long shadows over contemporary artists. At the same time that this historical past was codified, however, there developed an adversarial view of it as stultifying and inhibitive, encouraging artists to be self-consciously and deliberately unfettered to their heritage. It is precisely this tension between order and freedom, continuity and innovation, and tradition and novelty that existed around the turn of the century that incited the first appearances of the term neoclassicism.

My choice of beginning this study during the end of the nineteenth century is thus compelled by the necessity of providing a broad cultural environment for the origin of the term neoclassicism, and its explication occupies the first chapter. Once this background has been detailed, I proceed to outline the development of the term in Germany and France respectively during the decade that includes World War I. These first three chapters furnish the context for assessing the process by which neoclassicism came to be associated with Igor Stravinsky, the composer most frequently cited in connection with the term. The latter chapters analyze the circumstances which solidified this connection and produced the meaning of neoclassicism which matches its current usage, one whose evolution was complete by the end of the 1920s.

Acknowledgments

I wish to acknowledge the following individuals and organizations whose advice and aid were furnished during the research and preparation of this book. Initial thanks go to Glenn Watkins whose example as scholar and mentor furnished both the first and the continuing inspiration for the author. Professors David Crawford, Diane Kirkpatrick, and John Wiley provided expert counsel during the writing process. Marilyn Meeker graciously shared her collection of reviews of *Pulcinella*. Professor Richard Taruskin offered sound advice on Stravinsky. Mr. Paul Pisk kindly shared his recollections of Schoenberg with the author. Mr. Lawrence Schoenberg consented to the author's request to consult his father's correspondence housed in the Library of Congress. Mr. Wayne Shirley, head of the Music Division, made these and other materials easily accessible. Materials in the Arnold Schoenberg Institute were made available by its director, Leonard Stein, and its late archivist, Clara Steuermann. The staffs at the Music Library of The University of Michigan and at the Alma College Library expedited numerous requests for materials through their lending services. Finally, Mrs. Betty Ann Hall and Mrs. Pat McWilliams provided many hours of secretarial support.

1

Neoclassicism in France: 1870–1914

Fin-de-siècle Paris: Wagner and the French

Disorder, tumescence, and disintegration were signal features of a moribund, pre-war European culture that were often traded on during the 1920s by a generation seeking to sever its art from the corrupt, immediate past by utterly derogating it. Although propagandists may have considered themselves as fathers to the thought of a novel idiom, their characterization of it had appeared already, even as the trends which embodied the sense of decline took shape and expanded as the nineteenth century drew to a close. Recent cultural histories tend to qualify the decades which abut 1900 as a period of kinetic change rather than degenerate erosion. Barbara Tuchman has written thus: "Although *Fin-de-siècle* usually connotes decadence, in fact society at the turn of the century was not so much decaying as bursting with new tensions and accumulated energies."[1] In a more recent study on turn-of-the-century Viennese culture, Carl Schorske echoed this viewpoint: "In what seemed like ubiquitous fragmentation—Nietzsche and the Marxists agreed in calling it 'decadence'—European high culture entered a whirl of infinite innovation, with each field proclaiming independence of the whole, each part in turn falling into parts."[2] Too, the feeling of regression and excess was a phenomenon which tended to be limited to the milieu of authors and artists. Peter Gay has clarified this view by indicating that many in the nineteenth century reacted to the rapid changes around them with bewilderment, if not with actual despair: "In country after country, decade after decade, progressive and conservative voices alike lamented the unsettled, unsettling state of their age. They detected an alarming lack of anchorage, a universal anarchy of thought, an unhealthy speed of existence, a general uneasiness and vacillation in the very midst of irresistible scientific advance."[3]

During the *fin de siècle,* "decadence" became the archetypal exegesis of an era in which the exaggerated, overripe, and sometimes neurotic display of emotions appeared symptomatic precisely because such pessimism was rooted in artistic circles. Virtually any year during the two decades framed by the premieres of *Parsifal* in 1882 and *Pelléas et Mélisande* in 1902—perhaps the most crucial musical *loci* of the *fin de siècle*—could serve as the focal point to appraise the epoch. Authors of many recent studies in European literature and art have chosen a particular year during this period to introduce larger issues, believing that a cultural *Zeitgeist* can be graphically delineated by a precise historical moment. In a frequently cited book on the origins of the French avant-garde, Roger Shattuck isolated the death of Victor Hugo as a symbolic event:

> Artists sensed that their generation promised both an end and a beginning. No other equally brief period of history has seen the rise and fall of so many schools of cliques and isms. Amid this turmoil, the fashionable *salon* declined after a last abortive flourishing. The cafe came into its own, political unrest encouraged innovation in the arts, and society squandered its last vestiges of aristocracy. The twentieth century could not wait fifteen years for a round number; it was born, yelling, in 1885.[4]

Frederic Morton, in a study on the waning years of Imperial Vienna, used the period from July 1888 to April 1889 as his centerpiece: "Why just these ten months? Because they seemed representative of a watershed when the Western dream started to go wrong dramatically and the very failure was flooded with genius." In the standard work on post-impressionism, John Rewald chose 1886, because Seurat completed *La grande jatte* in that year, whereas Raymond Rudorff, in a study of Paris in the 1890s, picked 1889, the year of the completion of the Eiffel Tower.[5]

The year 1884 was particularly well-provisioned with works illustrating the themes of decadence. Verlaine's latest collection of verse, *Jadis et naguère*, included one poem, "Langueur," which began significantly: "Je suis l'empire à la fin de la décadence." In his *Essais de psychologie contemporaine*, which influenced Nietzsche and Spengler, Paul Bourget posed a rhetorical question (to which he would reply affirmatively): "If the advocates of decadence are inferior as purveyors of the grandeur of our country, are they not more superior as artists of the interior of their spirit?" Portions of Villiers de L'Isle-Adam's drama *Axël*, whose plot and imagery rely heavily upon *Tristan und Isolde* and the *Ring*, were first staged. Minor novels bore meaningful titles: *Le crépuscule des dieux* by Elémir Bourges, *Monsieur Vénus* by Marguerite Vallette (written under the pseudonym of Rachilde), and *Le vice suprême* of Joséphin Péladan, the first of a fifteen-volume cycle entitled *Etudes passionnelles de décadence*. Most important was the publication of Huysmans' *A rebours*, the Baedeker of the decadent movement. Huysmans' egregious hero, the Duc des Esseintes, defined the era by characterizing its leading lights: the artists Moreau and Redon and the poets Verlaine and Mallarmé. Of the latter he wrote:

In fact, the decadence of literature irreparably affected in its structure, weakened by the era of ideas, exhausted by the excess of syntax, sensitive only to the curiosities which inflame illness and also eager to express completely its decline, intent on restoring all the omissions of pleasure, devising the most subtle reminders of sadness on its bed of death; all this was incarnated in Mallarmé, in consummate and exquisite fashion.[6]

In painting, two important Salons inaugurated exhibitions. Redon helped to found the *Salon des indépendants* in Paris and, in Brussels, the "Group of Twenty" showed works by Ensor, Khnopff, Rops, and Whistler, and included a lecture on Wagner by Catulle Mendès.

With regard to music 1884 is also a trenchant year. On March 16, Charles Lamoureux conducted Act I of Wagner's *Tristan und Isolde* at a concert. The performance marked the first time that an entire act of a Wagner opera was heard publicly in Paris since the composer's youthful *Rienzi* on April 6, 1869, and before that, three disastrous performances of *Tannhäuser* in 1861. In the same year, the archconservative *Société des concerts* of the Paris Conservatoire, which even so orthodox a composer as Saint-Saëns had accused of being reactionary, and which had abruptly struck Wagner from its repertoire in 1870 after offering symphonic *morceaux* from *Tannhäuser* and *Lohengrin*, reinstated these pieces in January of 1884 as though receiving a cue.[7] In less than two decades from 1884, every major stage composition by Wagner received its Paris premiere or revival, with the exception of *Parsifal* because of a thirty-year limit restricting performance to Bayreuth.[8] Wagner's music had been virtually boycotted during the 1870s largely as a result of several literary squibs by him celebrating the German victory of 1871.[9] But the European-wide successes of the Bayreuth premieres of *Der Ring des Nibelungen* in 1876 and *Parsifal* in 1882, the death of the composer in 1883 (effectively eliminating the great obstacle of his fulsome person from French appreciation of his operas), and the appearance of a new generation of musicians (for whom the horror of the Paris commune was a childhood memory) triggered an idolatry of and prejudice for both his musical compositions and quasiphilosophical writings in France during the next quarter century. This fascination easily outdistances that for any other single figure and its rapacity is a clear indication of the overabundancy and self-indulgence which mark the era.

The near deification of Wagner during the *fin de siècle* and his identification with French avant-garde poetry and art was considerably aided by the advocacy of Baudelaire, *paterfamilias* of symbolism and the decadence. His reaction to *Tannhäuser* was verbalized in deliberately ambiguous synesthetic metaphors, providing a foundational influence for painters and poets alike.[10] Imagery from the *Ring* supplied inspiration for works by Redon, Doré, and Fantin-Latour. Wagner's music found less obvious admirers in Cézanne and Renoir.[11] The former belonged to a Wagner society in Marseilles with Emile Zola, and a painting of his from the 1860s is entitled *Overture to Tannhäuser*.

Renoir discussed impressionists in music with the composer himself in Naples in 1882 when Wagner gave him a sitting for his portrait. One year later, the symbolist poet and critic Jules Laforgue found an equivalency between Wagnerian orchestration and impressionist technique after he attended a Berlin art show in October: "In the little exhibition at the Gurlitt Gallery, the formula [of impressionism] is visible especially in the work of Monet and Pissarro . . . where everything is obtained by a thousand little dancing strokes in every direction like straws of color—all in vital competition for the whole impression. No longer an isolated melody, the whole thing is a symphony which is living and changing like the 'forest voices' of Wagner, all struggling to become the great voice of the forest."[12] A similar comparison was made by Van Gogh at about the same time. Writing to his sister circa 1888, he stated: "At present the palette is distinctly colorful, sky blue, orange, pink, vermillion, bright yellow, bright green, bright wine-red, violet. But by intensifying *all* the colors one arrives once again at quietude and harmony. There occurs in nature something similar to what happens in Wagner's music, which, though played by a big orchestra, is nevertheless intimate."[13] When Mallarmé declared of his verse, "We now *hear* undeniable rays of light, like arrows gliding and piercing the meanderings of song," he was, consciously or not, giving answer to the dying cry of the hallucinating Tristan: "Wie, hör' ich das Licht?"[14]

We may judge from this testimony that, for many of Europe's most avant-garde painters and writers of the 1880s, Wagner's music possessed a vividness and intensity which mirrored their own artistic aspirations and achievements. The composer's art had been discovered at a convenient time for French literary trends. *Gesamtkunstwerk* appealed somewhat vaguely to the sensibilities of a new generation of poets who sought to create a mystical union of words and musical effect, and leitmotifs seemed to have some connection with the plastic literary symbols being explored in the new French verse. The synesthetic interrelationship between tone and text is especially apparent when Mallarmé used musical terms to voice his poetic ideal, at times almost parroting the prose of Baudelaire.[15]

During the two decades between 1882 and 1902, one can find in excess of thirty titles whose contents deal exclusively with some aspect of Wagner's life and work.[16] The most ambitious literary effort was undoubtedly the *Revue wagnérienne*, planned during the summer of 1884 at a performance of the *Ring* in Munich and founded in February 1885, by Edouard Dujardin, a critic and novelist who had given up an early career in composition upon first hearing Wagner's music and who possessed a remarkably sensitive hand upon the pulse of artistic novelty.[17] Dujardin claimed pretentiously that the journal's contents were not designed to laud Wagnerian music, but to reveal the secrets of Wagnerian theory.[18] No clear picture of aesthetics emerged from this review however, for the contributors—including Mallarmé, Verlaine, Huysmans, Villiers,

Swinburne, Redon, and Fantin-Latour—were not prepared to admit that their interpretation of the composer's theory did not match his music and that, as amateurs, their knowledge of symphonic *morceaux* was not sufficient basis for the lucid explanation of dramatic form. Contributors not only found themselves forced to adumbrate Wagnerian theory, but actually to invent it.

The reaction of French composers to Wagnerian music dramas was as profound and immediate as that of their literary counterparts, differing in kind rather than intensity. Their enthusiasm and interest were primarily for the music, not for the perception of theoretical aesthetics. This attitude aroused considerable distaste at the *Revue wagnérienne*, and accusations of imperfect understanding were hurled at Chabrier and Massenet by Dujardin, at Debussy by Catulle Mendès, and at Saint-Saëns by Téodore de Wyzewa.[19] But it was precisely the composers who made the earliest pilgrimages to Bayreuth, and it was they who exhibited a rapture which is as impressive for its implausibility as for its hysteria. Paul Landormy reported in *La victoire* that the Belgian composer Guillaume Lekeu fainted at the end of the Prelude to *Tristan und Isolde*. In a speech to the *Concerts historiques Pasdeloup* on April 18, 1920, Vincent d'Indy stated that, before a performance of *Tristan und Isolde* at Munich, Chabrier burst into sobs of despair, asserting that he had been waiting fifteen years to hear the Prelude's opening A on the cello.[20]

The narrative debt owed to *Parsifal* and *Tristan und Isolde* by many French operas is obvious. Reyer's *Sigurd* (1883), Chabrier's *Gwendoline* (1886), d'Indy's *Fervaal* (1897), Debussy's *Pelléas et Mélisande* (1902), and Chausson's *Roi Arthus* (1903) are among the more celebrated French operas whose libretti are submerged in Wagnerian imagery. However, the influence on musical language was keener and more far-reaching than the mania that was publicly promoted among literary circles. Some composers permitted themselves a luxury when they ridiculed contemporary taste by quoting leitmotifs in ludicrous situations as when Debussy quoted the opening of *Tristan und Isolde* in "Golliwogg's Cakewalk" from *Children's Corner* (1908) or when Chabrier used themes from the same opera for his quadrille, *Souvenirs de Munich* for piano four hands (1885–86). Their private responses, however, were genuine and serious. Debussy's letter of October 2, 1893, to Chausson is undoubtedly the most quoted testimony of the influence of Wagner, "the ghost of old Klingsor," whose presence during the writing of *Pelléas et Mélisande* forced the composer, after a sleepless night, to destroy part of the score.[21] Chabrier's letter to his wife after a Bayreuth performance of *Parsifal* is an even more spectacular confession: "Here on Sunday, July 21, 1889, I heard *Parsifal* for the first time; I have never in my life experienced a similar artistic emotion; it is *astonishing*; one (at least me) emerges after each act absolutely bewildered with admiration, amazed, distraught, streaming with tears. It is worse than *Tristan* in 1880. In short, what would you have me say? I have heard nothing to equal it. It is sublime from start to finish."[22] The chromatic harmony of Wagner's music was both new and fascinating to Parisian composers and an example not easily outdistanced. The recurrence of even so obvious a case as the opening motive from *Tristan und Isolde,* invariably labeled *Sehnsucht* or *Désir* during the late nineteenth century, is striking for the subtle variety of its appearance in otherwise very different French compositions (see ex. 1.1).

We may conclude from this evidence that Wagner's sway was clearly considerable, even fundamental, for many avant-garde tendencies in *fin-de-siècle* Paris. His prose served partially as a theoretical underpinning for literary symbolism, his imagery echoed in poetry and painting, and his musical language provided a precedent so vibrant that even Debussy felt it a threat to his independent creativity. Despite what nearly amounted to a wholesale and eventually chic fetish during the 1880s and 1890s, the admiration for Wagner was short-lived. Even as the infatuation reached its zenith, a reaction was swiftly finding its expression in a growing belief that the artistic products of the nineteenth century were bloated and redundant and, at least among Parisian thinkers, that this excess was the responsibility of the northern, Teutonic mentality. Such exclusive myopia was consistent with gradual political tensions between France and Germany.[23] Yet a burgeoning Gallic nationalism was congruent with the emerging dissatisfaction with *fin-de-siècle* pessimism and decadence. These stimuli nourished and at times provided a rationale for each other. The extent to which one might have felt that the nineteenth century was a corrupt artistic era was not infrequently measured by the degree to which the northern spirit had had a mortifying effect upon it.

Wagner was frequently singled out as the initial and principal target of the response because his influence appeared so endemic to French intellectual circles that Wagnerism was considered the sympathetic, if not chronologically exact, musical equivalent to impressionism in art and symbolism in literature.[23] But the reaction is especially crucial in the consideration of music because, of all artists, French composers at the turn of the century were acutely aware that the nineteenth century appeared to be a vast lacuna in their musical tradition and that the era more aptly characterized its most cherished icons in Germanic terms. Even as the popularity of performances of orchestral and chamber compositions in Paris during the nineteenth century grew before the Franco-Prussian War, German works clearly dominated; Beethoven, Mozart, Mendelssohn, Haydn, and Weber accounted for half of all the pieces heard.[25] The connection between the conservative agenda in much of French public life and the rise of cultural nationalism is a crucial one to establish, because the anti-German slant of French musical politics is fundamental if we are to understand the emergence of the first meaning of the term neoclassicism. In France, more so than in other European countries, an expanding nationalism helped to foster inspiration from native, pre-romantic antecedents, and incipient neoclassicism was born from a disbelief among artists in different genres that the progeny of decadence and symbolism could any longer supply useful models for creative expression.

French Reaction to Wagner: The Return to Tradition

For the *fin de siècle,* symbolism represented an aesthetic parallel to Wagnerism in music. The term symbolism had received a widely publicized birth in a manifesto by the poet Jean Moréas in *Le Figaro* on September 18, 1886. For the rest of the decade, Moréas was considered one of the most prominent advocates of the symbolist movement and his verse rivaled that of Verlaine in popularity.[26] Thus, a second manifesto issued by him in 1891 came as a complete surprise because its author suddenly professed opposition to the ideas which he had so recently championed. Moréas defined a new group of poets, the *Ecole romane,* whose verse was deliberately patterned after earlier, specifically French models.

> The French *Ecole romane* reclaims the fundamentally Greco-Latin principle in literature, which flourished during the eleventh, twelfth, and thirteenth centuries with our *trouvères,* in the sixteenth century with Ronsard and his school, in the seventeenth century with Racine and La Fontaine. . . . It was romanticism which perverted the principle in conception as well as in style, thus frustrating the French Muses of their legitimate heritage. . . . The *Ecole romane* renews the Gallic bond, broken by romanticism and its parnassian, naturalistic, and symbolist descendants. . . . Symbolism, which only has an interest as a transitory phenomenon, is dead.[27]

Moréas himself provided the embodiment of this new poetic ideal in his next collection of verse, *Eriphyle,* and he found it necessary to place himself at a distance from his earlier work when it was reprinted, calling the preface to *Pèlerin passionné* (published in 1890 and reissued in 1893) useless and stating in the second edition of *Les syrtes* (first published in 1884 and reissued in 1892):

> My instinct was not slow to warn me that it was necessary to restore a true classicism and a true antiquity and, at the same time, a most austere traditional versification. And in full symbolist triumph, I separated myself from my friends, who bore me malice for a while. Today, I take pleasure in stating that the whole world turns to classicism and antiquity.[28]

By 1894, a variety of works by members of the *Ecole romane* had appeared: *Le chemin de paradis* of Charles Maurras, *La métamorphose des fontaines* of Raymond de la Tailhede, Ernest Raynaud's *Le bocage,* and *Etudes lyriques* of Maurice de Plessys. Like Moréas, these poets emphasized repeatedly that their emulation of prototypes in early French verse was a self-conscious response against the sterility and pessimism of symbolist literature and a renewal of a "classic" order, clarity, and simplicity, terms which, although perhaps vague descriptions, were seriously put forward as legitimate characteristics of the French race.[29] Indeed, as Europe hurtled towards war, "classicism" in

Example 1.1. The *Sehnsucht* Motive in *fin-de-siècle* French Music

a. Richard Wagner, *Tristan und Isolde*, Prelude

b. César Franck, Sonata for Violin and Piano, First Movement

c. Claude Debussy, *Cinq poèmes de Baudelaire*, "La mort des amants"

contemporary literature and nationalism in public life were sometimes treated as equivalent phenomena. In 1913, Henri Clouard asserted that the "classical Renaissance" in French letters was commensurate with conservative political action. Clouard considered *vers libre* in *fin-de-siècle* poetry to be comparable to liberalism in the social order, and he praised Moréas for rejecting the "hypocrisy, sumptuousness, and sensationalism" of symbolist verse.[30]

d.   Emmanuel Chabrier, *Le roi malgré lui*, Act III "Entr'acte"

e.   Vincent d'Indy, *Fervaal*, Act III, Scene 2

While no group of painters coalesced in the deliberate and official manner of the *Ecole romane*, one can find several otherwise very different artists who were dissatisfied with the impotency of general trends and who took refuge, in part, in the examples of a pre-nineteenth-century French tradition. Renoir had declared that, by 1883, impressionism had become too complicated an affair and that working directly from nature ultimately produced monotonous results. His exploitation of museum pieces in paintings of the late 1880s was his attempt to effect a dry and precise style. As a young man, Renoir had been "carried away by the kind of passionate fluidity" of Wagnerian music. However, he grew to detest his experience at Bayreuth, and came to prefer the music of Couperin and Grétry which he likened to fine "drawing."[31] When one critic who viewed his *Grandes baigneuses* in 1887 declared it to be "a more solid, classical art," the painter approved.[32] If observers guessed at an older source of inspiration in such a work by labeling its author "classical," subsequent scholarship has shown that, in this case, Renoir had based his painting on works by Girardon and Boucher.[33]

In like manner, the work of Cézanne from the 1890s which utilized the same subject of bathers was, on occasion, considered classical in composition by his younger advocates such as Maurice Denis, whereas modern analysis has demonstrated that the figures were sometimes modeled after examples to be found in the work of Poussin.[34] Denis himself had been a champion of symbolism in 1890, but in the new century, when a critic accused him of structuring his work after Ingres, Denis did not deny the allegation. Rather, he insisted that his response to the negative effects of symbolism was a natural and inevitable reaction to a trend which had degenerated into facile and amorphous products. He emphasized further that the revival of an older French method and spirit did not exclude the ability to create art that was modern, progressive, and new.[35]

We may conclude from these examples that the term classicism tended to act as the embodiment of a number of aesthetic attributes which, even taken together, do not necessarily constitute for us an accurate basis for defining artistic style: clarity, simplicity, austerity, sobriety, pure construction, precision, discreet harmony, and formal perfection.[36] Such words have validity to the extent that artists themselves found them to be comprehensible and useful descriptions. The crucial point is that these terms could be represented as fundamentally nationalist traits, that is Gallic, Hellenic, Latin, and southern—a claim which took in a rather large and diffuse geographical and cultural area. Equally suspect is the rationale which could determine that the avatars of decadence were essentially German, Teutonic, and northern. Yet the fact that French artists derived fresh inspiration and insight from older, native sources by taking a quantum leap over the preceding century confirmed for them that the evolution of art was cyclic in matters of style and chauvinist in matters of aesthetics. The optimistic view that a wholesale reaction against German music in general, and Wagner in particular, would bring about a renascence of French music which would mirror the glory of earlier centuries had a large circulation in contemporary French histories of music as well. Charles Lalo was a typical voice in stating: "Now the Wagnerian age seems to us to have fulfilled all the characteristics of romanticism; and after romanticism, there can follow, according to all the analogies which have been offered from the twenty-five centuries of history, only decadence—or a renewal."[37]

Such a response among musicians became general only after century's end, because Wagnerian models had exerted a more spectacular and lingering effect upon them. Two articles, both in the form of *enquêtes*, appeared during 1903 and 1904, and the virtual unanimity of opinion among the respondents confirms the thesis that pre-nineteenth-century French sources had emerged as viable expressive alternatives to *fin-de-siècle* Wagnerian themes. An article in *Mercure de France* was the sixth installment in a wide-ranging inquiry into the German influence on a variety of aspects of French public life.[38] A later article in *La revue bleue* was exclusively musical in subject, and the questions posed were more specific:

> What does being French consist of in music? Does a musical tradition exist which can be called French? Where does this tradition begin? Is it interrupted with Berlioz? If lost, is it rediscovered after him? and finally, where are we at present?[39]

Both articles share the distinction of presenting the opinions of the two most influential French composers at the turn of the century: Claude Debussy and

Vincent d'Indy. They agreed that, whereas the influence of Wagner was manifest, the reaction to him was as inevitable as it was necessary.

[Debussy] Is Wagner perhaps an example of domestication? Still, musicians will be able to belong to him, recognizing his having left an admirable document on the uselessness of formulas, Parsifal. . . . Wagner, if one can express oneself with a little of the grandiloquence which suits him, was a beautiful sunset mistaken for a dawn. There will always be periods of imitation or influence whose duration and nationality one cannot foretell—a simple truth and a law of evolution. These periods are necessary to those who love well-traveled and tranquil paths. They permit others to go much further.

[d'Indy] Indeed I believe that the actual tentative moves to emancipation would not have been able to occur unless they who call themselves promoters had not, as a start, studied assiduously the art of the author of *Parsifal*. It can therefore be concluded that everywhere and always the foreign influence has been beneficial, since it has, by a kind of necessary reactive filiation, almost always given birth to a new manner of national art.[40]

The similarity of their answers belies their contrasting backgrounds and musical languages and mirrors the power exercised upon otherwise disparate sensibilities by the nostalgia for the classical past of the French musical tradition.

[Debussy] French music is clarity, elegance, and declamation both simple and natural. Couperin and Rameau are those who are truly French! . . . It is necessary to rid music of all scientific apparel.

[d'Indy] The [French] tradition can be represented by the great names of Charpentier, Couperin, and Rameau, Grétry, and so on. . . . We desire completely, more or less consciously, to rest from too complex music, to return to simplicity, but not to poverty.[41]

The remainder of the composers, historians, and critics who provided their opinions is also impressive by their agreement. The hegemony of German music had passed, and the revival of the French tradition, interrupted during much of the nineteenth century, was providing a much-needed antidote to the excesses embodied in Wagnerian operas. Responses by Lionel de La Laurencie, Jean Marnold, and Alfred Bruneau, respectively reinforce this point.

[La Laurencie] The Germans complicate by enlarging; we [French] simplify by condensing and M. Mithouard [see note 36] has strongly and justly signaled the tendency of our art to become classic, in the large sense of the word, that is to say to curtail every useless element to its goal, to crystallize in its defined forms issued by the law of least effort.

[Marnold] Today, German music exists in a lamentable agony. It rattles sweetly along in Mendelssohn-Brahms neoclassic chloroform or is stupified by romantico-Wagnerian morphine.

[Bruneau] The young French school, fortified, regenerated, more and more the vigilant keeper of the highest and most beautiful qualities of our race, will be shortly, if they aren't already, the first of those who contribute to the glory of the new century.[42]

Even a Frenchman like Dujardin, who had displayed an innate sympathy with German music, found himself forced to recognize Wagner's decadence.

> Wagner is still the great love of my life, but perhaps in the pejorative sense which takes the word love when one speaks of a delicious and fatal vice which possesses the heart. This is how, if Wagner seems to represent excellently the German spirit, one is constrained to avow that the German spirit represents all the destructive things which the French spirit truly must purge from the air as its mission.[43]

Such statements were echoed several years later when *La grande revue* conducted a similar *enquête* among a group of younger musicians, for example, Albert Roussel and Louis Laloy.

> [Roussel] I add, in conclusion, that, concerning this question of influences, it is difficult to place aside the question of race, and it will be very fortunate that French music tries to personify in a manner more and more affirmatively and vigorously, the genius of our race, the qualities of clarity, sensibility, luminescence and pure joy, which form our artistic heritage.

> [Laloy] Romanticism is German, that is, complicated and metaphysical. Without doubt, there is indeed a new classical age which announces itself, more well-informed than any other besides, and voluntarily more refined. The passions of romanticism will be retained, but reduced in their compass, adapted to their object, reconciled with their nature; the subtle exactitude of impressionist notations will be applied to solid constructions and, in their way, made regular, exact, classical.[44]

The use of "classic" by La Laurencie and Laloy obviously benefited from Mithouard's articles mentioned earlier. Indeed, we may gather from all the previously cited appearances of the term classicism that it signified an object which displayed artistic beauty by its fealty to principles of formal perfection embodied in a national tradition. But Marnold's barbed squib, alluding to German music other than Wagner's as "neoclassic chloroform," indicates that the term neoclassicism implied an altogether dissimilar and derogatory connotation, supplying both the reminder that Wagner was not the only German composer needing to be flushed from the French spirit, and the suggestion that that which was "neo" was not necessarily new or natural. Our previous discussion has revealed that the French held a somewhat schizophrenic view of Wagner which alternated passion with brutality. For those in the latter camp, the terminology of a "new classicism" accounted for a consummate and authoritative quality of art embedded in a national tradition. We shall see that as the term neoclassicism was adapted, it conveyed a pointedly different meaning.

Néoclassicisme and *Nouveau Classicisme*

The period in the fine arts now called neoclassic was not so named at the time. The term rather originated at the turn of the nineteenth century when the style dubbed neoclassicism, especially that represented by the art of late eighteenth-century France, was distinctly out of favor. As such, the term neoclassicism had a generally pejorative undertone arising from the disdain for what some late nineteenth-century writers considered a colorless imitation of Greek and Roman art and a servile captivation with academic niceties. Its use at this time, however, was anything but common. In the fine arts, several authors have concluded that the term may have been introduced during the 1880s, but I have been unable to locate an appearance of it in a French text before 1912. In books about French art of the eighteenth century which were published around 1900, one is far more likely to find the expressions *l'art antiquisante* or *la retour à l'antiquité* rather than neoclassicism.[45]

In his introduction to *La fin du classicisme et le retour à l'antiquité*, written on August 13, 1896, Louis Bertrand came as close to a late nineteenth-century definition of neoclassicism as any writer, but without having recourse to use the term itself.

It is proposed to study here this movement of the return to antiquity which, arising from the second half of the eighteenth century, was propagated in literature and art up to the beginning of romanticism, rather than being limited to a few small, isolated groups and some particular works. This movement conforms to the essence of classicism itself, whose fundamental principle is imitation. This was favored due to various historical circumstances which will be examined, but it is above all in the growing paganism of morality and in the disappearance or weakening of the religious idea that one must seek the principle. It miscarried for various reasons, but particularly because the French of that time did not know or did not want to disengage themselves from the classical discipline which was established in the eighteenth century. They became too *personal*, too exclusively *French*; they did not succeed in escaping from it in order to recover and recreate in themselves the spirit of ancient civilizations; and moreover, they continued to see in completely exterior imitation the supreme law of art; they even exaggerated such as none of the true classics had ever done. Under these circumstances, a return to antiquity was a return backward; it laid claim to the complete recommencement of historical evolution. But as all retrograde movements, this one was not bound to lead anywhere. It revealed only impotency and sterility; and thus this return to antiquity, by its own defeat, only brought about the ruin of classicism.[46]

In 1903, Bertrand employed the term *néoclassique* to criticize contemporary writers who indulged in a sterile, exterior imitation of antiquity after the fashion of the eighteenth century: "It is ridiculous to believe that that which has been will ever be able to be reborn, and it is vanity to pretend to resuscitate a lost and dead form."[47] Bertrand rejected romanticism as "exotic, bizarre, and extravagant" and German culture as "indiscrete and chaotic." He condemned equally the slavish reproduction of subjects from antiquity. But he lauded writers who perpetuated "respect for the national tradition" and the "French classical spirit" which he described in jargon that is typical for the period: "intellectual discipline," "probity of being," and "harmony, composition, and order."[48]

The term neoclassicism with regard to music occurs with increasing frequency only after 1900. These references suffice to give neoclassicism a specific definition during the first decade of the twentieth century: an expression pertaining to nineteenth-century composers who perpetuated the forms of instrumental music made popular during the eighteenth century, but who sacrificed originality and depth of musical substance for the abject imitation of structure. Thus the term, when applied to music, had a derogatory meaning akin to its use in literature. Unlike the latter reference however, its sense in relation to music was aggravated by nationalist feelings, since neoclassicism was invariably used, as in the case of Marnold, by French writers to describe German musicians.

As the most celebrated German instrumental composer contemporary to Wagner, Brahms was the most obvious individual to be contrasted unfavorably with French composers of orchestral and chamber music. Brahms's music was performed rarely in Paris before 1900, and he became a target for French writers only several years after his death. Before the turn of the century, Brahms was first subjected to ridicule in comparison to French music by Hugo Wolf after hearing Saint-Saëns' Septet for trumpet, string quartet, and piano in 1886. Although Wolf did not use the term neoclassicism, his treatment of Brahms had an unmistakable pejorative shading in relation to his appraisal of Saint-Saëns.

> This shrewd moderation and pithiness is admirable, and absolutely not to be underestimated. How many a German composer might envy Saint-Saëns this virtue! It is common to all French composers, and to none more becoming, perhaps, than to Saint-Saëns, and who, well aware that brevity is the soul of wit, carefully avoids all sentimental chatter, and only once or twice touches a sensitive nerve. Even then, he is quick to return to his curiously iridescent manner of speech, a superficial mode of address, but not without spirit.
>
> Saint-Saëns is reckoned by the French, oddly enough, a classicist, as hard to digest, as a learned composer, and heaven knows what else. Saint-Saëns' classicism is rather like Brahms's, with the distinction that with Saint-Saëns it is a natural outgrowth of his musical development (he was for some time an organist) while with Brahms it serves simply to disguise his creative impotence.[49]

Paris only occasionally heard Brahms's music during his lifetime, but the end of 1902 brought concerts of all of his major orchestral works and reaction ranged from tepid to openly hostile.[50] After a performance of the Third Symphony at the *Concerts Colonne* on November 9, Romain Rolland wrote:

> This is an excellent neoclassical work (if it is ever possible to be neo-anything and excellent as well). As is the case with Brahms, the passages of grace are infinitely preferable to those of force, and style is superior to feeling.[51]

By 1908, Rolland's opinion had deteriorated considerably, asserting that Brahms's neoclassicism was ravaged by a pedantry which had become the plague of German art.[52] Paul Dukas obviously had Brahms in mind when comparing anonymous neoclassicists to César Franck:

Franck's classicism is not purely that of form; it is not a mere filling in, more or less sterile, of scholastic outlines, such as resulted by the hundreds from the imitation of Beethoven, and later of Mendelssohn, and continue to grow every year out of respect for useless traditions. [Franck's compositions], like bodies in which the function creates the organ, are as widely different from the schematicism of most of the neoclassicists as a living organism from an anatomical model.[53]

That Dukas considered Brahms to be a neoclassicist can be gleaned from tracing his declining opinion of the latter in his critical writings. He expressed qualified admiration for the Second Symphony in 1892 and for the Third Symphony in 1893. By 1903, however, his estimate had greatly cooled. In characterizing post-Beethovenian orchestral music, Dukas felt that works with "neoclassic tendencies," that is the work of Schumann and Brahms, "represented nothing essential in the domain of the symphony."[54] D'Indy drew a similar analogy between Brahms and Saint-Saëns several years later.

Musical composition, according to Saint-Saëns, is always very classical; sometimes, one encounters in his works certain juxtapositions of tonalities which can only be explained with difficulty; but he always knows how to give these awkward neighbors a correct and elegant solution, which is never common with the oppressive tonal clumsiness so frequent in the works of Brahms and the German neoclassicists.[55]

Favorable acceptance of German music by French composers became increasingly inadmissable after 1900, abetted by the atrophying political relationship between the two countries. Mahler, in receiving the mantle of the German orchestral legacy, also inherited the French criticism of it as well as the label of neoclassicism. A case in point was a performance of the Fifth Symphony conducted by the composer at the first music festival of Alsace-Lorraine in Strasbourg from May 20–22, 1905. The entire program had been organized in an effort to re-establish cultural cordiality between France and Germany, symbolically taking place in a traditionally disputed area.[56] The outcome infuriated the French participants and supplied Rolland with the occasion to excoriate Mahler as he had Brahms.

This heaping up of music both crude and learned in style, with harmonies that are sometimes clumsy and sometimes delicate, is worth considering on account of its bulk. The orchestration is heavy and noisy. The underlying idea of the composition is neoclassic, and rather spongy and diffuse. . . . The whole is like a showy and expensive collection of bric-a-brac.[57]

If Alma Mahler is to be believed, when Mahler arrived in Paris in April 1910, to conduct his Second Symphony, Debussy, Dukas, and Pierné walked out during the second movement: "They said later they had found the music too 'Schubertian,' and that Schubert, also, was alien to them—'too Viennese, too

Slavonic.' Whatever their objections, they did not make them plain."[58] To the extent that Debussy's few recorded observations on Schubert's music were uncomplimentary, Alma's recollection is not far-fetched. Too, he could conceivably have found the double forte entrance of the Eb clarinet—a favorite Mahler instrument eschewed in Debussy's scores—doubled by three flutes, three oboes, and first violins to be an orchestral effect that was, if not grotesque, in bad taste according to his sensibilities.[59] The French composers apparently did not notice that, if the theme of the second movement of the Second Symphony is indebted to any specific work at all, it appears to be borrowed from a well-known Minuet from Bach's *Notebook for Anna Magdalena Bach*.[60] After Debussy had traveled to Vienna in November 1910, to conduct a concert of his own music, he wrote to a friend in December warning against being "deceived by pretentious profundities or by the detestable German *Modern-style*."[61] He might as easily have said neoclassicism, for either he had recalled his encounter with Mahler's Second Symphony eight months earlier, or else he had intended to allude to Brahms, whose music had been clamorously received at a lengthy performance the day before Debussy's own concert.[62]

The acid opinions about contemporary German instrumental music by Frenchmen like Rolland and Debussy probably helped to contribute to a comparable temperament in the young Stravinsky, whose early tenure in Paris was spent in the company of such artists. A letter to Maurice Delage on December 15, 1913, regarding Mahler's Eighth Symphony, reveals that Stravinsky's judgment was analogous to that of his colleagues.

> What can I say about the music of this German *Kolossalwerk*? I find that the only quality of this symphony is the rigidity of an absolute, bare-faced dullness. This is terrible, old friend! Imagine that for two hours you must comprehend 2 times 2 equals 4 and all this accompanied by a *FFFFF* in Eb-major performed by 800 people.[63]

The appraisal by French musicians and other intellectuals of the work of any German writer or artist prior to World War I seemed to be dependent upon the extent to which he appeared sympathetic toward the presumed goals of a national, classical renewal. Nietzsche's diatribes against Wagner and for Bizet, and his characterization of decadence and classicism in racial terms found a readily appreciative audience in Paris.[64] By contrast, when the paintings of Arnold Böcklin were exhibited in the capital, they drew unanimous condemnation from d'Indy, Debussy, and Stravinsky, all of whom likened the painter to Richard Strauss and with equally low regard.[65] Although composers can hardly be counted upon to be astute art critics, in this instance these observations are telling because they are mutual. Further, while French composers used garish colors of German art as a metaphor for their aversion to German instrumental works, this same analogy was employed by German musicians to represent their desire for effects possible only with an immense orchestra.[66]

To judge from the origin of the term neoclassicism, as evidenced by these pre-war appearances, its usage was different from our contemporary understanding of its meaning. In the prose of French composers and critics in the decade before World War I, neoclassicism represented the most banal and stifling treatment of the past by German musicians. Up until this point, the infancy of the term neoclassicism, its French paternity, and its emergence as a response to *fin-de-siècle* German music have been examined primarily through its rhetoric. Indeed, if the semantic fineness which distinguishes between *un néoclassicisme* and *un nouveau classicisme* supplied the limit of observations to be made about the term's early appearances, there would be justification in concluding that the sum of the evidence equaled little more than a case of over-heated sloganeering. However, a variety of examples in composition, academia, and performance practice support the thesis that a pre-war aesthetic existed attended by the French expression *un nouveau classicisme*, and that the derivation of its terminology was not merely the toy of journalism.

The New Classicism and French Musicology

The frequent declaration of a renewal of a pre-nineteenth-century artistic heritage in France circa 1900 was considerably buttressed by the parallel development of that country's musical scholarship. The period which embraced the rise of a nationalist spirit also witnessed the increasing availability of modern editions of early compositions and the opportunity to hear them performed by newly organized ensembles. Flourishing French musicology provided a key link in the formation of a French classicism *redivivus*.

Although the writings of Alexander Choron (1771–1834) and François-Joseph Fétis (1784–1871) supply evidence of the vitality of French lexicography during the 1800s, a serious interest in the systematic study of an older tradition did not occur until around the turn of the century. At the Paris Exposition in 1900, an international congress of academicians furnished Louis Bourgault-Ducoudray, then professor of music history at the Conservatoire, with the occasion to declare both the novelty and significance of French musicology:

> If the study of music history has excited certain individuals of every era, it is one of the honors of our own epoch to have instilled this scientific movement with a freshness and completely new importance. Speaking only of the French movement whose development I have been able to follow step by step, if I compare the actual progress of our studies with the state where they languished twenty years ago, I cannot resist a feeling of patriotic pride. Twenty years ago, it would have been scarcely possible to find ten people in Paris interested in musical archaeology. Today it can be said that the study of the musical past has entered education and, up to a certain point, artistic practice.[67]

Bourgault-Ducoudray's chronology is perceptive. The final decades of the nineteenth century exhibited the most explicit instance of Wagnerian influence on French thought, a susceptibility which is equally apparent among a generation of French historians generally born before 1860. This is the case with Albert Lavignac (1846–1916), a professor at the Conservatoire from 1875; Lionel Dauriac (1847–1923), professor of musical aesthetics at the Sorbonne between 1896 and 1903; Charles Malherbe (1853–1911), archivist at the Opéra from 1898; and Julien Tiersot (1857–1936), librarian at the Conservatoire between 1910 and 1920. An exception in this generation is Marie Bobillier who, under the pseudonym of Michel Brenet, wrote widely on early music before 1900.[68]

A definite change of sympathy can be found in a slightly younger group of writers, particularly those who were pupils of César Franck: Henry Expert (1863–1952), who succeeded Tiersot as librarian at the Conservatoire; Henri Quittard (1864–1919), who succeeded Romain Rolland as professor of music history at the Sorbonne; and Jules Ecorcheville (1872–1915). Three other French historians of this generation also warrant mention. Two studied with Bourgault-Ducoudray at the Conservatoire: Lionel de La Laurencie (1861–1933), who helped to found the *Société française de musicologie*; and Maurice Emmanuel (1862–1938), who succeeded his mentor as professor of music history at the Conservatoire in 1909.[69]

Among French musicologists born in the 1860s, Romain Rolland (1866–1944) is exceptional. He was similarly adept in the instruction of art history, but he achieved his most lasting fame as a novelist. The ambivalence which charges his writings on the music of France and Germany typifies the equivocal posture of many European intellectuals of this generation toward the polar attractions of decadence and classicism. As a product of nineteenth-century literary traditions, Rolland was firmly committed to the concept of the individual, divinely inspired artist-hero, yet he felt that the only living composer to whom he could accord such an honor, Richard Strauss, had brought a patina of excess to the cult of genius. Conversely, as a Frenchman, Rolland believed that the inherent classical spirit of his country's music would supplant the over-wrought emotionalism of German art, but he could not bring himself to characterize any French composer as more than a mere talent.[70] This fluctuant attitude can be found not only in the guise of the composer Krafft, the main character of *Jean Christophe* (1904–12), Rolland's *magnum opus*, but also informs his choice of subjects in music history. He wrote with authority on opera before 1750, but his biographies are of German composers, Beethoven (1900) and Handel (1910). The breadth of his learning and the force of his personality, rather than his example as a scholar, exerted an influence upon a younger generation of French musicologists and made his lectures at the Sorbonne second only to those of Henri Bergson in popularity.[71]

The influx of instruction in early music became a commonplace only after 1900. Although classes in music history were established at the Conservatoire in 1871, they were not made mandatory for all students until 1903. During the *fin de siècle,* the cultivation and dissemination of early music were not initiated by any of the established educational institutions of Paris, but rather were the consequence of a new school, the *Schola Cantorum.* Originally founded as a society for sacred music by Charles Bordes, Alexandre Guilmant, and Vincent d'Indy on October 6, 1894, the *Schola Cantorum* was transformed into a school for the restoration of music of the past on October 15, 1896. A measure of its influence on French cultural life can be taken from the number of its students and the performances its ensembles gave between 1896 and 1903. During these seven years, enrollment increased from 21 to 260 pupils; concerts in Paris totaled 149; and the *Chanteurs de Saint-Gervais,* a choir founded by Bordes in 1892 and incorporated into the school, gave 200 performances in 130 French cities.

The philosophy of instruction at the *Schola Cantorum* derived from a rich and not entirely compatible amalgam of enthusiasms of its founders. Bordes contributed his consuming interests in Gregorian chant and Palestrinian counterpoint. Guilmant's training as an organist supplied the concern with Bach and early keyboard music. The passions of d'Indy provided the most important factors to both the curriculum and the general outlook of the *Schola.* The repertoire included the lyric theater of Monteverdi, Rameau, and Gluck as well as the nineteenth-century instrumental lineage of Beethoven, Wagner, and d'Indy's teacher, César Franck. To this music was grafted the deeply spiritual and almost mystic hauteur endemic to the Franck coterie. D'Indy himself added a virulent disregard for the mundane academic program of the Conservatoire and an ill-concealed anti-semitism which he contrasted with the lofty goals of a pedagogy steeped in music of the Catholic Church, French folk song, early opera, and modern cyclic forms—all calculated to preserve the vitality and integrity of the French tradition. For d'Indy, music was a mission, not a *métier.*

> And this, then, will be the task of professors: no longer to exercise the fingers, the larynx, the writings of students, and the method of familiarizing them with the tools they will have to use, but to form their spirit, their intellect, their heart. Finally, these tools should be employed to sane and elevated work, and the means acquired can thus contribute to the grandeur and development of musical art. My dear friends, do not mistake that which we ought to seek in our works of art. It is not profit. Leave this trade to the too numerous semites who encumber music, since it is susceptible to becoming a business. It is not even for personal glory, an ephemeral and unimportant result. No, we ought to aim higher, we ought to see farther. The true goal of art is to teach, to elevate gradually the spirit of humanity, and, in a word, to *serve,* in its sublime sense: *dienen*—that which Wagner put into the mouth of the repentant Kundry in Act III of *Parsifal.*[72]

Plainsong and Wagner, early opera and Beethoven: these would appear unlikely partners upon which to erect a course of musical study. But in stating the artistic *Credo* of the *Schola,* Bordes connoted what compositions from these divergent sources might have in common: the immaterialization of movement, a rhythm which is composed of accents succeeding one another freely in time and unfolding in infinite variation or *melopée continue*, a suggestive and mysterious game, the freedom of the musical phrase, and an assurance of an artistic training contained among a cadre of adepts.[73] Such language more closely approximates the jargon of symbolism than an espousal of a classical ideal. Indeed, these remote abstractions furnish a rare point of contiguity between the *praxis* of the *Schola* and the aesthetic of Debussy. In the same year that Bordes issued the *Credo*, d'Indy, one of the few Europeans acquainted with the operas of Monteverdi, found a spiritual sympathy, if not a actual stylistic parallel, between *Orfeo* and *Pelléas et Mélisande*.[74]

The meridian of influence outlined by the *Schola Cantorum* lasted only about a decade. By World War I it had acquired the sterile, academic character it was originally designed to combat. But during the early years of the new century, it acted as the most significant institutional conduit for the publication and performance of early music in Paris. Despite the oddly alloyed repertoire of its curriculum, its expressed goal remained the triumph of French music and its cult.[75] *Cult* is the critical word because, although the *corpus* of old music revived by the *Schola* was prodigious and without precedent in France, the hieratic mien and insular outlook of its architects also produced some harrowing by-products. There remained a large gap in the secular tradition because d'Indy deeply mistrusted the philosophical underpinnings of Renaissance humanism.[76] D'Indy preferred to think of the evolution of art as a continually progressive and self-renewing spiral. As a result, the performance of early music in its original and authentic guise was irrelevant and out of date.

> I will not linger upon the truly puerile objection composed of saying that our modern performance is not an exact reproduction of that of the sixteenth century. This is undeniable, while we do not conjecture about that which could be the original rendering of a Gluck or Rameau opera, and that even the manner of creating a performance of the *Damnation of Faust* from the time of Berlioz is something completely ignored by our generation. But what difference does it make? And is this [a modern interpretation] not new proof of the vitality of beautiful works and that there is this power to rediscover a new youth in every age?[77]

This hermetic attitude also extended toward the performance of early keyboard music. When Bordes announced plans to have the *Schola* artists perform the complete music for *clavecin* by Rameau, he declared that, like the music of Bach, it should be played on the piano in order to "break faith with the supposed tradition which shackles the flight of an entire literature and which diminishes it, by always wanting to preserve the scale of a medium that is charming, but slim and passé."[78]

One of the house pianists whom Bordes encouraged to participate in these concerts was a young Polish virtuoso, Wanda Landowska. When she arrived in Paris in 1900, Landowska had already acquired a formidable technique and an admiration for pre-romantic music from studies in Warsaw and Berlin, as well as a background in research techniques from her husband, Henry Lew, an expert in Hebrew folklore. Her entry into the circle of scholars at the *Schola* helped to nurture her single-minded fascination for the revival of the keyboard literature of the seventeenth and eighteenth centuries. But her scrupulous fidelity to performance on authentic instruments ran counter to the prevailing attitude at the *Schola*. She could hardly have been enthusiastic over Bordes' proposal in a letter of July 13, 1903, which may have contributed to her decision to introduce a harpsichord into one of her recitals in that same year.

> I want to put you to a big task, one which may become for you a splendid specialty. Play all the works of the harpsichordists, *but not on the harpsichord*; enough of the 'cage for flies' which reduces superb and often large-scale works to the size of its tiny, spindly legs. Therefore, harpsichord [works] on the piano, like those of Bach; but you will have to work hard on Couperin, Chambonnières, and Rameau. I would like to give a whole series of concerts with you this winter, at the *Schola*, to build up your name in this repertoire. And I am already organizing three concerts in Geneva. We must absolutely discuss this.[79]

Landowska demurred, but her reputation became established quickly. In 1908, Albert Schweitzer wrote of her admiringly: "Once one has heard Wanda Landowska play the *Italian Concerto* on her wonderful Pleyel harpsichord which adorns her music room, it would be inconceivable that one could ever reproduce it on a modern piano."[80]

Landowska promoted the vitality of early music as a polemicist and a performer concurrently. From her first essays, she asserted that the essence of keyboard music before 1750 was constituted in the purity and logic of its polyphonic structure whose interpretation demanded "the art of phrasing and of bringing out voices, individually or simultaneously." She argued that modern pianism was irrelevant to the performance of this repertoire because of its "noisy virtuosity, thick sonority muddled with too much pedaling, exaggerated tempi, contraction, and distortions of the lines."[81] Contemporary performance practice was mired in the cultural aesthetic of romanticism, producing "an increasingly sickish feeling" which was alien to the precision and clarity which the music required and which only the harpsichord could provide. Landowska treated the contrast between piano and harpsichord with the same language that her French contemporaries represented the difference between the legacy of nineteenth-century German neoclassical works and their own artistic heritage.

> We have been congested for too long by all that is bulky, fat, huge, loud, and forceful, by this entire museum of monsters and wild beasts . . . so polished that our spirit does not long after the more tender and refined images, after this *paradis galant* where all that is brutal can be curbed. We have been dazed for too long by roaring seas, torrents and cries of theatrical passion, so that our fatigued spirit does not find repose in sweet quietude of this [other] serene, lucid, masterly, majestic, and divinely naive music.[82]

While Landowska continued to be the most significant force in the promotion of authentic performance practice in France after World War I, she was anticipated in her revival by several musicians in Paris before 1900. The *grand-père* of this renewal was Louis Diémer (1843–1919), a piano virtuoso for whom Widor, Saint-Saëns, and Lalo all wrote pieces and, from 1887, a professor at the Conservatoire. Early in 1889 Diémer assembled a group of musicians to perform two concerts of the music of Marais, Leclair, Handel, Legrenzi, Rameau, Milandre, Loeillet, Couperin, and Daquin on early stringed instruments and harpsichord. Their favorable reception stimulated Diémer to organize a further series of recitals of eighteenth-century French music for the Paris Exposition later that year. The ensemble consisted of viola d'amore and viola da gamba reconstructed by Gand-Bernardel and Chardon and a 1769 harpsichord by Pascal Taskin loaned to Diémer by the maker's grandson.[83] The ambience, however, did not prove conducive for a judicious appraisal of the merits of either the works or their performance.

> These concerts were given in a new hall constructed in the roof of the Trocadéro, up to the fourth stage, under a glass window which, on warm days, established in the hall a hot temperature greatly appreciated by those denizens of the tropics actually in Paris whereas on days when it is cold, an open staircase lets into the hall a current of air which makes the good seats uninhabitable. Further, the hall is entirely covered in a material on which the sound is muffled as soon as it is uttered and whose beef-blood colored reflections are not absolutely favorable to the beauty of the spectators. But to proceed, the musicians are used to these things. It is said that the Trocadéro will be fatal to them.[84]

Despite these circumstances Diémer and his colleagues continued to perform. In 1895, they organized the *Société des instruments anciens*, and concertized widely throughout Europe for several years until the deaths of several of its members curtailed further activity.

Their example led to the formation of a second group, the *Nouvelle société des instruments anciens*, founded by Henri Casadesus (1879–1947) in 1901.[85] During the next decade the reputation of the new society eclipsed that of its predecessor, a tour of Russia in 1909 being particularly noteworthy. In St. Petersburg the group was heard by the poet and Francophile, Alexandre Benois. He was so charmed by the music of Montéclair that he suggested to his colleague, Serge Diaghilev, that Casadesus arrange several of the pieces for a ballet. Diaghilev vetoed the project because Casadesus insisted that the music be performed on the original instruments which the impresario considered inadequate for a large concert hall.[86] Although the idea remained stillborn for the next fifteen years, it was Diaghilev's introduction to the possibility of creating ballet music by reconstructing works from the eighteenth century. In 1913, he was planning ballets based on the music of Bach and Scarlatti, again at Benois' proposal.[87] The Montéclair ballet achieved realization only after World War I, in the wake of the successes of *Les femmes de bonne humeur* and *Pulcinella*, when Casadesus arranged pieces for the 1924 production of *Les tentations de la bergère, ou l'amour vainqueur.*

In common with the rise of French musicology and the resurgence of authentic instrumental performance was the appearance of editions of a pre-nineteenth-century repertoire. In many cases these multivolume monuments still serve as resources to be tapped by both scholar and performer. These works often stressed the nationalist quality of the revival of the French lineage. Théodore Michaelis, whose publications of French opera enjoyed the editorship of Franck (three works of Philidor) and d'Indy (*Les éléments* of Destouches and *Les bayadères* of Catel), declared that his work was designed as "an imperishable edifice which we propose to elevate to the glory of our *Great French Masters*"; while Henri Expert, in his preface to his series of French Renaissance composers, asserted that the music was a mirror of its times "where the characteristics and intimate energies of our race are exalted and deployed."[88]

Among individual composers, the two whose music sustained the greatest rehabilitation during the surge of French historicism at the turn of the century were François Couperin and Jean-Philippe Rameau. The earliest appearance in the nineteenth century of the *Pièces de clavecin* of Couperin was in 1862, in the fourth volume of a massive twenty-three tome collection of keyboard works from Merulo to Schumann, *Trésor des pianistes* (1861–72), edited by Aristide and Louise Farrenc. There followed in 1871 the first autonomous publication of Couperin's complete works in four volumes since their original issue in the 1700s. The emergence of this version carries with it a certain degree of irony since its editors were Friedrich Chrysander and Brahms, the latter treated with considerable derision by many French contemporaries who were either unaware of the composer's participation in revising the works of one of their country's most hallowed musicians, or who preferred to ignore it for the purposes of an anti-German campaign. Aside from their motives, the French had to wait until after 1900 to boast of an indigenous version of the *Pièces de clavecin* when, in 1905, Durand printed Diémer's edition of the complete keyboard works.[89] Shortly thereafter, in 1908, the same publisher issued Couperin's chamber pieces, *Les goûts réunis*, edited by Dukas.

Unlike Couperin's *Pièces de clavecin*, the *Oeuvres complètes* of Rameau was the progeny of an exclusively French community. The project was begun in 1895 under the direction of Malherbe and Saint-Saëns and, with its completion in 1911, boasted the participation of several of the most distinguished composers of the period: Saint-Saëns (keyboard works, 1895; chamber works, 1896; cantatas, 1897; motets, 1898 and 1899), d'Indy (*Hippolyte et Aricie*, 1900; *Dardanus*, 1905; *Zaïs*, 1911), Dukas (*Les indes galantes*, 1902; *La princesse de Navarre*, 1906), Guilmant (*Les fêtes d'Hébé*, 1904; *Le temple de la gloire*, 1909), and Debussy (*Les fêtes de Polymnie*, 1908).[90] This list not only suggests the fascination exercised upon the French mind at the turn of the century by the works of Rameau, but also indicates that their legacy furnished a rare point of aesthetic propinquity for composers whose artistic creeds were otherwise at great distances and who, in several instances, disliked each other intensely.

To summarize: toward the end of the nineteenth century, French composers found themselves confronted with contemporary German musical traditions which constituted, on the one hand, the libidinous stridency of Wagnerian opera and its close association with the malaise of the decadent sensibility and, on the other hand, the massive instrumental edifices of Brahms and Mahler, whose neoclassicism was defined and frequently belittled by the French for its stereotypical structures and vapid thematic content. Debussy gave a cogent resume of the situation in 1903: "One side is blinded by the last rays of the Wagnerian sunset, and the other frantically holds onto the neo-Beethovenian formulae bequeathed by Brahms."[91] In seeking compelling alternative models, many French artists, fortified by a milieu of increasingly vociferous nationalism, were drawn to their preromantic past which was construed to embody a purity inherent in their race. The call for a revival of this heritage by polemicists who reckoned a disparity between its new classicism and German neoclassical compositions received clamorous support from musicians and found practical expression in changes of school curricula and in the appearance of editions and performances of a hitherto scarcely familiar repertoire. We may now turn to the works of contemporary French composers at the turn of the century in order to discover the extent to which their scores echoed this rhetoric.

The New Classicism and French Music: Saint-Saëns, d'Indy, and Others

If the renewal of the classical past of French music was a manifest intellectual trend before World War I, its influence upon specific works was necessarily apposite in order to invest that tendency with a significance beyond mere fashion. The new classicism acquired even greater acuity when compositions reflected the slogans of contemporary criticism. To be credible, the French had to practice in their music what they preached in their prose.

The earliest pieces which bear an affiliation with a pre-nineteenth-century tradition do so as much in name as in substance. Instrumental compositions entitled "in the ancient style" first appeared after the Franco-Prussian War, implying a connection between a sympathy for the past and a more coeval nationalism. This relationship is further suggested by the coincidence of the first such work, the *Cinq pièces dans le style ancien* by Alexis Castillon, receiving its premiere on November 25, 1871, at the inaugural concert of the *Société nationale*, an organization bearing the motto *Ars Gallica* and devoted to the exclusive performance of new French music.[92] Although the movements of this work—"Prelude," "Ronde," "Adagietto," "Fantasie," "Saltarello"—indicate an affinity with the romantic era as much as any other period, the title of the composition possibly fathered a handful of offspring during the next thirty years: *Six airs de danse dans le style ancien pour la scène du bal* (1882) by Léo Delibes, written as incidental music for Hugo's *Le roi s'amuse*; *Suite en ré dans le style ancien* for trumpet, two flutes, and string quartet (1886) by d'Indy; *Suite d'orchestre dans le style ancien* (1892) by Albéric Magnard; *Pastorale variée dans le style ancien* for flute, oboe, clarinet, trumpet, horn, and two bassoons (1894) and *Ballet de cour. Six airs de danse dans le style ancien* (1905) by Gabriel Pierné; *Pièce dans le style ancien* (1893) by Cécile Chaminade; *Menuet antique* (1895) by Ravel; and *Air de danse dans le style ancien* (n.d., but before 1910) by Bourgault-Ducoudray. Castillon died in 1873 at thirty-five and his compositions whose titles imply a relationship with early music—gavottes and minuets—always remained in close proximity to other, more contemporary dance types—waltzes and scherzos—with both groups achieving only the status of salon music.[93]

The first major French composer to utilize the dance idioms of the seventeenth and eighteenth centuries was Saint-Saëns. As has been observed previously, Saint-Saëns' interest in music before Beethoven was great, although the composers whom he knew best—Bach, Handel, Gluck, and Mozart—were equally familiar to the romantic generation of Berlioz. Several of Saint-Saëns' compositions mirror in their titles and instrumentations an association with pre-nineteenth-century models: *Suite pour orchestre* (1877); Septet for trumpet, string quartet, and piano (1882); and *Sarabande et rigaudon* for string orchestra (1892). The Septet was commissioned by a chamber society, *Le trompette*, which accounts for its uncommon ensemble. Despite the titles of its movements—"Prélude," "Menuet," "Intermède," "Gavotte en final"—the treatment of thematic material conveys an eclecticism of sources that Saint-Saëns characterized as the foundation of his style.[94]

The main theme of Saint-Saëns' "Gavotte en final"—its square phrasing in duple time, moderate tempo, and commencement on the upbeat—suggests, if only broadly, an affinity with the earlier gavotte type. Further, the proximity of its melody to that of a sonata by Jean Marie Leclair implies a self-conscious allusion to the eighteenth century on Saint-Saëns' part, although he would have had to have familiarity with Leclair's music in manuscript since it only appeared in a modern edition, *Les maîtres violonistes de l'école francaise du xviiie siècle*, compiled by Guilmant in 1905 (see ex. 1.2). Elsewhere in the Septet, theme, structure, and even formal plan connote a closer relationship to Saint-Saëns' own century. The "Prélude" bears a textural similarity to the opening of the first movement of Schumann's Quintet in Eb for piano and strings in the same key. The resemblance is surely more than fortuitous since Schumann's quotation of his theme in the coda of the final movement—a unifying structural device of nineteenth-century invention—is copied exactly by Saint-Saëns (see ex. 1.3).[95]

Example 1.2. Melodic Reminiscence: Leclair and Saint-Saëns

a.   Camille Saint-Saëns, Septet, "Gavotte en final"

b.   Jean Leclair, Sonata, op. 1, no. 9 (Edited by Alexandre Guilmant)

Another example of the apparent discontinuity of eighteenth-century title and nineteenth-century source in Saint-Saëns' music is the "Allegro quasi minuetto" from his *Album pour piano* (1884), wherein the Schumannesque octaves of the left hand seem to have been borrowed from "Wichtige Begebenheit" from *Kinderszenen*, op. 15.

    The instrumentation of the Septet may have served as the model for d'Indy's *Suite en ré dans le style ancien* (1886) for trumpet, two flutes, and string quartet although its commission by *Le trompette* as well can account for the similarity in part. Like the Septet, d'Indy's *Suite* displays a not entirely compatible amalgam of sources. In the "Sarabande," the descending dotted melody in the flute suggests a connection to the slow movement from the Bach Flute Sonata, BWV 1034, a work which d'Indy could have been acquainted with through performances by Paul Taffanel who had made the six Bach flute sonatas a regular part of the repertoire of the *Société des instruments à vent* which he founded in 1879. The accompanimental figure of the strings and trumpet, however, recalls the final movement of Brahms's Fourth Symphony, particularly the first variation in strings and horns. The chronology is also suggestive: the Fourth Symphony was premiered throughout Europe at the end of 1885 and the beginning of 1886, was published that year, and d'Indy composed his *Suite* during the spring of 1886. The resemblance may equally be a coincidence due to both compositions sharing an even earlier model, Bach's Passacaglia in C minor for organ, which d'Indy had known as early as 1873 when he played it on the organ of the *Thomaskirche* during a trip to Germany. During this same trip, d'Indy tried to meet Brahms but, according to his memoirs, *Impressions d'enfance et de jeunesse* (1930), was snubbed as Brahms disdained to look at Franck's *Rédemption* which the younger composer had brought with him. Léon Vallas disputes that there was no conversation by citing that, after his trip, d'Indy wrote in his copy of Berlioz's *Mémoires* several lines about valved horns which concludes: "Finally, there is the advice from Liszt and Brahms, who [Brahms] calls them *petits trompettes*."[96] Given his later virulent nationalism, d'Indy's recollection of 1930 is predictable. In 1886, however, he may still have had a sufficiently open mind to succumb to a Brahmsian influence. While the affinities shared by the Brahms and d'Indy excerpts might still be regarded as fortuitous, textural and chronological similarities also exist between the "Sarabande" and Franck's Symphony in D minor begun in 1886, which perhaps is less coincidental than a Brahms-d'Indy connection owing to the symbiotic nature of the personal and creative relationship between Franck and d'Indy.

The other three movements of the *Suite* also display a mixture of possible sources. A similarity of rhythmic motive and sequence exists between the "Entrée" and a Couperin harpsichord piece, "Les chérubins" from the twenty-first *Ordre*, and its repetitive four-bar phrasing recalls Baroque practice (see ex. 1.4). However, d'Indy's use of a single rhythmic cell in the "Ronde française" as the sole means of thematic development is a device which reflects his veneration of Beethoven, a relationship reinforced by the identical appearance of the dotted motive in the "Ronde française" and the first movement of the latter's Seventh Symphony (see ex. 1.5). By contrast, the stylization of phrasing, texture, and melodic cliché in the "Menuet" is possibly owing to d'Indy's familiarity with Destouches' *Les éléments,* which he edited in 1883 (see ex. 1.6a,b).

Saint-Saëns and d'Indy arrived at their compound uses of pre- and post-Beethovenian sources from different directions. Saint-Saëns, born in 1835, was sufficiently close in age to the first generation of nineteenth-century compos-

Example 1.3. Cyclic Procedure in Outer Movements of Chamber Works by Schumann and Saint-Saëns

a. Robert Schumann, Quintet, First Movement

b. Robert Schumann, Quintet, Fourth Movement

c. Camille Saint-Saëns, Septet, "Prélude"

d. Camille Saint-Saëns, Septet, "Gavotte en final"

Example 1.4. Recurrent Rhythmic Patterns: d'Indy and Couperin

a. Vincent d'Indy, *Suite dans le style ancien*, "Entrée"

b. François Couperin, "Les chérubins"

ers to be considered a transmitter, rather than a legatee, of its language. D'Indy, sixteen years his junior, forged a method dominated, like his pedagogy, by his sense of history. For him, Bach and Beethoven were not German musicians, but great universals, as fundamental to the evolutionary perfection of art as Rameau, Couperin and, inevitably with his ego, d'Indy himself. The inclusion of French

Baroque dance idioms among their models was as much a result of a belief in the legitimacy of their national tradition as a mistrust of the ascendant *outre-Rhin* styles contemporary to them. The employment of earlier genres was significant in furnishing inspiration for younger composers as well. The similarity of practice among several generations of French musicians expresses a durability in the aesthetic premise of incorporating elements of a remote past into a fresh context. For example, the opening measures of d'Indy's "Menuet" may have served as the basis for the first movement of the *Suite brève* (originally composed in 1900 for two pianos and orchestrated in 1913) by Louis Aubert, since a striking affinity exists between the theme of the latter and d'Indy's melody (see ex. 1.6c) True, Aubert could as likely have found an earlier source directly from the eighteenth century without relying on d'Indy's "Menuet" as an intermediary. Yet the resemblance emphasizes the continuity of a coherent treatment of a pre-nineteenth-century dance idiom in the development of a neoclassic manner before World War I.

An analogous case derives from a comparison of the *Concert en ré* (1891) by Ernest Chausson and the *Suite pour piano* (1910) by Albert Roussel. Either Saint-Saëns' Septet or d'Indy's *Suite* could have provided the stimulus for Chausson's choice of instrumentation: solo violin, string quartet, and piano. The composer's incorporation in the second movement of the characteristic gestures of the sicilienne—the $\frac{6}{8}$ meter, the dotted figure in the melody, and the regular 16th-note pulse in the accompaniment—conveys a familiarity with the earlier idiom, if not necessarily a reliance upon a specific model. Considering Chausson's ensemble, the prototype could have been supplied by the slow movement of Bach's Violin Sonata in G minor, which the composer may have known from a printed edition, since several of his acquaintances—Franck, Bordes, and Guilmant—subscribed to the *Bach Gesamtausgabe*; or from a performance, since Eugène Ysaÿe, the Belgian violinist to whom the *Concert en ré* is dedicated and who premiered it, concertized regularly with the Bach violin sonatas (see ex. 1.7a,b). Chausson had been d'Indy's fellow Franckian acolyte during the 1860s and Roussel, born in 1869, fourteen years after Chausson, began studying composition with d'Indy in 1889. While Roussel's knowledge of the *Concert en ré* is contingent upon his sharing mutual artistic circles with its composer, the appearance of stylistic similarities between his *Suite* and Chausson's work arises from the nearly identical usage of the rhythmic and textural stereotype of the sicilienne in the middle movement (see ex. 1.7c). In addition to sharing the obvious, even superficial, metric, rhythmic, textural, and phrasing clichés of the sicilienne, the three examples in 1.7 resemble each other in their use of a stepwise bass motion which encompasses the octave, although harmonic considerations are widely different in each case. In the Bach Sonata, the harmonic progression from the tonic, C minor, through the minor subdominant, F minor, is determined by the linear descent of the bass line. With Chausson's second movement, a similar

Example 1.5. Recurrent Rhythmic Patterns: d'Indy and Beethoven

a. Vincent d'Indy, *Suite dans le style ancien*, "Ronde française"

b.   Ludwig van Beethoven, Symphony No. 7, First Movement

Example 1.6. Gestural Affinities in Minuets by French Composers

a. Claude Destouches, *Les éléments,* "Second menuet"

b. Vincent d'Indy, *Suite dans le style ancien,* "Menuet"

c. Louis Aubert, *Suite brève*, "Menuet"

Example 1.7. Gestural Affinities in Three Siciliennes

a. J. S. Bach, Sonata, BWV 1017, "Siciliano"

descending line (minus the pitches C and B♭ which are implied in measure 7) arises from harmonic considerations in which F and A are treated as competing tonic poles resulting, in turn, from the congruence of pitches shared by F major and A phrygian. In Roussel's work, the ascending collection of pitches, D–E–F#–A–B–C#, anchors a sequence of arpeggiated parallel chords, which acts as a nonfunctional coloristic contrast to the larger harmonic motion—G# to C#—which frames it. The contrasting harmonic service to which each bass line is put illustrates how individual and extensive were the uses of the past by French composers during the *fin de siècle*.[97]

Although composers around 1900 often avowed their allegiance to the seventeenth and eighteenth centuries, their selection from that repertoire remained largely dependent upon the circumstances surrounding each individual's awareness of specific works, particularly before that music, especially the oeuvre of Rameau and Couperin, was widely available around the turn of the century. During the efflorescence of French musicology in the 1900s, the treatment of pre-nineteenth-century compositions was still subject to the congeniality of the material within the composer's personal style. For example, although Dukas participated extensively in editing early music, when he chose to write variations on a minuet by Rameau in 1903, the result was not a set of *doubles* in the manner of the *clavecinistes* but, owing to the romantic legacy, was an expansive work which Debussy characterized as "festooned with so much gilt that at times Rameau himself would not have been able to find his theme."[98]

b. Ernest Chausson, *Concert en ré*, "Sicilienne"

Example 1.7 (continued)

c. Albert Roussel, *Suite pour piano*, "Sicilienne"

Despite the teaching careers of d'Indy and Roussel at the *Schola Cantorum*, works such as the *Suite dans le style ancien* and the *Suite pour piano* clearly were exceptional departures from their preponderant pre-war language. Only after 1920 did their output suggest a greater reliance upon early sources. In these instances, Roussel's *Suite en fa* (1926), Concerto for small orchestra (1926–27), and *Petite suite* (1929); and d'Indy's *Diptyque méditerranéen* (1925–26), Concerto for flute, cello, and strings (1926), and Suite for flute, string trio, and harp (1927) appeared as sequels to a European-wide trend in addition to renewals of a stylistic thread which had surfaced before 1914. The relationship between the emergence of early French music via pre-war musicology and contemporary composition is more appreciable in works by Debussy and Ravel than in those by an idealogue like d'Indy, even though they were estimated, paradoxically, as the more revolutionary musicians before World War I.

The New Classicism and French Music: Debussy

Debussy began using the names of Baroque dances in his first multimovement keyboard pieces: *Petite suite* (1888–89), *Suite bergamasque* (1890–1905), and *Pour le piano* (1894–1901). With regard to musical content, the young composer found his models not in prototypes from the seventeenth or eighteenth centuries, but rather in pieces with similar classicizing titles by his older contemporaries. One can even argue that the generation of French composers before Debussy

Example 1.8. Harmonic Similarities in Sarabandes of Debussy and Satie

a.   Erik Satie, *Première sarabande,* mm. 16–25

b.   Claude Debussy, *Pour le piano*, "Sarabande," mm. 51–55

exerted the greatest sway over his music before 1890. James Briscoe has asserted the following: "At each main element of style . . . the French group provided the essential influence upon the formative compositions of Debussy. Virtually all of the innovative stylistic traits present in the formative compositions had occurred previously among that group. From the beginning, Debussy recombined some-what isolated traits that he sensed as most liberating, explored them in the formative compositions, and began the personal synthesis that would culminate in his mature production."[99] A frequently cited example of this influence is the harmonic language of the "Sarabande" from *Pour le piano*, written in 1894, whose parallel and non-functional chords of the seventh and ninth may have been inspired by their analogous treatment in the *Trois sarabandes* (1887) of Erik Satie[100] (see ex. 1.8). The three simultaneities starting in the second measures of both examples are almost identical although spelled differently. The large harmonic motion is exact: toward Eb-major in measure 20–21 by Satie and to D#-major in measure 55 by Debussy. The introduction of a chord of the ninth, on Gb/F#, is also proximal in both examples.

Example 1.9. Gestural Affinities in Minuets by Debussy and Saint-Saëns

a.   Claude Debussy, *Petite suite*, "Menuet"

b.   Camille Saint-Saëns, *Menuet*, op. 56

An instance of motivic likeness occurs in a comparison of the "Menuet" from the *Petite suite* to the *Menuet*, op. 56 (1878) by Saint-Saëns (see ex. 1.9). The introductory flourish of sixteenth notes by Saint-Saëns in measures 2 and 4 is mirrored by Debussy in measures 3 and 7. Saint-Saëns alternates these roulades with units of three quarter notes in measures 1, 3, and 5; Debussy vaguely echoes this treatment in measures 1–2 and 4–6 and repeats it exactly in measure 8. There is also a shared melodic gesture between measures 9 and 11 of the Saint-Saëns *Menuet* and measure 10 of the Debussy "Menuet" although the latter has reversed the rhythmic ordering of the note values.

An analogous allusion occurs in the "Passepied" from the *Suite bergamasque*. Seventeenth- and eighteenth-century passepieds are in triple time, yet Debussy has chosen a duple meter. An example of a passepied in $\frac{4}{4}$ does appear, however, in Delibes' *Six airs de danse dans le style ancien* (1882) (see ex. 1.10). In addition to the metric likeness, the broken staccato bass patterns resemble each other closely. Circumstantial evidence also suggests that Debussy could have known Delibes' music. The latter was performed, the year before the *Suite bergamasque* was begun, in 1889 at the Paris Exposition which Debussy is known to have frequented. The "Passepied," in the words of one critic, so charmed its listeners that it had to be encored.[101] Taken separately, the metric, rhythmic, and circumstantial affinities are inconclusive indications in arguing for a case of modeling. Taken in conjunction, and together with the other two examples, they furnish persuasive testimony that Debussy's earliest awareness and treatment of his pre-nineteenth-century musical heritage was distilled through his acquaintance with sources from his contemporary purview.

When Debussy was composing the keyboard works of circa 1890, his access to editions and recitals of early music was almost nonexistent. The tide of French musicology which surged into the new century, reawakening interest in this largely moribund repertoire, attracted the composer almost immediately. The first performance of a Rameau opera since the eighteenth century occurred at the *Schola Cantorum* on January 22, 1903, when d'Indy conducted a complete concert version of *Castor et Pollux*. Debussy attended the premiere and, under the guise of *Monsieur Croche*, not only wrote admiringly of the particular work and its composer, but also launched into a wholesale panegyric on the true French tradition.

We have, however, a purely French tradition in the works of Rameau. They combine a charming and delicate tenderness with precise tones and strict declamation in the recitatives—none of that affected German pomp, nor the need to emphasize everything with extravagant gestures or out-of-breath explanation, the sort which seem to say, "You are a singular collection of idiots who understand nothing and would easily believe that the moon was made of green cheese!" At the same time one is forced to admit that French music has, for too long, followed paths that definitely lead away from this clearness of expression, this conciseness and precision of form, both of which are the very qualities peculiar to French genius. I've heard too much about free exchange in art, and all the marvelous effects it's had! It is no excuse for having forgotten the traditions founded in Rameau's work, unique in being so full of wonderful discoveries.[102]

In a letter to Durand shortly after the appearance of his essay, Debussy confessed to having failed to do justice to his subject in this article.[103] In the above excerpt,

Example 1.10. Gestural Affinities in Passepieds by Debussy and Delibes

a. Claude Debussy, *Suite bergamasque*, "Passepied"

b. Léo Delibes, *Six airs de danse dans le style ancien*, "Passepied"

however, one can discern several favorite themes to which the composer would often return during the next twelve years in his career as a music critic: the great esteem in which he held Rameau, one of the very few composers who merited unqualified approbation; the characterization of his eighteenth-century legacy as constituting uniquely French attributes of clarity of expression and concision of formal values; the regret at the contemporary failure to emulate these traits; and the ruthless denigration of foreign, "cosmopolitan" influences.

The composer closest to Rameau's era whom Debussy considered inimical to the inherently French sensibility was Gluck. A performance of *Alceste* later in 1903 supplied Debussy with the opportunity to make a withering denunciation addressed directly to the shade of the composer. Having decried Gluck's pomposity, Debussy indicated the nature and extent of his stultifying legacy.

> But despite the "deluxe" side of your art, it has had a great influence on French music. One finds it first in Spontini, Lesueur, Méhul, and so on, but, worst of all (you will see why later on), you contain the seed of many of Wagner's ideas. And between you and me, your prosody is awful: you turn French into an accented language when it is really a language of nuances. (Yes, I know you're German.) Rameau, who helped to form your genius, had some examples of fine and vigorous declamation that could have been of use to you—but I will not bother you with what a marvelous musician Rameau was, lest you suffer by comparison. We must acknowledge that it was you who made the action of the play predominate over music. But was that such a good thing?[104]

Debussy, however, blithely ignored his declination to compare Rameau to Gluck and instead rejected the latter because Rameau was "more Greek"; his lyricism was rediscovered only in Debussy's own time and perhaps, by implication, by the composer himself.

Debussy retired *Monsieur Croche* at the end of 1903 and did not return as a regular critic until 1912. In the interregnum he offered an occasional interview or essay for publication and Rameau continued to resurface. Anticipation of the revival of *Hippolyte et Aricie* at the Opéra under d'Indy's direction on May 13, 1908, furnished the composer with the premise to renew several cherished ideas.

> We cannot foresee what the performance of *Hippolyte et Aricie* at the Opéra will be like. It is a venture that is more daring than one would readily suppose. Rameau was a musician of old-time France, and if he was obliged to concern himself with spectacle he felt no need to give up his right to compose real music. That may seem natural enough, but we don't seem to be able to do it anymore. We have adopted a frenetic way of shaking up the orchestra as if it were a salad, so that any hope of real music must be completely abandoned. The beauty of this frenzied way of doing things is so deep that it is difficult to perceive.
>
> I fear that our ears have thus lost their power to listen with the necessary delicacy to the music of Rameau, in which all ungraceful noises are forbidden. Nevertheless, those who do know how to listen will be afforded a polite but warm welcome.
>
> It is annoying that we should have forgotten these ways which were once our own, replacing them with our barbarous attitudes. We can be neither too respectful nor too moved. Let us listen to Rameau with our full attention, for a voice more thoroughly French has not been heard for many years at the Opéra.[105]

At the end of 1912 Debussy's friend André Caplet asked him to furnish for an American journal an article on Rameau which was never published in the composer's lifetime. Debussy wrote to Caplet of the difficulty in according the subject the proper esteem in so limited a forum but the essay remained consistent with the themes of 1903.[106] When Debussy returned to criticism on a more frequent basis for the *Bulletin de la société internationale de musique* (*SIM*) in 1912, he still perceived the French heritage as being ignored in favor of Wagnerian models.

> Why are we so indifferent toward our own great Rameau? And toward Destouches, now almost forgotten? And to Couperin, the most poetic of our harpsichordists, whose tender melancholy is like that enchanting echo that emanates from the depths of a Watteau landscape, filled with plaintive figures? When we compare ourselves to other countries—so mindful of the glories of their pasts—we realize that there is no excuse for our indifference. The impression with which we are left is that we scarcely care at all for our fame, for not one of these people is ever to be seen on our programs, even at this time of year when we make a point of coming closer to our relatives. On the other hand, we do find *Parsifal*.[107]

Not surprisingly, World War I brought an increased acerbity for the same subject.

> In fact, since Rameau, we have had no purely French tradition. His death severed the thread, Ariadne's thread, that guided us through the labyrinth of the past. Since then, we have failed to cultivate our garden, but on the other hand we have given a warm welcome to any foreign salesman who cared to come our way. We listened to their patter and bought their worthless wares, and when they laughed at our ways we became ashamed of them. We begged forgiveness of the muses of good taste for having been so light and clear, and we intoned a hymn to the praise of heaviness. We adopted ways of writing that were quite contrary to our own nature, and excesses of language far from compatible with our own ways of thinking. We tolerated overblown orchestras, tortuous forms, cheap luxury and clashing colors, and we were about to give the seal of approval to even more suspect naturalizations when the sound of gunfire put a sudden stop to it all.[108]

"Overblown orchestras" and "tortuous forms" might refer to Mahler, while "cheap luxury" and "clashing colors" could suggest Strauss. "Suspect naturalizations" might then indicate Schoenberg, although there is disagreement on whether Debussy was familiar with Schoenberg's compositions. On October 24, 1915, he wrote to Stravinsky:

> In these last years, when I felt the Austro-German miasma extending into the arts, I would have liked to have more authority, in order to cry out in distress and warn of the danger confronting us . . . !
>   How did we fail to see that these people were attempting to destroy our art, as they prepared the destruction of our countries? And especially with that old racial hatred, which will end only with the end of the Germans! Will there ever be a last German? I remain convinced that German soldiers beget German soldiers.[109]

Debussy's fondness for early French music in general, and Rameau in particular, was a recurrent topic in the prose and correspondence of the post-*Pelléas* decade. The encomiums were not merely critical lip-service: the second book of *Images* (1905) contains a movement entitled "Hommage à Rameau." About the same time he accepted the task of editing a Rameau opera, *Les fêtes de Polymnie*, for the *Oeuvres complètes* even though there existed a deep animosity between him and Saint-Saëns, the series' general editor. Thus by 1908 when the volume was published, Debussy had acquired an acute knowledge of Rameau's music through performances and editions of the operas engineered by the emergence of French musical historicism.

Debussy did not return to using classicizing titles until the sonatas of 1915, but aspects of his late style suggest that he benefited directly from his infatuation with early music which had been nurtured during the past dozen years. The composer had originally projected a set of six sonatas for various combinations of instruments and, although he only lived to write three, his attraction toward a chamber music idiom was almost unprecedented in his published works since the string quartet of 1893. One can only speculate whether the projected ensembles (oboe, horn, and harpsichord; trumpet, clarinet, bassoon, and piano; and several instruments including double bass) would have emphasized the trio sonata texture implied by their scoring. If Debussy's interest in considerably reduced ensembles can be construed as an impatience with the demands of immense orchestral forces which dominated the *fin de siècle,* France's entry into World War I surely heightened the composer's already existent nationalist sympathies. In a letter to Durand on August 19, 1915, Debussy labeled himself as a *musicien français*, a self-proclaimed badge of honor which also appeared on the title pages of the three sonatas.[110] On October 24 of that same year he wrote to Stravinsky that "I have only written pure music, 12 Etudes for piano, and two sonatas for various instruments—in our old form, which, mercifully, did not impose tetralogical auditory efforts."[111]

The most likely French source for Debussy's sonatas would naturally seem to be the Rameau opera for which he served as editor. One need search no further than the opening page of *Les fêtes de Polymnie* to compare its "Prologue" with the first gesture of the earliest of the three sonatas, for cello and piano, which is also entitled "Prologue" (see ex. 1.11). Debussy's incorporation into the melodic line of three triplet figures (the third group in measure 4 repeated immediately) is directly analogous to the three triplet runs in measures 4–6 of the Rameau excerpt. Although triplet groups appear in Debussy's music throughout his career, they are invariably used as either rhythmic ostinati (*Seconde arabesque*, 1888) or else they define a nontonal melodic ambit intended to create a pseudo-exotic effect ("Pour la danseuse aux crotales" from *Epigraphes antiques*, 1915). In the case of example 1.11, the triplets are employed as decorative *agréments* moving toward important tonal points. Although the first two groups are *doubles* (three rising pitches in the triplet) rather than the *tirades* (three descending pitches in the triplet) of Rameau, the third run is pitch equivalent. The harmonic motion to the major subdominant is also proximal, given the

Example 1.11. Rhythmic Reminiscence: Debussy and Rameau

a.   Claude Debussy, Sonata for Cello and Piano, "Prologue"

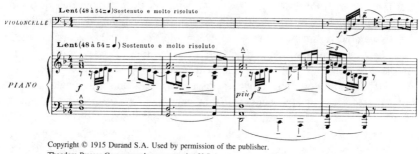

b.   J.-P. Rameau, *Les fêtes de Polymnie,* "Prologue-overture" (Edited by Debussy)

disparity of mode. The Rameau "Prologue" in D major is I ^{7}–V $^6_5$–I (I ^{6})–IV and with Debussy, in D minor, is i–iv ^{9}–v ^{7}–i (III)–IV.

A distinct rhythmic likeness occurs between the "Prélude" to Act I of Rameau's opera and the "Tempo di minuetto" of the Sonata for Flute, Viola, and Harp, also from 1915. The recurring dotted figure of the opening phrase used by Debussy (motive x in ex. 1.12) is mirrored in the work by Rameau almost intact in measure 1–2 and identically in measures 2–4. Note that Debussy's removal of the dotted figure from Rameau's beat one to beat two, while visible, is not audibly testable because of the static pedal. These two examples suggest that the French spirit of Debussy's late sonatas was more than merely a result of reduced instrumentation. The composer also profited from his admiration for Rameau and from his experience, albeit brief, as an editor of his music.

Example 1.12. Motivic Similarities: Debussy and Rameau

a. Claude Debussy, Sonata for Flute, Viola, and Harp, "Tempo di minuetto"

b. J.-P. Rameau, *Les fêtes de Polymnie,* Act I, Scene 1, "Prélude" (Edited by Debussy)

Debussy's fondness for Couperin, the other towering figure of the French eighteenth-century heritage, did not occupy as grand a position in his criticism. Couperin is first mentioned only in general terms in 1908, the year in which Dukas's edition of *Les goûts réunis* appeared.

> Why do we not regret the loss of these charming ways in which music was formerly written, so lost that it is now impossible to find the least trace of Couperin's influence? His music was never superfluous, and he had great wit—something we hardly dare show these days, considering it to lack grandeur. But grandeur is something that often stifles us without our ever achieving it.[112]

By 1913, however, his knowledge of the repertoire was specific, implying that perhaps recently issued volumes of Couperin's music had come to his attention.

> We should think about the example Couperin's harpsichord pieces set us: they are marvelous models of grace and innocence long past. Nothing could make us forget the subtly voluptuous perfume, so delicately perverse, that so innocently hovers over the *Barricades mystérieuses.*[113]

The affinity shared by Debussy and Couperin was observed in general terms almost immediately after the former's death. In an introduction to an edition of Couperin's *Les folies françaises ou les dominos*, published around 1919, d'Indy stated that many of the harpsichord pieces "are so truly musical images, sometimes rather enigmatic, that in our times Claude Debussy has attempted to revive them by applying all their charm to his own personal style." A possible instance of a compositional relationship between the two occurs between the "Pastorale" from the Sonata for flute, viola, and harp and a passage from the *Septième concert* of *Les goûts réunis* (see ex. 1.13). In addition to the similarities of key and rhythmic gesture, one fragment of the melody, Ab–F–G–Eb (in brackets), is remarkably alike in both examples. In addition, the temporary harmonic compromise between C minor and F minor in the Couperin excerpt, which arises due to the clash of E♮ in the continuo and Eb in the violin, is echoed by Debussy by his use of E♮ in the flute and Eb in the viola.

The development of French musicology between Debussy's early piano pieces and his late sonatas was relevant to the composer's evolving style. Before 1900, Debussy found his models for the French classical tradition through works of his contemporaries, whereas the emergent presence of musical historicism nurtured an aesthetic already disposed towards that legacy. Debussy discovered in Rameau and Couperin those characteristics that were congenial to his style. He found traits of the eighteenth century which he accomodated to his own language and, at the same time, confirmed the legitimacy of his cultural heritage.

Example 1.13. Gestural Affinities: Debussy and Couperin

a. Claude Debussy, Sonata for Flute, Viola, and Harp, "Pastorale"

b. François Couperin, *Les goûts réunis*, *Septième concert* (Edited by Paul Dukas)

The New Classicism and French Music: Ravel

An equivalent relationship between expanding scholarship and maturing style, although not with as conspicuous an effect, is demonstrable in the music of Ravel. Like Debussy, his senior by ten years, Ravel had recourse to classicizing titles in his early keyboard works: the *Menuet antique* (1895), the *Pavane pour une infante défunte* (1899), and the "Mouvement de menuet" from the *Sonatine* (1903–5). Also like Debussy's youthful pieces, these compositions owe less to the eighteenth century specifically than to older contemporaries. In Ravel's case, the significant figure appears to be Chabrier, as Ravel himself indicated in criticizing the *Pavane*: "I perceive too easily its faults, the too flagrant influence of Chabrier and the rather poor form."[114] Ravel's biographers have confirmed this connection with greater definition by identifying affinities between Chabrier's *Menuet pompeux* (1881) and the *Menuet antique*, and between "Idylle" from the *Dix pièces pittoresques* (1881) and both the *Menuet antique* and the *Pavane*, or else by suggesting a more general influence of Fauré and Debussy.[115] Too, the sense of an association with the past in a work such as the second movement, "Mouvement de menuet," of the *Sonatine* is equally due to the relative difference between the narrow compass of the keyboard in which it is written and, in Ravel's phrase, the "transcendental pianism" of the compositions which frame the *Sonatine* chronologically: *Jeux d'eau* (1901), *Miroirs* (1905), and *Gaspard de la nuit* (1908).[116]

In a manner similar to Debussy's career, Ravel's interest in evoking pre-nineteenth-century music was temporarily submerged during the decade after the *Sonatine*. Ravel's return to the employment of names linked to Baroque dance idioms occurs around the beginning of World War I in the third movement, "Passacaille," of the Trio for violin, cello, and piano (1914) and *Le tombeau de Couperin* (1914–17). If Ravel had a particular source in mind for the "Passacaille," its genesis is unclear. The structure of the movement is a series of eleven eight-measure phrases, each of which varies the opening monophonic theme. The first three statements, each by a different instrument, are recapitulated in the last three repetitions, which gives the design a balanced, tri-partite structure. In this respect it does not resemble pieces designated "Passacaille" by Couperin in the second and eighth *Ordres*, and by other *clavecinistes* who preferred a form alternating a homophonic refrain with several *couplets*. This theme-and-variation treatment rather recalls Bach's Passacaglia for organ even though the melodic contour is dissimilar. Too, the same observation might be made for works by composers whose style and aesthetic were uncongenial to Ravel, and the composer's biographers have tendered Saint-Saëns and Mozart, as well as Bach, as candidates for the inspiration for Ravel's "Passacaille."[117]

If the identification of a possible source for the "Passacaille" remains shrouded, the recognition of models which underlay *Le tombeau de Couperin* secures the premise that Ravel's return to the use of classicizing titles displayed a more intimate acquaintance with his eighteenth-century legacy than his early compositions. In the spring of 1914, Ravel mentioned in a letter to Cipa Godebski that he was transcribing a "Forlane" by François Couperin ostensibly because certain fashionable circles in Paris had chosen to substitute the forlane for the tango due to a public decree which banned the latter's performance.[118] Although the original reason for doing so does not seem very serious, Ravel apparently later on thought highly enough of the effort to begin an entire *Suite française* which would incorporate a forlane of his own composition.[119] Couperin's "Forlane" was taken from the *Quatrième concert* of the *Concerts royaux,* which had appeared in an edition by Georges Marty before 1908. While this version may have served as Ravel's source, this particular movement also appeared in an essay, "La Forlane," by Jules Ecorcheville in the April issue of *La revue musicale de SIM*. Inasmuch as the date of the article is very close to that of Ravel's letter to Godebski and given that essays by the composer appeared regularly in the same journal at this time, including the April issue, Ravel could equally have found Couperin's "Forlane" there. Ravel's response to his model resembles the general attitude of his contemporaries toward their eighteenth-century tradition to the extent that the most overt sense of similarity derives from the recurrence of a rhythmic gesture (see ex. 1.14). In addition, Ravel's "Forlane" has also acquired the *rondeau* design of refrain and *couplet*. The key is also the same although Ravel's treatment of mode and tonal function is dictated by his personal harmonic language.

Ravel stated that the homage implicit in *Le tombeau de Couperin* was "in reality less to Couperin alone than to French music of the eighteenth century."[120] While this remark seems to support existing evidence that Couperin's "Forlane" was the composer's only specific prototype, one is encouraged to seek additional sources. Indeed, close affinity occurs between the "Rigaudon" and the "Premier tambourin" from the *Troisième concert* of Rameau (see ex. 1.15). Again the correspondence is articulated via the rhythmic gesture and, in addition, the melodic countour of the motive in both excerpts is proximal. Too, the forte outburst of sixteenth notes with which Ravel culminates the end of the phrase is analogous to the climactic repetition of the motive by Rameau. The difference in title of the two movements possibly argues against the conclusion of a self-conscious allusion on Ravel's part. Yet, the tambourin and rigaudon are both Provençal in origin and in the French Baroque style are both written in a vigorous duple meter. During the eighteenth century the distinction was hardly an acute one, and dances entitled "Rigaudon en tambourin" can be found in the work of Rameau.

The preceding discussion has dwelled exclusively upon the relationship between French music in the decades before World War I and the works of Rameau and Couperin. Clearly in the minds of Debussy and Ravel this legacy dominated the intepretation of their glorious past heritage. Despite this prominence, the influence of pre-seventeenth-century music is also detectable in their works after 1900. Occasionally, both composers effected in their music a general patina of archaism by employing parallel fifths and octaves. Ravel did so rather early in his career in "D'Anne qui me jecta de la neige" from the *Epigrammes de Clément Marot* (1899), and Debussy had frequent recourse to them in "La cathédrale engloutie" from the first book of *Préludes* (1910), "Ballade que Villon fuit" (1910), and the Preludes to both *Pelléas et Mélisande* and *Le martyre de St. Sébastien* (1911). After the premiere of Debussy's first opera, Louis Laloy went so far as to assert that there was "a persistence of certain forms of plainchant in *Pelléas*."[121] More explicit instances of allusion occur in reference to the chanson repertoire of the sixteenth century. The rapid reiteration of a motive among

Example 1.14. Gestural Affinities in Forlanes by Ravel and Couperin

a. Maurice Ravel, *Le tombeau de Couperin*, "Forlane"

b. François Couperin, *Concerts royaux, Quatrième concert,* "Forlane"

Example 1.15. Rhythmic Similarities: Ravel and Couperin

a. J.-P. Rameau, *Troisième concert,* "Premier tambourin" (Edited by Saint-Saëns)

Example 1.15 (continued)

b.   Maurice Ravel, *Le tombeau de Couperin*, "Rigaudon"

several voices which appears in Debussy's "Quant l'ai ouy le tabourin," the
second of his *Trois chansons de Charles d'Orléans* (1908), is used frequently by
Janequin in his programmatic chansons such as *La guerre*, a work which Debussy seems to have known (see ex. 1.16). After a performance by the *Association
chorale professionelle* in March 1914, Debussy wrote that Janequin's
"marvelous masterpiece . . . conveys all the hubbub and the rough way of life at
an army camp. It is noted down shout by shout, noise by noise: the sound of the
horses' hooves mingles with the fanfares of trumpets in a subtly ordered tumult.
Its form is so direct that it would almost seem to be 'popular music,' so accurate
and picturesque is the musical representation of these events."[122] Ravel's *Trois
chansons pour choeur mixte sans accompagnement* (1915) also derives partial
inspiration from Janequin's habitual use of rapidly repeated pitches for programmatic effect (see ex. 1.17). Debussy's *Trois chansons* may also have furnished Ravel with a model for his *Trois chansons*, at least with regard to one
phrase of triplet figures in parallel motion underlaid by a "la, la" refrain (see ex.
1.18).

Example 1.16. Recurrent Rhythmic Patterns: Debussy and Janequin

a. Clément Janequin, *La guerre* (Edited by Henri Expert)

b. Claude Debussy, *Trois chansons de Charles d'Orléans*, "Quant l'ai ouy le tabourin"

Example 1.17. Rhythmic Patterns and Nonsense Syllables: Ravel and Janequin

a. Clément Janequin, *Le chant des oiseux* (Edited by Henri Expert)

b. Maurice Ravel, *Trois chansons pour choeur mixte sans accompagnement,* "Nicolette"

Example 1.18. "La-la" Refrains in Works by Ravel and Debussy

a. Maurice Ravel, *Trois chansons pour choeur mixte sans accompagnement*, "Ronde"

Example 1.18 (continued)

b. Claude Debussy, *Trois chansons de Charles d'Orléans*, "Quant l'ai ouy le tabourin"

The Legacy of the Pre-War Generation

We have seen that many French composers, artists, and writers before World War I felt that symbolist rhetoric and German music were turgid and luxuriant, qualities which were to become fashionable anathemas to the post-war spirit. Living in a milieu politicized by fervent nationalist sympathies, composers, educators, and performers in France before 1914 had sensed the desirability for the simplification of the material resources of style and technique and the purification of the aesthetic foundation of subject and model. In their intent to betoken a reverence for the classical past in their works, French composers had recourse to the employment of recognizable conventions derived from a pre-nineteenth-century repertoire. The familiar rhythmic or melodic gestures effected a correspondence to an earlier manner: the users of these readily identifiable clichés could count on their audiences to make the appropriate musical and cultural connections.

Yet if the adoption of the matter of their eighteenth-century antecedents was congenial at times to their contemporary musical goals, the treatment remained far too disparate to permit their elevation to the level of a dominant artistic trend, least of all one called neoclassic. Those elements of the pre-war tendency toward neoclassicism did not coalesce into the semblance of an integrated mode of expression because the uses of that material were different for each composer. The term neoclassicism is not acceptable for the historical unity of the first two decades of the twentieth century; individual styles resisted placement in historical closure, especially in an era where novelty was the prized hallmark. None of the works cited before 1920 that are in an arguably neoclassic manner can be construed as their composers' most spectacular musical utterances, even though we can recognize in retrospect the aesthetic alloy which they form.

How then did elements of this concept, nurtured in a pre-war atmosphere, find their way into the 1920s, only to have the tag of neoclassicism hung around them? Our study now must determine the extent to which the premise for the appropriation of early music in pre- and post-war composition was a shared affinity between generations. The need to attach to a tradition and to enter its mainstream seems to have pulled strongly upon both parties although the agenda for their uses of the past may not have been identical. The term neoclassicism needed to go through some sort of aesthetic rehabilitation for it to arrive at its post-war meaning and, as we shall see, the French could not claim exclusive rights for that change.

2

Neoclassicism in Germany: 1910–1925

Thomas Mann and *Neue Klassizität*

In tracing German terms which are related to neoclassicism, and in comparing their origin and usage with contemporary French expressions, similarities occur which suggest that a schizophrenic quality in European high culture attended the appearance of the term neoclassicism before World War I. Nineteenth-century music and its philosophic underpinnings both repelled and attracted artists, and the lure of Wagner in particular was frequently counterbalanced by a nostalgia for a pre-romantic past. Although Wagner's nationality was not the issue in Germany that it was in France, the composer's musical language and aesthetic notions also sparked an ambivalence among German and Austrian musicians.

In Mahler's symphonies, for example, an apocalyptic, visionary aspect reminiscent of *Götterdämmerung* and *Parsifal* occurs in company with banal references to Haydn and Schubert. In 1910, as he was composing the Tenth Symphony, Mahler arranged four movements from Bach's orchestral music into an orchestral suite. Reger's *Konzert im alten Stil*, op. 123 (1912) has a first movement that clearly pays homage to the *Brandenburg Concertos* which the composer edited in 1905–6, yet the second movement loiters in the dense chromatic sonorities characteristic of several of Wagner's works. The close proximity of two compositions by the young Schoenberg—a Gavotte and Musette for string orchestra with the title "in the old style" written in March 1897, and a fragment of a symphonic poem, *Frühlingstod*, after a poem by Lenau written in July 1898—suggests an "inner conflict between the apparently inimical worlds of Wagner and Brahms."[1] Strauss's *Der Rosenkavalier*, which premiered in Dresden on January 26, 1911, appears to represent a *volte-face* from the composer's *Salome* (1905) and *Elektra* (1908). But for every critic who recognized characters which suggested *The Marriage of Figaro* or noticed musical allusions to *The Magic Flute* in this evocation of Maria Theresa's Austria, there were others who detected references to several Wagner operas. Whereas some contemporary reviewers compared the Marschallin to the

Countess, likened Octavian to Cherubino, and asserted that the final duet was based upon a tune from *The Magic Flute*; other critics noted that the first scene of *Der Rosenkavalier* parodied the love duet from *Tristan und Isolde*, that the presentation of the rose resembled the grail music from *Lohengrin*, and that Ochs's third leitmotiv was taken from "Steuermann, lass die Wacht" from *Der fliegende Holländer*.[2] The many citations of Mozart in contemporary reviews of *Der Rosenkavalier* may have been responsible for the "return to Mozart" mentioned by Egon Wellesz in 1911, although he felt that such a return would "not last in a copy of his style, but in a simplified means of musical expression which, in order to have artistic value, must create new values."[3]

The term neoclassicism occurred even more rarely in Germany than it did in France. In German, *Neoklassizismus* did not appear until after World War I when it was usually identified with French art and architecture of the late eighteenth century. Before 1914, histories of German literature often distinguished between *Klassizismus* and *Klassik* or *Klassizität*. The former invariably connoted an imitation of models—whether derived from the French Enlightenment or from Greek and Roman antiquity—that was frequently stilted and pale in its subservience to the originals. With this derogatory association, *Klassizismus* was equivalent to the English "pseudo-classicism." The latter terms, however, referred to works that, even when inspired by the past, were exemplary in their own right and were invariably connected with Goethe and Schiller.[4] Likewise with regard to music, the more the term *Klassik* came into use at the turn of the century in connection with Haydn, Mozart, and Beethoven, the more it contrasted with *Klassizismus*.[5]

If *Klassizismus* had a pejorative connotation and if *Klassik* was limited to a narrow historical period, how could a German writer before World War I satisfactorily describe contemporary music that would approach an exemplary character that might counter the prevailing mood of the *fin de siècle*? During the summer of 1911 two music journals published an essay by Thomas Mann which offered a solution.[6] The novelist, confronted by the powerful influence of Wagner, ambivalent toward the underlying principles of his music dramas, and ultimately placed in an artistic crisis over his philosophy, employed the term *eine neue Klassizität* in a way that resolved the semantic dilemma.

For a long time the Bayreuther's name stood over all my artistic thoughts and deeds. For a long time it seemed to me that all the artistic yearning and desire of our times flowed from this powerful name. But at no time, not even when I didn't miss any performance of *Tristan* at the Munich Hoftheater, was my profession about Wagner equal to a profession in Wagner. As a spirit, as a character he seemed to me suspect, as an artist irresistible, even if deeply equivocal with respect to the nobility, purity, and healthiness of his method. Never had my youth yielded to him with the complete trusting abandon with which it affixed itself to other poets and writers.

My love of him was love without faith because it always seemed to me pedantic: love without knowledge or belief. It was a relationship that was skeptical, pessimistic visionary, nearly malicious, and moreover entirely passionate and indescribably alluring. Wonderful hours were spent deep in lonely happiness amidst the theater crowd, hours full of paroxysm and short bliss, full of delights of the nerves and the intellect, full of insights of moving and great importance: if only this gave way to an overreaching art.

In truth, in the superior youth of today who are instinctively if silently distrustful and even admittedly immaterial, much Wagner criticism is anti-Wagnerian. And how could it be otherwise? Wagner is nineteenth-century through and through. Indeed, he is the representative German artist of his epoch whose survival in the thought of mankind will perhaps be as great and certain as it will be unfortunate.

But I think about the masterpiece of the twentieth century and something occurs to me that differs very importantly and, as I believe, very favorably from Wagnerism—something that appears logical, structural, and clear; something that is equally austere and serene; something not from so petty a will as his, but from a fresher, nobler, and healthier spirituality; something which finds its greatness not in the Baroque or colossal, nor its beauty in frenzy—a new classicism, it seems to me, must come.

But still, when an unexpected sound or a related turn of Wagner's work strikes my ear, I cry out for joy, a sort of nostalgia for youth and country overcomes me, and further, as before, puts my spirit under the old bright and thoughtful yearning and cunning magic.[7]

Mann's characterization of "a new classicism" is strongly akin to the French *nouveau classicisme*, both in the language used to describe the two terms and in their counterposition to Wagner. It is worth dwelling upon Mann's motivation for using the term as well as the semantic implications because its appearance in 1911 was triggered by the same kind of cultural crisis that prompted the French to distinguish between *un nouveau classicisme* and *un néoclassicisme*.

At the end of March 1911, Mann wrote: "I am so worn out in mind and body that I am on the point of retiring to a trustworthy naturopathic sanatorium for several weeks."[8] He elected to travel to Italy, and during a stay in Venice from May 26 to June 2 he composed the Wagner essay after receiving a request from the editor of *Der Merker* for a contribution to a commemorative Bayreuth issue. Venice, of course, has several connections to Wagner. There the composer had written part of *Tristan und Isolde* and had spent his last months there as well. Mann knew Wagner's impassioned and melancholy Venetian diary written to Mathilde Wesendonck which had already appeared in two editions by 1911.[9]

Mann's sojourn also inspired the novella *Der Tod in Venedig*. Aschenbach, the work's protagonist, is a quasi-autobiographical creation, a successful Munich novelist who suffers an artistic crisis and decides to journey to Venice. Wagner's death in Venice was certainly known to Mann, although he acknowledged that his physical description of Aschenbach was patterned after the likeness of Mahler. Mann learned of that composer's death on May 18, a week before his arrival on the Lido.[10] Aschenbach's vision of the city appears in language unmistakably similar to Wagner's description in his diary: an unreal place of uneasy silence, overgrown with exotic vegetation, full of fantastic buildings sinking into the lagoon. Venice becomes Mann's metaphor for the kind of dreamlike beauty, cultural decay, and spiritual oblivion that he discerned in

Wagner's operas. Mann's description of "a landscape, a tropical swampland under a heavy, murky sky, damp, luxuriant, enormous, a kind of prehistoric wilderness" is similar to Klingsor's magic garden in *Parsifal*.[11]

Aschenbach's destruction comes as his contemplative and Platonic love for a young boy devolves into physical lust. His image of Tadzio disintegrates from a connoisseurship of the grace and charm of Greek statuary to an obsession filled with "fugitive, mad, unreasoning hopes and visions of a monstrous sweetness."[12] Aschenbach, whose writing style had hitherto showed "a new austerity, a lofty purity, symmetry, and simplicity which gives his work the stamp of classicism and of conscious and deliberate mastery," experiences an almost orgiastic ecstasy when he is inspired to write of the boy's beauty.[13] The syntheses of love with death and destruction with ecstasy clearly suggest the climaxes of *Tristan und Isolde* and the *Ring*. Further, while Mann was writing *Der Tod in Venedig* he attended a performance of *Götterdämmerung* which left him with "an inner resistance" to Wagner's music.[14]

Mann's increasing antipathy toward Wagner, the representative German artist of the *fin de siècle*, as revealed in *Der Tod in Venedig*, the Wagner essay, and the correspondence, is similar in kind if not intensity to the vociferous opinions in France. Mann's attitude, however, was not shaped by the French but rather was derived from Nietzsche, who had often accused Wagner's music of irrationality and decadence. Aschenbach's constant comparisons of Tadzio to Greek statues is indebted to Nietzsche's interpretation of the dual nature of art as Apollonian and Dionysian. In his "Geist und Kunst" notes, Mann wrote: "Besides Nietzsche, there is still no other Wagner criticism. . . . There is no doubt that there is more to learn from Nietzsche's criticism than from that of Glasenapp, Wolzogen, etc."[15]

Just as Mann used Wagner as his artistic symbol of the decadence of the nineteenth century, he had in mind Goethe when speaking of the regenerative qualities of *neue Klassizität*. Mann had already contrasted Wagner's "suspect modernity" with the "sublimity and purity of Goethe" before writing his essay and, shortly after its appearance, he confessed that he would like to have every German choose between Goethe or Wagner.[16] In 1925, Mann related how he daily read several pages of Goethe's *The Elective Affinities* before writing *Der Tod in Venedig*, and it has been argued that the former work was fundamental to Mann's conception of the new classicism in his essay of 1911.[17]

We can conclude that Mann's representation of the qualities of the new classicism was catalyzed by negative feelings toward Wagner. In this respect, he resembles many French contemporaries who were led to use the term *nouveau classicisme* by a similar antipathy to Wagner's operas as symbols of the decadence of *fin-de-siècle* culture. As French artists, writers, and composers defined the new classicism in terms of the regenerative and paradigmatic features which they discerned in their national tradition, so too did Mann use Goethe as the foundation for his idea of *neue Klassizität*. Thomas Mann was not alone in his regard of Goethe. Indeed, it is a measure of the latter's stature that, like Bach among composers, he exercised an attraction for writers whose artistic aims were otherwise antithetical.[18] Goethe is signficant in the discussion of the origins of neoclassicism in the twentieth century because, just as he lay behind Mann's formulation of *neue Klassizität*, he provided the inspiration for Ferruccio Busoni's creation of the term *junge Klassizität* which, after World War I, played a signficiant role in shaping the concept of neoclassicism.

Ferruccio Busoni and *Junge Klassizität*

At the time when Thomas Mann was wrestling with his Wagnerian demon, Ferruccio Busoni was crisscrossing Europe at a dizzying pace as a keyboard virtuoso. As a composer, he cherished the rapid stylistic changes in contemporary music, and his own works helped bring tonality to its furthest reaches. As an amateur aesthetician, he wrote favorably of the most extreme methods of composition at that time, including microtones and new sound sources (the latter deriving from his awareness of Thaddeus Cahill's invention of the telharmonium). As World War I began, however, Busoni made a crucial decision to retreat from public life to Switzerland, preferring artistic isolation to residency in one of the belligerent countries. The insular years of the war exercised a profound effect upon Busoni as revealed in a letter of August 19, 1917: "This evening I dreamed about a journey to Paris. My thoughts always return there: I have a nostalgia for big cities, traveling, freedom of movement. Actually I do not budge. I write often, I play sometimes, I am truly alone—so alone—socially and morally."[19] So acute was Busoni's sense of alienation that, after the war's end, his overriding concern was to return to the mainstream of European culture. He did so in grand and symbolic fashion by organizing a series of five concerts with himself as soloist, designed to illustrate the history and continuity of the piano concerto from Bach to the present. The performances occurred from February to April of 1919 with the Zurich Tonhalle Gesellschaft under the direction of Volkmar Andrae.[20]

On May 12, shortly after the completion of these performances, Busoni wrote a draft of an essay in which he looked back upon the evolution of musical composition.

I have spent my life during a time in which the musical world was dominated, spiritually by Beethoven and practically by Wagner. . . . We abandoned, little by little unknowingly, the domain of music, in order to resort to Philosophy: we lost our joy in pure art and became saturated with "profundity," we made efforts to admit that which was wearisome—and all this was cemented by a severe control and rigid judgement. Wagner's hard won victory has been delayed by us beyond its time, from whence our backwardness in progress. . . . It is now a question not of disparaging but of establishing permanent values. We need a new classic art.

> That is classic which is beautiful, great, simple, impressive: that is to say a stable, enduring
> work. All the attempts of the beginning of the twentieth century must be gathered together to be
> incorporated in the definite creation which is to come.[21]

Busoni's dislike of the Wagnerian style had been expressed by him before World
War I in his pamphlet, *Entwurf einer neuen Aesthetik der Tonkunst* of 1907. His
formulation of *eine neue klassische Kunst* in the 1919 draft is a new concept. The
definition of this phrase is reminiscent of Mann's treatment of the term *neue
Klassizität* in his 1911 essay, although only the latter's appearance in two
well-known music journals, to which the composer was a contributor, suggests
the possibility that Busoni was aware of it.

Busoni broadened the contents of the draft in the form of an open letter to
Paul Bekker, music critic of the *Frankfurter Zeitung*, and dated January 20,
1920. The beginning of the letter indicates that Busoni was writing in sympathy
with Bekker's article, "Impotenz oder Potenz," which had appeared in the newspaper on January 15, and which was intended as a polemical response to Hans
Pfitzner's *Die neue Aesthetik der musikalischen Impotenz* (1920). Pfitzner's
book is a generally violent condemnation of "anti-German" elements in music
such as "atonality, internationalism, Americanism, German pacifism," and in
turn is more specifically a vitriolic attack on Bekker's *Beethoven* (1912). Busoni
and Pfitzner had engaged in a similar aesthetic exchange: the latter's *Futurist-
engefahr* of 1917 took exception to the former's *Entwurf* of 1907, and Busoni's
rebuttal appeared in the *Vossische Zeitung*, June 3, 1917. Busoni's letter of
January 20 was printed in the *Frankfurter Zeitung* on February 9, occupying the
three columns of the bottom of page one of the first morning edition.[22]

In his letter, Busoni used *neue Klassizität*, the term employed by Mann in
1911, and introduced a new expression, *junge Klassizität*. The former term
appeared in the context of a discussion on the recent evolution of art. The 1880s,
he argued, was a decade marked by creative stagnation on the part of musicians
bound by tradition. The emergence of a number of experiments, rebelling against
tradition, though a natural appendage to artistic development, had increased to
such a degree in the past fifteen years that the present scene was marred by
exaggeration and extravagance.

> But the general growth of excess, with which the beginner today already makes his debut, is
> becoming general and portends the end of such a period; and the next step is that which leads
> toward a new classicism (which opposition is bound to stimulate).[23]

In the very next sentence, however, Busoni switches to the term *junge
Klassizität*.

> By "young classicism" I mean the mastery, the sifting and the turning to account of all gains of
> previous experiments and their inclusion in strong and beautiful forms.[23]

Although the contexts for both terms, "new classicism" and "young classicism," appear to be similar, Busoni's preference for the latter can be inferred from evidence other than that the phrase "young classicism" appears a second time in the letter and that it was coined by the composer.[25] The crucial difference between the two terms was stated clearly by Busoni in a letter to a pupil, Gisella Selden-Goth, on February 7, 1921.

> *Regeneration*—an architectonic *terminus technicus*—signifies, as you know, the slimming down, the simplification of the line. (For that reason not *new* classicism, against which I restrain myself because this sounds like a return, but *young* classicism.) This one can observe in the growth of trees, from which that architectonic principle stems, because the trunk is an imitation of constraint which serves as support for the branches in the most primitive form.[26]

On June 18, Busoni expressed a similar opinion in a letter to his son:

> Already more than two years ago, as you know, I brought the term "young classicism" into the world and at that time predicted popularity for it. It seems therewith strange to me, because today the term is circulated save that nobody still knows who coined it. So occasionally it is said that Busoni also follows the new classicism! One does not have to be a prophet to desire it. After a questionably long series of experiments and initial "secessions," out of which counter-secessions and ultimately only separate groups in swarms redivided themselves downwards, the necessity of a comprehensive certainty of style must announce itself. But—like everything else—I was also misunderstood with this, in which the masses conceived of classicism as some kind of reaching backwards. This is confirmed in painting—for example in the rehabilitation of Ingres who, a master himself, is a forbidding standard of dead forms. (The view here is stamped harshly on purpose.) My idea (much more a feeling of personal necessity rather than a constructed principle) is young classicism: consummation as perfection and consummation as an ending, a conclusion to the previous experiments.[27]

Busoni felt that *neue Klassizität* implied a mere imitation of the past. He employed the term *junge Klassizität* because it suggested that musical evolution embodied an ongoing, rejuvenative process, which he likened to organic growth in nature.[28]

The foundation for Busoni's analogy of "young classicism" with the organic development of plants, as well as the source for many of the composer's essays on aesthetics, derives from the writings of Goethe. Busoni always held the highest admiration for the poet whom he considered a standard by which to measure the quality of other authors. In a letter to his wife on June 25, 1900, Busoni praised Poe as "Goethe-like in his clarity of style and in his powers of description," and in a letter of September 21, 1913, he wrote that he had purchased a copy of Goethe's complete works in fifty-five volumes, even though he already owned a set.[29] Busoni's artistic declarations which share the strongest affinities with those of Goethe stem from the post-war period, 1919–24, a time in which the composer used six Goethe texts as bases for compositions.[30] Busoni's definition of *junge Klassizität* in his correspondence bears more than a fortuitous resemblance to Goethe's discourse on style, a term the poet used to indicate the highest level of artistic creativity: "Style rests on the most profound foundations of knowledge, on the essence of things, insofar as is permitted us to recognize it in visible and comprehensible forms."[31]

Busoni's fondness for explaining musical evolution in terms of natural growth, which can be found throughout his writings, is undoubtedly based upon Goethe's analogy of plant development and poetic invention.[32] For Goethe, art was a mirror of nature, and the eternal laws which motivated the latter emerged in the expression of the former. "The laws of art lie just as truly in the nature of creative genius, as the great universal nature preserves the organic laws in eternal activity."[33] Busoni had arrived at the same view as early as the *Entwurf* of 1907.

> *Let music be naught else than Nature mirrored by and reflected from the human breast*; for it is sounding air and floats above and beyond the air; within man himself as universally and absolutely as in Creation entire.[34]

Modern composition developed organically and inevitably from all worthy music of the past and, as in nature, it tended toward simplicity and beauty. As Busoni stated in a letter of February 7, 1921, "economy" was the necessary endeavor and final achievement of the composer. *Junge Klassizität* could never be an antecedent, only a consequent.[35]

For Busoni, a composition was "classic" if it possessed those qualities of artistic value which would in time be perceived as forming a perfect art-work. There could be no such thing as an instant classic, nor did novelty necessarily qualify a composition to be a good one any more than age did.[36] Such a view is also derived from Goethe. According to the poet, an art-work was classical, not because it was old, but because it was strong, fresh, joyous, and healthy, and he extended his analogy by considering romanticism as bad art because it was sick and enervated. In like manner, Busoni, in a letter to Selden-Goth, February 3, 1921, characterized musical excess and its renunciation as symptoms similar to sickness and convalescence. He also classified Beethoven as a romantic because his individuality was a portent of "modern nervousness." For Busoni, a musical composition was good not because it was new, but because it appeared with form and beauty.[37]

Just as Goethe influenced Busoni's formulation of "young classicism," so too did the poet provide the source for the three criteria by which the composer defined this expression. The first of these postulates was the idea of unity or *Einheit*. By this characterization, a musical composition possessed no inherent theatrical, religious, or symphonic qualities which gave it meaning other than the setting in which one placed it, the title affixed to it or the text to which it was set.

> I mean the idea that music is music, in and for itself and nothing else, and that it is not split up into different classes; apart from cases where words, title, situations and meanings which are brought in entirely from outside, obviously put it into different categories.[38]

Busoni's belief that music could not represent moral conditions nor embody ethical qualities is one that has a rich tradition among nineteenth-century thinkers, most notably the Viennese critic Eduard Hanslick who was most responsible for popularizing this view in his *Von musikalisch-Schönen* of 1854: "As a consequence of our mental constitution, words, titles, and other conventional associations (in sacred, military, and operatic music more especially) give to our feelings and thoughts a direction which we often falsely ascribe to the character of the music itself."[39] Among the philosophers, both Schopenhauer and Nietzsche held this opinion, and Busoni quoted both of them in this connection. While it is true that Busoni considered music incapable of representing abstract concepts or of interpreting the specific causes of definite emotion, the inner essence of those emotions could be expressed, because human moods, unlike social conditions, were part of the eternal harmony. In the *Entwurf* he wrote: "To music, indeed, it is given to set in vibration our human moods . . . likewise, the inner echo of external occurences which is bound up in these moods of the soul."[40] This opinion is drawn from Schopenhauer: "Music never expresses the phenomenon, but only the inner nature, the in-itself, of every phenomenon, the will itself. Therefore music does not express this or that particular and definite pleasure . . . but their essential nature, without any accessories, and so also is without the motives for them." Busoni's concept, however, falls short of Hanslick's central thesis of musical autonomy: "Definite feelings and emotions are unsusceptible of being embodied in music."[41]

Busoni's idea of *Einheit* was founded on the concept that all music proceeded from a single source. An "eternal harmony" sounded throughout the universe, and all art-works existed within it. Any musical composition was an imperfect transcription of the idea, because that music existed before its tones sounded and after they died away, complete and intact.[42] In order to characterize this music, Busoni invented the term *Ur-musik*, borrowed from the *Ur-ei* which Goethe used to designate the infinite source of all poetry and which, in turn, he had developed from the term *Ur-pflanze* to show the kernel from which all matter evolved.[43] It was left to the creative genius of the artist to realize an individual art-work. Busoni insisted on the word *Gestalter* to identify the composer because, as with Goethe, the artist did not invent; he shaped and brought works which had always existed to a level of human perception. *Gestalt* suggested the endless process of becoming, rather than the self-contained state of being. Ultimately, this theory of *Einheit* led Busoni to Goethe's world-view that an individual object mirrored an ordered totality and that it was a copy of all past members of a species which nevertheless existed as a wholly unique creation.[44]

The second characteristic of *junge Klassizität* was that musical composition should be generated by horizontal elements as opposed to vertical progressions.

With "young classicism" I further include the definite departure from what is thematic and the apprehension again of melody—not in the sense of a pleasing motive in a pleasing instrumentation—but melody as the ruler of all voices, all impulses, as the bearer of the idea and the begetter of harmony, in short: the most highly developed (not the most complicated) polyphony.[45]

Busoni had earlier hinted at the preferred place melody held in the hierarchy of composition in a letter to his wife, March 15, 1911, which he entitled: "Melody belongs to the future."[46] The composer also echoed the opinion of his correspondent, Paul Bekker, who had identified the tendency in contemporary music as

a melodic style which is equal to the old polyphonic art with respect to formative power, without copying it, which is related to it in kind only according to principle, and now, intrinsically suggested through the formal richness of polyphonic as well as harmonic art, a new type of form-building power brought forth from within itself.[47]

Finally, Busoni argued against the use of tone-painting and overripe harmonies, which had become increasingly evident in music since the death of Wagner.

A third—no less important—idea is the denial of the "sensuous" and the renunciation of subjectivity. . . . The substance of what is artistic relates only to proportions, to the limits of what is beautiful, to the preservation of taste—it means above all: an art which does not express propositions which lie beyond its nature (for instance in music: description).[48]

Busoni decried recent music that was subjective, descriptive, exaggerated, metaphysical, sensual, and vertically governed. In its place he advocated a conception of composition that was objective, absolute, serene, distilled, pure, and horizontally generated.

If the above quotation were taken out of the context of Busoni's complete aesthetic *oeuvre*, it could be construed that he championed a revival of the spirit of eighteenth-century compositional practice and rejected out-of-hand the indulgence in excessive chromatic language and the overwrought imagery inspired by contemporary literary movements. Busoni did indeed object to the hysteria and temperamental gestures of what he called "neo-expressionism."[49] He repudiated a composition, not because it might employ all possible harmonic combinations or an accumulation of different rhythms, but because these experiments had not been applied intelligently within the structure and their proportions had not been distributed artistically throughout. Any possible combination of tones was valid so long as it contributed to the perfection of the art-work. All new resources were available to the composer with the realization that their arbitrary use would result in anarchy.

Busoni's letter generated no immediate response, although a letter to Selden-Goth on February 12, 1920, suggests that he anticipated one.[50] The first reaction came in the form of a gloss by Hermann Scherchen when portions of the letter were reproduced on July 16, 1920, in the new music journal, *Melos*. (*Melos* began publication in Berlin on February 1, 1920, and appeared fortnightly thereafter with Scherchen its founder and general editor from 1920–21.) Scherchen considered it incredible that hardly any member of the European musical community had taken notice of the essay. He interpreted the document to be both an explanation of what Busoni considered to be the goal of music and a self-confession of his stylistic transformation in his most recent works, despite the fact that nowhere in the letter did Busoni refer to his compositions. While Scherchen deemed Busoni's letter an admirable reflection of his evolution, he did not feel that the composer had clarified or understood the true direction of contemporary music. Scherchen wrote that artistic vitality could be recaptured

> not by new classicism, not by either Schönberg or Béla Bartók—above all not by this art; refined and sick by reason of too much cerebral intensity. The future of music will be a new, simple, monumental creation that grows from deepest mutual feeling and established firmly in folksong.[51]

As a prediction of the course of music in the 1920s, this bit of commentary has proven to be incorrect. Indeed, based upon Scherchen's career as a conductor, it is questionable that he really believed this statement, but that he was, for once, prone to editorial hyperbole.[52]

If the sincerity of Scherchen's gloss is problematic, there were readers who accepted its contents at face value and, in doing so, helped to promulgate the term *neue Klassizität*. On October 16, again in *Melos*, Adolf Aber used the above quotation by Scherchen as a motto for the beginning of an article in which he agreed with Scherchen's "redeeming words, found by one who hardly places himself in word and deed with the youngest in art."[53] Aber thus assumed that Scherchen had repudiated his patronage of modern music. The latter now had reason to regret his gloss, for a letter to his wife on November 6 indicates that it had become popular within a few weeks.

> Moreover, it is a nuisance that Aber's quoted line in *Melos* has found such wide dissemination, so that one might be tempted to make use of it as a sign for the fact that even I have converted from Saul to Paul.[54]

If the quotation to which Scherchen refers in his letter had this "wide dissemination," it follows that the term *neue Klassizität* was likewise circulated at the end of 1920. The term *neue Klassizität* did appear in a spirited defense of Busoni that same month: "For the benefit of Diesterweg's news, must the maestro compose as soon as possible a Ninth Symphony as proof of the new classicism?"[55] (Adolf Diesterweg was a conservative critic for the *Allgemeine Musik Zeitung* who had attacked the composer's aesthetic position.)

During 1921 it became increasingly common to find Busoni associated with the term *neue Klassizität* rather than his own *junge Klassizität*. In January 1921,

Musikblätter des Anbruch, the house organ for Universal Edition and Vienna's best known propagandist for modern trends, devoted a special double issue to Busoni in which the *junge Klassizität* letter was reprinted. In an essay on the composer's recent evolution, Philipp Jarnach used the term *neue Klassizität* in both the article and its title.

> This great mind has slipped off the chains of established convention from himself without apparent effort; his solemn art, from pure feeling and inexhaustible invention, is classic in the complete, profound sense of the word; into it flows the result of a great evolution, which does not create immutable rules, but no doubt points out unending trends. No formal schema rules it; but a form turned spirit, form as style, as experience. It realizes the synthesis of that which Busoni calls the new classicism—with this term the reawakening of a characteristic concept, which will forever gain acceptance over all other manifestations.[56]

Similarly, Edward Dent, the composer's English biographer, labeled Busoni an "Italian Neo-Classicist" after hearing a performance of the *Rondo arlecchinesco*.[57]

The frequency with which the term *neue Klassizität* appeared in connection with Busoni in 1920 and 1921, and the fact that the association arose due to journalistic accident, undoubtedly rankled the composer as his correspondence demonstrates. He attempted to rectify the misattribution publicly as well. In 1922, he arranged for the letter to be reprinted again in a collection of his essays and the appearance of *junge Klassizität* in the title leaves no doubt as to his insistence upon the term. Also in 1922, Busoni's pupil and close friend, Gisella Selden-Goth (to whom the composer had emphasized the difference between *neue Klassizität* and *junge Klassizität* in a letter of February 7, 1921) wrote a biography of the composer which characterized the disparity between the two terms. Given the close relationship between the biographer and her subject, it is conceivable to credit Busoni with the following concept:

> The expression *junge Klassizität* has been frequently misunderstood. It appears to many as an acknowledgment of sin of the mature Busoni who, growing out of the frenzy of experimenters himself, tries to tie back together the arbitrary, disconnected strands of tradition and, at the same time, desires to approach at times in his recent compositions an awareness of archaic forms, to motivate his reaching back to older, even "classic" aesthetic art styles. He perceives an artistic natural law, according to which a classicism must be shortly born again; not a historical one like a revival of the Bach-Mozart-Beethoven style, but an aesthetic one in understanding, as a change from disunion to harmonization, from symbolism of the refined to its clearer, more temperate, and technically more complete statement.[58]

The terms *neue Klassizität* and neoclassicism were associated with Busoni only briefly. By 1924, the year of Busoni's death, new works by other composers, notably Stravinsky, had arrived on the international scene and those compositions were identified with the term neoclassicism. Articles in 1924 invariably called Busoni the inventor of *junge Klassizität*, and one year later, in a major early treatise on modern German painting, Franz Roh asserted that Busoni's *junge Klassizität* letter was one of the first documents to foresee the neoclassicism of contemporary artists such as Georg Schrimpf.[59]

In many respects Busoni's aesthetic of *junge Klassizität* was characteristic of the era. While its rudimentary formation had been shaped in the composer's essays and letters during the first fifteen years of the century, the urgency for its complete statement became manifest in the aftermath of World War I. Thus Busoni's writings parallel, in part, French thought to the extent that the qualities of *nouveau classicisme*, which furnished attractive alternatives toward Wagnerian models before 1914, acquired a tangible sense of necessity in the post-war atmosphere. Too, global conflict implied a threat to the fundamental basis of Busoni's theory: that all music was a derivative of an eternal harmony. The composer turned to Goethe, Mozart, and Bach with intense affection at the same time because their work was a confirmation that art mirrored a universal order.

In this regard, Busoni also reflects a common and especially German theme of the 1920s in relying on Goethe as the cultural underpinning for his aesthetic conception, because the poet was an enormous influence upon German artistic thought during this decade. Hauer used Goethe's *Farbenlehre* as the philosophical basis for his post-war theory of composition in *Vom Wesen des Musikalischen* (1920). That Schenker's theory of an *Urlinie*, first mentioned by him in 1920, has a philosophical basis in Goethe's *Ur-pflanze* may be deduced from Schenker's frequent quotations of the poet and by his constant comparisons between musical development and the natural growth of plants and animals. In his discussion of the concept of the background in *Der freie Satz* (1935), Schenker stated: "Because these comparisons [e.g. between music and life] are of a biological nature, and are generated organically, music is never comparable to mathematics or to architecture, but only to language, a kind of tonal language."[60] Krenek used Goethe texts for his opp. 43 and 47 (1926), and opp. 56 and 57 (1928). Webern employed Goethe's verse for his op. 12, no. 4 (1917) and no. 19 (1926), and sketches for several songs with texts by Goethe occur between 1917 and 1930. Further, Webern claimed on several occasions that his manipulation of combinatorial properties of the row was indebted to Goethe's theory of the organic processes of nature and art. Mann's reliance upon Goethe for his conception of *neue Klassizität* has been detailed earlier. Paul Klee spoke of painting in terms of Goethe's theory of organic growth in his *Creative Credo* (1920) and much of his work of the 1920s demonstrates the latter's influence.[61]

The relationship between Busoni's music and his aesthetic is more elusive than that between that aesthetic and the culture that produced it, partly because he did not compose very much after World War I. Krenek and Varèse, a generation younger than Busoni and associated with him at this time, felt that his music did not equal the imagination and vision of his prose.[62] Toward the end of his life, Busoni himself became increasingly pessimistic that the perfect artistic expression could ever be achieved, and that circumstances of time and place worked to hinder the creative genius from reaching that end. Significantly, those musical portions of *Doktor Faust* which remained incomplete upon his death, but which were finished by his pupil, Philipp Jarnach, were the vision of Helene, the embodiment of perfection, and Faust's death and apotheosis at the end of the opera.[63] A great deal of his time was instead taken up with arrangements and editions of the music of Bach and Mozart. Busoni's edition of Bach's keyboard music was completed in 1920, and between 1919 and 1923 he arranged eighteen works of Mozart. Although Busoni's fondness for these composers is apparent before World War I, his deep involvement in their music during the 1920s, like his affection for Goethe, reflects his intense nostalgia for the eighteenth century. Mozartean melody and phrase structure are detectable in the Concertino for clarinet and small orchestra (1919) and the Divertimento for flute and orchestra (1921). Similarly, the *Toccata: Preludio, Fantasia, Ciaccona* (1921) is indebted to Bachian counterpoint.

On occasion, Busoni's music influenced compositions of his younger contemporaries. The example of his *Toccata* is reflected in Krenek's *Toccata and Chaconne* (1922) and Weill's *Fantasia, Passacaglia, Hymn* (1922). In one case, a similarity occurs between a *junge Klassizität* composition by Busoni, the first of the *Sechs kurze Stücke zur Pflege des polyphonischen Spiels* (1923), and a work that was considered a typical example of neoclassicism, the third movement of the Sonata (1924) by Stravinsky. The latter had heard Busoni's pieces in August, 1923, when he went to Weimar to see the Bauhaus production of *Histoire du soldat*. A letter to Ansermet on September 9 indicates that Stravinsky liked the pieces.[64] The resemblance between the two works is as likely fortuitous, however, inasmuch as both compositions share an affinity with a common model, the Prelude in E minor from Book I of *The Well-Tempered Clavier*.

The importance of this comparison lies less in proving that Busoni influenced Stravinsky than in suggesting that the aesthetic premises that underlay the methods of both composers were contemporary and even sympathetic developments. The essential difference between Busoni and the post-war generation is that he did not possess its historical cynicism. The term neoclassicism, as it was understood in the 1920s, denied organic evolution in art, insisting rather that each composition created its own logic, discrete and unrelated to every other work. For Busoni, musical composition remained an act of faith, affirming the belief that creativity always developed toward the sublime.

3

Neoclassicism in France: 1914–1923

The War and Changing Attitudes

As often as the terms *nouveau classicisme* and *néoclassicisme* were distinguished from each other before 1914 by language that underscored nationalist feelings, those sentiments were greatly intensified during World War I. As the French and English were allies on the battlefields, so too were they sympathetic voices in music criticism. During the war years it was common to find Germans accused of "destroying the clarity of the eighteenth century," and to find French music equated with "the anti-sentimental trend"; characterized by "grace, vivacity, certain forms of politeness, colour and wit"; made up of "more conciseness, more logic, more clearness" than before; intolerant of "fatiguing prolixities, tediousness, redundancy, sterile agitation"; returning to "the taste for clear thought, formal purity and sobriety, the disdain for the big effects"; and representative of "order and architectural structure."[1] To use such prose for nationalistic descriptions of exclusively French art was to ignore its applicability to a good deal of German music as well. Among English writers, Ernest Newman's voice was a rare one when he observed in 1917 that

> it is the circumstances, not racial germs, that have determined the different ideals that French and German music have set before them. The danger of selecting a few mental traits and elevating them to the dignity of national characteristics is that composers may feel it their duty to try to live up to them, to the damage of their own originality which may really have quite a different orientation.[2]

The problem for critics who were responsive to French music was not to find a rationalization for describing it in arguably vague terms, but to determine which composer to celebrate as its leader. Debussy's last sonatas and Ravel's Trio and *Le tombeau de Couperin* encouraged a few writers to place them in the vanguard. Shortly after Debussy's death in 1918, Georges Jean-Aubry claimed that the composer was more obsessed with the French tradition than any of his countrymen. In the following year, Camille Mauclair declared that "Debussy affirms a particular formula which is far indeed from shutting in so profound and subtle an art, only in order to demonstrate clearly his desire to be, despite his reputation, a neoclassic, a child of the *clavecinistes* of the eighteenth century, a descendent of Rameau." Ravel's *Le tombeau de Couperin* was similarly considered by René Chalupt to be "simplified to the extent that it becomes refined and reties the broken thread to our old *clavecinistes*" and "a direct reaction against romanticism, against gothic and medieval taste and against all anti-renaissance prejudices." Roland-Manuel found the Trio to be "the most eloquent illustration . . . against false pictoriality and flabbiness of expression" and "classic, in the sense where classicism is taken to be concise perfection."[3] Egon Wellesz, one of the few composers to have an acquaintance with novel trends emanating from both Paris and Vienna, and to have noticed the influence of French musicology on contemporary music as early as 1911, asserted that Debussy's final sonatas pointed to the neoclassical style. He likewise felt that Ravel's Trio and *Le tombeau de Couperin* demonstrated a "wonderful clarity . . . a new classicism, a harmonious balance between form and content which can only be formed among Latin peoples, without having the stamp of academicism."[4] The above-mentioned views of Debussy and Ravel during the immediate post-war years is similar to the pre-war descriptions of contemporary French music to the extent that they were considered to be linked to a national style inherited from the eighteenth-century *clavecinistes*. Wellesz's use of *neue Klassizismus* may have been drawn from an awareness of Thomas Mann's Wagner article, but for Camille Mauclair to have employed the term neoclassic in a way that was not pejorative suggests that the pre-war distinction between a new classicism and neoclassicism deteriorated after 1918. This is true up to a point. As will be seen, the term neoclassicism was not used in a positive sense regularly until the middle of the 1920s. In the half-dozen years before that it more commonly retained its derogatory meaning.

While the music of Debussy and Ravel from the war years was, on occasion, called neoclassic and with praiseworthy intent in 1919 and 1920, the composers' reputations suffered from some contemporary criticism. Leigh Henry, an advocate of *Les Six,* felt the "anemic neoclassicism" of *Le tombeau de Couperin* "threatens to become the musical tomb of Ravel."[5] For many artists, the European-wide pallor of despair brought about by World War I created the image of an insurmountable wedge between the leading currents in musical composition which preceded it and the ascendent creative impulses which followed. For many, the end of World War I created a growing perception of a new spirit in the arts which clearly distinguished itself from the trends before 1914. Some propagandists of contemporary art tended to disavow any kinship with pre-war styles which, with few exceptions, they generally regarded as corrupt in one way or another. For these artists and critics, Debussy was the avatar of impressionism; the composer of *Pelléas* and *La mer*. Likewise Ravel was associated with a gaudy romanticism and the fact that *La valse* was his first post-war work encouraged that assessment.

Jean Cocteau and the "New Simplicity"

The primary responsibility for shifting critical approval away from Debussy and Ravel belongs to Jean Cocteau. His pamphlet of aphorisms, *Le coq et l'arlequin*, appeared in 1918 and, along with the *succès de scandale* of *Parade* the previous year, served to vault Erik Satie into prominence as the leading French musician among composers and writers with avant-garde sensibilities. The language which Cocteau used to promote Satie's music in *Le coq* is remarkably close to pre-war descriptions of *nouveau classicisme*. For Cocteau, however, it was Satie alone who "pursued his little classical path" before 1914; who "cleared, simplified, and stripped rhythm naked"; and who, "sick to death of flabbiness, fluidity, superfluity, frills, and all the modern sleights-of-hand, voluntarily abstained in order to remain simple, clear, and luminous."[6] Although this prose resembles that used to describe the music of many French composers before and during World War I, Cocteau set Satie apart from either pre-war trends or remote national traditions. The "classical path" of clarity which Cocteau accorded Satie was a solitary one that did not reach back into the past. The "new simplicity" of Satie (reiterated by Cocteau in a lecture of 1920) was both "classic" and "modern"; "a French music" that did not recall any other French music.[7]

Le coq presents a paradox, or perhaps a confusion, between the praise of certain aesthetic attributes that suggest a rational order and the partisanship of artistic novelty. This peculiar tension between continuity and innovation suggests that Cocteau may have been influenced by Apollinaire's *l'esprit nouveau*, which the poet had discussed in the year immediately preceding the writing of *Le coq*. For Apollinaire, the new spirit meant "inheriting from the classics a good solid sense . . . the sense of duty which denudes the sentiments and limits them or rather contains their manifestations." Yet it also meant "to explore the truth, to search for it, as much in ethnicity, for example, as in imagination."[8] One biographer of Apollinaire considers the contents of his essay as presenting "a dilemma . . . between order and adventure," and this description fits the language of *Le coq* as well.[9] Elsewhere Apollinaire wrote of the painter Derain in a manner strikingly similar to Cocteau's description of Satie: "With unequaled daring, he went beyond the most audacious forms of contemporary art in order to rediscover simplicity and freshness, the principles of art and the discipline which stem from such an exercise."[10]

Cocteau may have intended a deliberate irony in using the slogans of earlier criticism to describe his contemporary aesthetic while, at the same time, ruthlessly denigrating the composers with whom that commentary was previously associated. In *Le coq et l'arlequin*, Debussy is the only French composer criticized by Cocteau, although Wagner comes in for a large share of ridicule. In 1920, Cocteau was responsible for a series of four broadsheets entitled *Le coq* in which Ravel was attacked. The judgment that Cocteau's use of pre-war rhetoric was self-consciously ironic is perhaps overly generous insofar as his musical acumen is concerned. If his relationships with composers in the years leading up to the writing of *Le coq* are examined, it can be concluded that he measured the value of music in terms of its capacity to scandalize and that *Le coq* itself was as much a self-promotion as a characterization of a new artistic spirit.

Cocteau's first relationship with a composer resulted in a notably disappointing collaboration: *Le dieu bleu* with music by Reynaldo Hahn and staged by the *Ballets russes* in 1912. Its failure was magnified by the sensational premiere of *The Afternoon of a Faun* two weeks after the Cocteau-Hahn ballet. That same year Diaghilev had urged Cocteau to "astonish me," and when *Le sacre du printemps* appeared in 1913, Cocteau witnessed just the sort of *succès de scandale* that he believed Diaghilev wanted and which he himself wished to achieve. One biographer of Cocteau has written: "What Cocteau did not consciously comprehend as he listened to the *Rite*—and his failure in this respect was to mark much of his minor work—was how little the creation of masterpieces and the desire to astound have to do with each other."[11] Cocteau's inability to understand Stravinsky's music in any terms other than its riotous reception emerged in his harassment of the composer during 1914 in an effort to secure Stravinsky's collaboration in a new ballet, *David*. Cocteau's attempt to interest the composer in this aborted project can be traced in their correspondence.[12] By the summer of 1914 Cocteau had abandoned any hope of Stravinsky's participation; his communications with the composer were sufficiently annoying to provoke several letters of apology during 1915 and 1916 in an endeavor to reach a rapprochement, although their acquaintance had not been close enough to justify Cocteau's feeling that an artistic break had occurred. In 1915, possibly in a further effort to shore up the relationship, Cocteau wrote about Stravinsky as though he were the only composer worthy of attention and contrasted him with Schoenberg, even though it is highly doubtful that Cocteau had ever heard the latter's music.

Two figures rise up among composers: a Russian, Igor Stravinsky; an "Austro-German," Arnold Schoenberg.

The masterpiece of Stravinsky, *Le sacre du printemps*, appears now to those who were unsettled by it without snobbism or anti-snobbism, as a prelude to war. . . . Those who were at this spectacle, and whose emotions were isolated by the incomprehensible and completely natural uproar, will not forget that final scene, the polyphony of a factory machine which has gone out of order, where the young victim, offered to the earth, is consumed with horror and resignation. . . . Schoenberg fights against the old notes and, whereas the dispassionate lucidity helps Stravinsky to free himself from an oriental poetry, Schoenberg calculates, dislocates, and limits himself. He is angry with himself for liking *Tristan und Isolde*, he composes like a machine, he adjusts his spectacles like that of an intellectual and a "Herr Professor! . . . " Schoenberg, on account of his fear of the stereotyped, creates a new stereotype. In order to be free, he imprisons himself in formulas and what of the naive disciples he condemns to captivity!

Long live the healthy, rich, and youthful music of Stravinsky.[13]

Cocteau wrote about Stravinsky with unqualified adoration until he was intro-duced to Satie at the end of 1915 and secured his agreement to collaborate on *Parade* the following year.[14] The premiere of *Parade* in 1917 gave Cocteau exactly the scandal he wanted and its success, coupled with his new liaison with Satie, resulted in the viewpoint of *Le coq et l'arlequin*. Now Satie was the only composer of the moment, and Stravinsky was relegated to a lesser role.

> The profound originality of Satie provides young musicians with a teaching that does not imply the desertion of their own originality. Wagner, Stravinsky, and even Debussy are first-rate octopuses. Whoever goes near them is sore put to it to escape from their tentacles; Satie leaves a clear road open upon which everyone is free to leave *his* own imprint. . . . I consider *Le sacre du printemps* to be a masterpiece, but I discern in the atmosphere created by its produc-tion a religious complicity existing among the initiated, like the hypnotism of Bayreuth.[15]

Cocteau could not have calculated less complimentary pairings than Wagner and Stravinsky or Bayreuth and *Le sacre*.

It is with this background that Cocteau's description of Satie's *petite route classique* ought to be evaluated. His choice of the term "classic" may have been intended to provoke a response, in kind if not in size, that was reminiscent of the reaction to *Parade*. The pairing of the Satie of *Parade* and classicism might be reckoned to have a sensational impact upon readers in 1918. Although Satie's "new simplicity" was described by Cocteau in terms that were very similar to pre-war descriptions of French music, he continually emphasized that it owed nothing to a national tradition. Nostalgia for the past found a place in Cocteau's post-war world only when he became sufficiently aware that the artists he admired like Picasso and Stravinsky were able to be inspired by their predeces-sors without sacrificing their originality. Cocteau's *Plain-chant*, modeled on sixteenth-century French verse, and his adaptation of Sophocles' *Antigone* come from 1922, after Stravinsky's *Pulcinella* and *Mavra* and Picasso's numerous drawings and paintings with themes taken from the antiquities of Greece and Rome. Toward the end of his life, Cocteau continued to admit only Stravinsky and Picasso as the living artists whom he cherished. In a journal entitled *Le passé défini*, which he kept between 1951 and 1963, he wrote: "With Stravinsky, with Picasso, I feel comfortable. I feel at home with them."[16] The dependency of Cocteau's aesthetic upon his loyalties of the moment is underscored by the effusive praise he accorded Stravinsky in a lengthy addendum to *Le coq et l'arlequin* when it was reprinted under a new title, *Le rappel à l'ordre*, in 1926, just as Cocteau was writing the libretto for Stravinsky's *Oedipus Rex*. In 1918, however, Cocteau's emphasis was on Satie and the immediacy of art, rather than upon its heritage, and it was that angle which attracted attention to *Le coq*.[17]

The Breakdown of Pre-War Terminology

Although Cocteau's treatment of *classique* and *une nouveau simplicité* may have been prompted by a motivation other than aesthetic conviction, the appearance of such terms was not uncommon in the immediate post-war years. In 1921, the Italian ex-futurist artist Gino Severini published a treatise, *Du cubisme au classicisme*, in which he employed the term *nouveau classicisme* to describe a new trend in the visual arts. Severini characterized this tendency as based upon geometric principles of proportion, as opposed to what he considered the personal whim of impressionism and the experimental nature of cubism.

> The most intelligent of artists, however, are beginning to realize that it is not possible to construct something solid based on caprice, fantasy or good taste, and that, in sum, nothing good is possible without the School.
>
> One can begin to comprehend the pressing necessity in rebuilding the School, not an old School patched up and repainted with fresh Impressionist colors, like the *Ecole des beaux-arts*, but a *Building*, a monument that is completely new, from top to bottom, entirely generated by eternal laws of construction, which we rediscover at the foundation of art of all times, *those which do not prevent others from remaining different*. . . . One does not become classic by feeling, but by understanding; the work of art ought not to begin by a study of its *effect*, but by a study of the *cause*, and one does not *construct* without method, basing everything on the eyes and on good taste, or on vague general notions.
>
> I have the greatest respect and interest in the experiments which go on around me, and in which I participated with faith and enthusiasm for more than ten years. The discipline which they show constitutes already a step on the true path, and the tendency toward construction will state itself precisely without doubt on the day when artists will avail themselves more of measure and number. . . . I sincerely believe that cubism, constituting entirely the only interesting tendency from the point of view of discipline and method and, this being so, being the foundation for a new classicism which is in preparation, is nevertheless still today in the final stages of impressionism. And, it follows, one will effectively be able to surpass this intermediary period of art and construct truly according to the rules only when artists have absolute understanding of those rules: they will be in geometry and numbers, as will be shown in this account.[18]

Severini was careful to distinguish between the "dead formulas" taught by academies and the "eternal laws of construction," although he did not clarify the precise nature of the difference other than suggesting that art schools had succumbed to the fashion of teaching superficial methods of impressionist technique. Although clearly wrong about the end of cubism, Severini's treatise was reminiscent of Cocteau's *Le coq et l'arlequin* insofar as the former's "new classicism" and the latter's "classic route" might be similarly described as contrasting with their perception of impressionism as the prevalent *fin-de-siècle* artistic trend.

Similar in intent was Maurice Brillant's use of the term *nouveau classicisme* in an essay on contemporary art in 1921. The new classicism was a style which emphasized "great care of construction, a great austerity, and a sobriety pro-voked by renunciation of impressionist colors." Brillant found the tendency to "eliminate recent audacities" and to "stick to a highly respectable sobriety" to be common to all the arts. Musicians who were polytonalists and poets who were either anarchists or "neoclassicists" (by which he meant conservative, academic writers) were now calling themselves "classic."[19] The most important painter whom Brillant mentioned as a representative of *nouveau classicisme* was André Lhote. Perhaps it is no coincidence that when Cocteau was in Le Piquey, a village retreat on the bay of Biscay, during August 1917 (that is, between the first performance of *Parade* and the writing of *Le coq*), his only acquaintances were Lhote and Severini.

If the term *nouveau classicisme* was still laudatory in 1921, as late as 1922, *néoclassicisme* characterized a style with which artists did not want to be associated. Like Severini, the painter Giorgio de Chirico had sensed the need to draw back from the dream-like, visionary quality of his pre-1918 work and to achieve a "more solid" method. De Chirico's solution was to study Roman antiquities and Renaissance art treatises and paintings. In an open letter to the poet André Breton he emphasized that this connection to the past was not a matter of slavish imitation or of academic restoration. De Chirico's letter was precipitated by the controversy that his recent work was generating among the surrealists who considered his *Pittura metafisica* style one of the foundations for their movement and who, consequently, viewed his new allegiance to the past with alarm and derision.

Now it's necessary above all that I clarify one point for you: the point which has to do with my recent painting. I know that in France (and even here) there are people who say that I am making museum art, that I have lost my path, etc. This was fatal and I expected it. But I have an easy conscience and am full of inner joy, for I know that the value of what I am doing will appear sooner or later even to the most blind.

And now, my dear friend, I am going to speak to you about my present painting. You must have noticed that a while ago something in the arts changed; let us not speak of neoclassicism, revival, etc. There are some men, among them probably yourself, who, having arrived at a limit in their art, have asked themselves, where are we going? They have felt the need of a more solid base; they have renounced nothing. This magnificent romanticism which we have created, my dear friend, these dreams and visions which troubled us and which without control or suspicion we have put down on canvas and paper, all these worlds which we have painted, drawn, written and sung, and which are your poetry and that of Apollinaire and a few others, my paintings, those of Picasso, Derain and a few others—they are always there, my dear friend, and the last word has not been said about them. Posterity will judge them much better than our contemporaries and we can sleep peacefully. But a question, a problem, has tormented me for almost three years: the problem of *métier*. It's for that reason that I began to make copies in museums, that at Florence and Rome I spent entire days, summer and winter, studying and copying fourteenth- and fifteenth-century Italians. I dedicated myself to the reading of ancient treatises on painting and I have seen, yes I have seen at last, that terrible things go on today in painting and that if the painters continue on this route, we will approach the end.[20]

Here again is the disavowal of an artistic relationship to the immediate, pre-war period. Unlike the Cocteau of 1918 (though not the Cocteau of 1922) de Chirico found that the study of a remote tradition was a legitimate recourse for creative inspiration, although he was quick to distance himself from the term *néoclassicisme*.

Néoclassicisme suggested to de Chirico a quality of uninspired and banal imitation. For Georges Auric, in an essay appearing in the same month as de Chirico's letter, the term had an equally pejorative implication of "fatigued and impractical architectures." Auric disavowed any connection with the term.

> Nobody takes as seriously maintained certain declarations and certain manifestations of which the letter and the spirit are for us equally dead. We know that truth and intelligence cannot be among that which takes part in a certain form of art condemned by its very same principle. It is necessary that one knows that not one of us, I think, will agree to figure—even by means of some equivocation—among the defenders of neoclassicism.[21]

These quotations by de Chirico and Auric indicate that, as late as 1922, the term *néoclassicisme* still had a derogatory connotation for some, although it did not necessarily have the association with German music that was normal in French criticism before World War I. By contrast, the term *nouveau classicisme* had a laudatory meaning, even if it was not always specifically connected with a national tradition, as was usual before 1914. If the evidence suggests that the effect of World War I did not drastically and suddenly alter the use of this terminology, one cannot find an event or occasion by which the treatment of the term neoclassicism was irrevocably changed. By 1922 the use of the remote past as a model for contemporary art was rife, and between 1922 and 1923 the use of the term neoclassicism became smudged: while it was still used to indicate a link between present and past, that relationship was no longer necessarily negative.

Auric had insisted that he and his colleagues (by "we" he probably meant those composers known as *Les Six* since 1920) not be associated with the term neoclassicism insofar as it connoted a reversion to academic formulae. Yet scarcely weeks later, the music critic for *Le Figaro* identified these musicians as "reacting against the excess of misunderstood romanticism and against an amorphia which would risk their falling into musical impressionism whose most illustrious model is Debussy. Each of *Les Six* interprets in his own way this conception which could pass as a sort of neoclassicism, and no other artistic bond connects the adherents of the group."[22] Milhaud's music was singled out for its qualities of "construction, logic, and detachment," the kind of vague description that had long been used by French critics to characterize the new classicism. Of course, each critic did not read every review, nor did each one necessarily know what he was talking about. The appearance of *néoclassicisme* in connection with a group of composers scarcely a month after one of their number disavowed any relationship with that term, however, suggests that its use was becoming too capricious and erratic to permit its previous meaning to survive.

In 1923, the term neoclassicism appeared in several contexts that were not pejorative but were arguably whimsical. To that year belongs the publication of an anthology of art reproductions and criticism, *Le néoclassicisme dans l'art contemporain*. The essays were French translations of articles that had first appeared in the periodical *Valori plastici* between 1918 and 1921, and were devoted largely to the work of the newest generation of Italian painters, especially de Chirico and Carlo Carrà. The choice of the term neoclassicism for the collection is peculiar on a number of accounts. The term does not appear in any of the essays chosen for the 1923 volume, although it is used in other articles printed elsewhere in the periodical between 1920 and 1921.[23] Some articles contradict others in their evaluation of using the art of the remote past as models for contemporary painting. Alberto Savinio, de Chirico's brother and a composer as well as a painter, criticized the "fossilized academicism" of *le dernier classicisme*. Carrà, however, declared it necessary "to return to the Italian idea of the natural solidity of things," and he preferred "the return to the painting of the past" to the avant-garde trends of pre-war art.[24] The lack of any sustained consistency of thought in this anthology is due to the fact that both Carrà and de Chirico were undergoing a considerable change in their style and aesthetic during the precise years that *Valori plastici* was being printed. Savinio was describing the work of these painters from before 1919, when their art was dominated by hallucinatory and cryptic imagery that suggested anxiety, fear, and alienation.[25] By 1921, however, Carrà was following the lead of de Chirico, who had begun to use Italian Renaissance paintings and Roman antiquities as models for some of this work in 1919 and 1920, and who frequently wrote about his change of direction.[26] Thus the term neoclassicism, as it appeared in the title, *Le néoclassicisme dans l'art contemporain*, had no necessarily visible connection to the original articles that made up the collection, but it did have relevance to the most recent art of the painters who were discussed in its contents. Despite de Chirico's disavowal of the term neoclassicism in 1922 because he feared its retrogressive connotations, one year later it was associated with him in a positive sense via the anthology.

In that same year, 1923, Michel Georges-Michel, a writer, arts reviewer, and acquaintance of members of the *Ballets russes*, published an anecdotal history of the troupe. In it, he quoted Diaghilev's response to critics who were marking the end of cubism and futurism with his production of *Sleeping Beauty* in 1922: "But no, good heavens, one does not revive. . . . One evolves toward neoclassicism, as Picasso evolves toward Ingres. . . . My god, is it still necessary to explain such things?"[27] If this quotation is accurate, Diaghilev considered revival and evolution to be different. Although the distinction is not explicit, one possible interpretation is that, for Diaghilev, the former connoted a restoration or imitation of the past whereas the latter suggested the ability to interpret the past in a fresh light and so develop one's art into something new. The appearance of the term neoclassicism is surprising in this context for, prior to 1923, it would have been more common to associate it with revival in negative terms, whereas here its meaning is clearly laudatory.

Of further interest is that, for Diaghilev at least, the evolution toward neoclassicism was an obvious fact by 1923. That he should use as a metaphor the relationship of Ingres and Picasso is also noteworthy and requires some explanation. Nonabstract figuration had been abandoned by Picasso around 1907, but eight years later, he suddenly produced drawings of Max Jacob and Ambroise Vollard which are almost naturalistic in their realism.[28] A variety of non-abstract figural styles existed simultaneously with his more familiar cubism until 1924, when it disappeared from his paintings, although it occasionally resurfaced in his graphic work. Within this period a number of stimuli can be detected. Some group figures are indebted to sixteenth-century Italian mannerists, while others recall the antiquities he first viewed on a trip to Rome and Naples in February and March of 1917. These months were spent with members of Diaghilev's circle—Stravinsky, Cocteau, and Massine—and the nonabstract figuration of Picasso's drawings of them is jarring when compared to his cubist set and costume designs for *Parade* that same year. Another series of works appears to have been inspired by the frescoes of Fontainebleau, where Picasso spent the summer of 1921.[29]

Neoclassicism was a term rarely associated with Picasso between 1915 and 1924, but his connection with Ingres was observed often and usually by people who had their portraits drawn in a style that recalled Ingres. Stravinsky wrote to Ansermet on August 22, 1922, that Mozart was for him what Ingres was to Picasso; Cocteau wrote to Valentine Gross on May 1, 1916, that Picasso was "beginning an 'Ingres' head of me"; in an essay from the March 1915, issue of *Le petit messager des arts et des industries d'art*, Apollinaire quoted a letter from an anonymous correspondent that Picasso "has outdone Ingres in his admirable drawings without even trying"; and one year later, Picasso drew Apollinaire's portrait in his "Ingres" style.[30] A measure of the frequency of associating Picasso and Ingres is suggested by Arsène Alexandre's juxtaposition of the latter's *La source* with the former's *Femme nue vendue* of 1907 in *La renaissance de l'art français et des industries de luxe*, July 1921. Picasso's part-time adherence to nonabstract figuration was a powerful attraction to many. De Chirico's biographers generally agree that Picasso's example helped to stimulate him toward his own rediscovery of the past. Similarly, Apollinaire wrote to Picasso shortly before his death in 1918 that he was writing poetry that was "more in line with your own preoccupations of the moment. I am trying to renew my poetic tone but within the classical rhythm." So frequent was the connection between Picasso and Ingres that the relationship was even subject to satire, as in the case of Picabia's drawing, *La feuille de vigne*, of 1922.[31]

Although Picasso had begun non-abstract figural drawings in 1915, his attachment to the *Ballets russes* was surely a further incentive for developing that style, and Diaghilev would undoubtedly have been aware in 1923 that Picasso's intensified interest in the past and his professional liaison with the troupe were almost chronologically exact.[32] For Diaghilev to use the term neoclassicism in connection with Picasso may have been exceptional in 1923, but its appearance again suggests that, by 1923, the term had lost the derogatory connotation it once possessed.[33]

Having traced the evolution of the term neoclassicism in the half-dozen years after World War I, we may conclude that its meaning gradually changed. As public life achieved a degree of normalcy in the post-war years, many writers, painters, and composers were attracted toward the stabilizing reentry into the mainstream of European art and a nostalgia for the past which that return implied. Contemporary to that tendency, however, was a perception that an alliance with the past might compromise creativity and that it was wise to remain a cultural orphan. The tension between freedom and order in post-war art seemed to incite the desire for a terminology to explain it. In that atmosphere neoclassicism was transformed so that it might account for both innovation and tradition. The term enjoyed a renewed life beginning in 1923 because it was associated with Stravinsky for the first time in that year, and that relationship would prove decisive in securing a meaning for neoclassicism that was different from what it once had.

4

Neoclassicism and Stravinsky: 1914–1923

Introduction

In the first decade of the twentieth century the terms *nouveau classicisme* and *néoclassicisme,* each with its own separate meaning, became commonplace. A half-dozen years after World War I, the definitions of these expressions had become thoroughly indistinct. As the first writer to apply the term *néoclassicisme* to Stravinsky in 1923, Boris de Schloezer was constrained to admit that it had lost its original, pre-war meaning:

> Art is always in a condition of motion, a condition of becoming, its equilbrium is unstable, but in the case of music, such instability, such a *complexio oppositorum,* is never lasting. I envy those critics, those aestheticians who succeed in unraveling the dominant tendency, who foresee the direction to be taken, and who proclaim that we move undeniably toward a denuded, stripped-down style, whereas others announce to us no less categorically that we march toward a greater complexity. M. Wiéner is personally inclined toward Stravinsky and that which one would be able to call neoclassicism, if this term had not been distorted from its original meaning.[1]

This review of a concert organized by Jean Wiéner marks the first occasion on which the term neoclassicism was employed in a manner which matches current usage both in its characterization as a musical idiom and in affiliation with its most frequently cited practitioner, Stravinsky. The appearance of the article in February 1923, represents a fortuitous coincidence of a term which signifies a compositional style and the work which is most often regarded as the watershed for that style, Stravinsky's Octet, completed in May of the same year. Although Schloezer's usage of the word neoclassicism was a novelty in connection with Stravinsky, the author admitted that the term had existed previously with a different meaning. His explanation refers to the fact that, while *néoclassicisme* connoted an attachment to the past by the use of the surface design of eighteenth-century forms or melodic and rhythmic gestures, it was initially a pejorative term associated with German instrumental music, particularly that of

Brahms and Mahler, around 1900. Because that original definition had been corrupted, Schloezer may have permitted himself the liberty of employing it here.

The sixty-year association of the term neoclassicism with Stravinsky has produced a relationship that is convenient, if not indispensable, when considering the composer's music during the thirty-year period beginning after World War I. Scholars do not agree on which Stravinsky opus is most appropriate to label as his first neoclassic composition; the majority opinion is divided between *Pulcinella* and the Octet.[2] The expression, however, never appeared in reviews of the premieres of these works, and its attachment in 1923 to Stravinsky may have seemed random, occurring just at the moment when the terminology needed a composer of sufficient stature upon which it could be grafted in order to sustain its continued use. In hindsight, aspects of these compositions appear to be a gradual departure rather than a radical shift from Stravinsky's post-*Sacre* work. If there is a degree of stylistic continuity in the composer's music in the decade before the Octet, is there a similar thread to be gleaned from the aesthetic pronouncements which surrounded this repertoire, and in what ways were reactions to Stravinsky's major compositions joined to a neoclassic tendency before the term was specifically identified with him? An examination of the critical response to Stravinsky's works as well as the composer's own prose during the period 1914–23 (when the meaning of the term neoclassicism was transformed) can determine the link between his musical style and the aesthetic which attempted to define that style.

Regardless of which term was employed by the architects of the avant-garde during the decade between *Le sacre du printemps* and the Octet, the definitions for *nouveau classicisme* and *néoclassicisme* invariably contained a common vocabulary: abstract, absolute, architectural, pure, concise, direct, and objective. Opposed to these apparently sane and healthy tendencies were characteristics deemed more common to the pre-war era: illustrative, metaphysical, sentimental, symbolic, prolix, vague, and subjective. Stravinsky used this rhetoric as often as any of his contemporaries; its increasing frequency in his writings after *Le sacre du printemps* reflects his shifting personal allegiances as much as his gradually changing compositional style. Stravinsky's public and private opinions of the artistic scene in which he lived were also held by those with whom he shared that milieu; his language was theirs and it was easily accommodated to the term neoclassicism in 1923. Whereas the veracity of Stravinsky's prose can be tested against the research and analyses of the past sixty years, the question of the composer's motives is a more elusive problem to solve. If, as Robert Craft suggests, Stravinsky was becoming more preoccupied with aesthetics immediately after World War I, he was also becoming more adept at carefully stage-managing his own publicity.[3] Too, at times the line between personal artistic conviction and public stance is sometimes so fine as to be indistinguishable. Yet if some of Stravinsky's prose strikes us today as the product of a *poseur*, there is little to suggest that what he said was taken with anything other than absolute seriousness by his contemporaries. Where possible, the criteria for judging the degree of genuine feeling in the composer's public pronouncements rests with the corroborative detail which can be brought to bear by the reappearance of his statements in private correspondence and the consistency of a given statement at other times.

The critical response to Stravinsky's music in the decade before the Octet, as well as the composer's own prose, can be classified into four general topics: 1) simplicity—the reaction against obscurity, density, and size; 2) youth—the belief that spontaneity, freshness, and vigor could often be best characterized by evoking the childlike condition; 3) objectivity—the response to the notion that intensely personal utterances led to either distortion or rank sentimentality; 4) cultural elitism—the posture that the previous elements were all inherent in non-Germanic peoples. Each of these categories will be discussed in turn; their invocation by both the composer and his advocates appeared with each new work even before they coalesced under the single rubric of neoclassicism.

Simplicity—The Example of Satie

Possibly Stravinsky's earliest pronouncement which indicates his keen awareness of shifting tastes in European culture occurs in an interview with Carl Van Vechten before August 1915:

> I want to suggest neither situations nor emotions, but simply to manifest, to express them. I think there is in what are called "impressionist" methods a certain amount of hypocrisy, or at least a tendency towards vagueness and ambiguity. That I shun above all things, and that, perhaps, is the reason why my methods differ as much from those of the impressionists as they differ from academic conventional methods. Though I often find it extremely hard to do so, I always aim at straightforward expression in its simplest form. I have no use for "working-out" in dramatic or lyric music. The one essential thing is to feel and to convey one's feelings.[4]

Part of this statement might strike one today as confusing, inasmuch as the first and last sentences are equally applicable to musicians who were assumed to be remote from Stravinsky's aesthetic at the time.[5] The composer's espousal of an anti-impressionist method, however—his contrasting of "vagueness and ambiguity" with "straightforward expression in its simplest form"—became typical of the post-war period. Like Cocteau in *Le coq et l'arlequin*, Picasso was also fond of the term "simplicity" as a code word for the anti-romantic bias of avant-garde Paris, and Stravinsky similarly described *Mavra* to Ramuz on August 18, 1921, as "music [that] is *very simple*, even more so than that of *Histoire du soldat.*"[6] The composer's attitude was influenced in part by new friendships. More so than his acquaintance with Cocteau, whom he met in 1914 and quarreled with the following year, was the composer's liaison with Erik Satie.

Stravinsky was introduced to Satie by Debussy in 1910. By 1916 their friendship was close enough for Stravinsky to encourage Diaghilev to support Satie.[7] Satie dedicated to Stravinsky the third of his *Trois mélodies,* "Le chapelier," which he completed on April 14 of that year. Of their early encounters, Stravinsky recalled:

> He was certainly the oddest person I have ever known, but the most rare and consistently witty person, too. I had a great liking for him and he appreciated my friendliness, I think, and liked me in return. . . . He spoke very softly, hardly opening his mouth, but he delivered each word in an inimitable, precise way. His handwriting recalls his speech to me: it is exact, drawn. His manuscripts were like him also, which is to say as the French say, *"fin".* . . . I met him in 1913, I believe, at any rate I photographed him with Debussy in that year. Debussy introduced him to me and Debussy 'protected' and remained a good friend to him. In those early years he played many of his compositions for me at the piano.[8]

Sixteen sets of keyboard pieces, all written between 1912 and 1914, constitute the works by Satie which he likely played for Stravinsky. Shortly before his interview in 1915 Stravinsky composed the "Waltz" from the *Three Easy Pieces,* the manuscript dated March 6, and dedicated to Satie as "a souvenir of a visit to him in Paris" and intended "to portray something of his *esprit.*"[9] That Stravinsky should have chosen the idiom of waltz in order to pay homage to the French composer is not surprising, for that genre figures prominently among Satie's compositions during the period: the "Valse" from *Sept danses du "piège de Meduse"* (1913); "Españaña" (August 1913) from *Croquis et agaceries;* the "Valse du chocolat aux amandes" from the first set of *Enfantines* (October 1913); and especially the *Trois valses distinguées du précieux dégoûté* (July 1914). This latter work may have been intended as a satire of Ravel's *Valses nobles et sentimentales* (1911). In addition to the similarity of melodic rhythm between Ravel's second waltz and a passage from Satie's waltz, "Sa taille" (see ex. 4.1), the latter also imitated Ravel's penchant for preceding his music with a literary quotation.[10] Too, among Satie's characteristically humorous commentaries which underpin the music is the line from "Sa taille": Does he not possess a tender heart?," a description of Ravel attributed to the poet of *Shéhérazade,* Tristan Klingsor. Satie's shaky relationships with both Debussy as well as Ravel at this time and his growing friendship with Stravinsky may have encouraged the latter to write publicly about his aversion to impressionism. It is possibly not coincidental then that the friendship between Stravinsky and Debussy was strained at this same time. Robert Craft suggests that a letter from Debussy to Robert Godet on January 4, 1916, implies that the French composer was aware of Stravinsky's interview with Van Vechten. Stravinsky's criticism·of *Le mar-tyre de Saint Sébastien* in a letter to Diaghilev on November 16, 1916, was repeated to Debussy, and Cocteau's letter of August 11, 1916, encouraged the rift between the two composers.[11]

Stravinsky wrote or sketched eight waltzes within five years after his ac-quaintance with Satie, a frequency that is noticeable in comparison to the relative scarcity of waltzes in the pre-war ballets. The *Valse des fleurs*, is dated Septem-ber 30, 1914, two months after Satie's *Trois valses*. A fragment of one of three waltzes sketched in 1915–16 appears on a page with drafts for the *Valse des fleurs* and the Waltz from the *Three Easy Pieces* and, perhaps not coincidentally, it uses the same rhythmic idea as that in the examples by Ravel and Satie in example 4.2.[12] Such stylistic proximities suggest that Stravinsky's friendship with Satie encouraged the anti-academic, anti-impressionist stance of the former's interview in 1915, and that his fondness for "straightforward expression in its simplest form" was reminiscent of the tone which Satie himself would use in 1917 when he characterized *Socrate* "as white and pure as Antiquity."[13]

We have seen that Satie's *nouveau simplicité*—Cocteau's expression—had one important aesthetic difference that distinguished it from the *nouveau classi-cisme* of Ravel and Debussy, and attracted many among the Parisian avant-garde: Satie's "little classical path" did not lead back directly to the music of the French tradition of Rameau and Couperin. Nostalgia for the eighteenth century was an anathema to him, and he invariably couched his evocations of the past in ruth-lessly satiric terms. Satie's *Sonatine bureaucratique* (1917), for example, is a notorious burlesque of Clementi's Sonatina No. 1. In 1922, with the hearkening to tradition already common in French music, the composer wittily claimed: "I also want to pay my homage. . . . Debussy is taken, so are Couperin, Rameau, and Lully as well. . . . I want to compose a homage to Clapisson."[14] Satie was often described during the early 1920s with the vocabulary common to character-izations of the new classicism. Paul Landormy defined his music as "in sum, a very sober art, very stripped . . . a realist art, a simple art, a nude art." For Rollo Myers, Satie had attained "a classic elegance and purity of style." Charles Koechlin credited him with "the return to more civilized sentiments completed by returning to writing with more consistent purity." But it was not until after his death in 1925, at a time when neoclassicism had reached common currency, that that term was applied to him by H. H. Stuckenschmidt.[15] The absence in Satie's music of surface gestures or formal designs drawn from the eighteenth century is a significant distinction between his works and those of Debussy and Ravel from the war years. This difference may account for Satie's music being described as simple, pure, sober, and denuded, but not as neoclassic before 1925. Cocteau was probably the first to describe the difference between Satie and his French contemporaries thus:

Example 4.1. Twentieth-Century Waltzes

a. Igor Stravinsky, *Petrushka*, Third Tableau, "Waltz"

b. Maurice Ravel, *Valses nobles et sentimentales*, No. 4

c. Erik Satie, *Trois valses distinguées du précieux dégoûté*, "Sa taille"

d. Igor Stravinsky, *Three Easy Pieces*, "Waltz"

Example 4.2. "Easy Pieces" for Five Fingers

a. Florent Schmitt, *Sur cinq notes*, "Ronde"

b. Igor Stravinsky, *The Five Fingers*, "Allegretto"

To an epoch of refinement, only one opposition is possible: simplicity. Understand this; not a recollection, not a return to the old simplicities, not a pastiche of the *clavecinistes*. Satie furnished a new simplicity, upstart of all the refinements which preceded it. His music is finally a French music—a music so white, so delicate, that in hearing it one thinks of the phrase of Nietzsche: "The ideas which change the face of things come like the step of a dove."[16]

As will be seen later, similar language attended descriptions of Stravinsky's compositions before 1923. The view of Satie as standing apart from the French classical heritage may well have appealed to Stravinsky, who viewed himself as also removed from direct ties to the great historical traditions of German or French music, and is suggested by a letter from Robert Gaby to Stravinsky on April 19, 1929: "You were one of the first, perhaps *the* first— by the prestige of your authority—to draw attention to the essentially 'pure-music' quality of the music of Erik Satie."[17]

Youth—Children's Pieces

One manifestation of Stravinsky's claim to straightforward expression was the series of piano compositions of 1914–21 which were united by their evocation of childlike simplicity: Diaghilev's rudimentary piano technique triggered the creation of the *Three Easy Pieces*; the composer's children supplied the impulse for the *Five Easy Pieces*; and keyboard beginners in general furnished the motivation for *The Five Fingers*.[18] It could scarcely be coincidental that the contemporary French composers who were both Stravinsky's colleagues and personal friends had already established the child-inspired keyboard album for two or four hands as something approaching a cult, and which provided as potent an antidote to the hyperbolic musical excesses of the *fin de siècle* as those compositions inspired by a hallowed national tradition.

In his pioneering study on the origins of the avant-garde in France between 1885 and 1914, Roger Shattuck has described the impulse toward juvenalia as one of the fundamental characteristics of the era and a key legacy of an earlier period.

The first of these traits grew out of the cult of childhood established by the romantics. Wordsworth and Jean-Jacques Rousseau, Blake and Nerval reasserted the virtue and happiness of childhood as something inevitably stifled by education and society. Later generations began to perceive where the true challenge lay: in a revaluation of the very idea of maturity. Who is the complete man? There has been a series of answers, from the Greek devotee of *arête* to the Christian ascetic to the Renaissance courtier to the seventeenth-century *homme honnête*. In all of them, adult qualities of self-control preponderate over those of the child. But after romanticism, and starting long before Freud, a mood developed which reexamined with a child's candor our most basic values: beauty, morality, reason, learning, religion, law. With Rimbaud a new personage emerges: the "child-man," the grownup who has refrained from putting off childish things. Artists became increasingly willing to accept the child's wonder and spontaneity and destructiveness as not inferior to adulthood.[19]

This development of child-inspired literature is equally applicable to music. Although rudimentary keyboard pieces are almost as old as the piano itself, before the nineteenth century these works were either designed with an explicit pedagogical intent or more often were tailored for adult dilettantes.[20] As Shattuck has suggested, the artists of the romantic era were the first to offer the nostalgic evocation of the world of the child as a medium of artistic expression whose relative technical simplicity was equal in value to more labyrinthine keyboard compositions.[21] While youth-inspired piano compositions appeared among the *oeuvre* of Reger (*Aus der Jugendzeit*, 1895) and Bartók (*For Children*, 1909), during the *fin de siècle,* the repertoire was overwhelmingly dominated by French musicians. It is significant that the development of children's pieces among Parisian composers parallels exactly the revival of the French classical tradition. The earliest examples date from the post-Franco-Prussian War years and their number increases during the ensuing decades to include works by many of the major figures as well as several individuals of lesser stature. This immense popularity for the subject of childhood in French music in the dozen years beginning around 1907 is also mirrored in the country's arts and letters.[22]

Stravinsky's pre-war compositions attest to the important influence of contemporary French music.[23] Although Stravinsky's personal attachments to several of these musicians fluctuated at the time he was writing his keyboard works, his friendships are graphically revealed in the numerous exchanges of dedications between the composer and his French contemporaries.[24] Given Stravinsky's attraction to the novelty of French music early in his career and his friendship with the composers in Paris during his pre-war association with the *Ballets russes*, it would not be surprising to find him sympathetic to contemporary French music compatible with his own prevalent attitude.

The Waltz from *Three Easy Pieces* has already been cited as one possible instance of the relationship between Stravinsky and French piano literature whose technically simple musical material evokes a nostalgia for the world of the child. This rapport is more pronounced in *The Five Fingers*. Stravinsky's concept was "to confine each finger of the right hand to a single note and thus to limit myself to a five-note row."[25] It would be an extraordinary coincidence if the composer did not derive his idea and his title from Schmitt's *Sur cinq notes* (1907), also a set of eight pieces in which both hands of the *piano prima*, almost always doubling at the octave, are confined to a five-note diatonic collection in several transpositions. Although the fundamental concept may have been borrowed from Schmitt, the limitations of the correspondence between these two compositions are readily apparent when the rhythmic manipulation of these rudimentary scale patterns is compared. The first movement of each work is a brisk number in $\frac{2}{4}$ time utilizing a similar motive (see ex. 4.2). Schmitt's handling of the material is, without exception, restricted within regular four-bar phrasing.

Stravinsky, on the other hand, introduces a rhythmic ellipsis which upsets the sense of periodic uniformity and confounds the tonic–dominant implications of the F–C in the left hand.[26]

Stravinsky's fondness for eliding phrases, which in turn puts the harmonic direction askew, was characteristic of his treatment of ostensibly diatonic elements and was a compositional feature of his music that kept him distant from his French contemporaries. Among the latter, one popular gambit for communicating childlike simplicity was the repetition of the first five pitches of the C-major scale. The obvious pedagogical implication of this usage was exploited by Debussy in "Pour les 'cinq doigts' d'après Monsieur Czerny," the first of the *Douze études* (1915), which probably incited Casella to use a black-key distortion of the same pitch collection in his "Omaggio a Clementi" from the *Undice pezzi infantili* (1920). Whether or not these examples furnished Stravinsky with the idea to employ the same pattern in the "Allegro" of *The Five Fingers*, comparison of the three excerpts indicates that the asymmetric groupings brought about by eliding phrases were features not in evidence among his colleagues in Paris (see ex. 4.3).

Yet *The Five Fingers* is exceptional among Stravinsky's music at this time because several of the movements are composed of atypically regular four-measure phrases. In such places, Stravinsky appears closer to his contemporaries' children's pieces than at any other time. For example, the "Larghetto" employs the dotted rhythmic cliché of the sicilienne and the flatted leading tone contributes to a pseudo-antique effect. Modal and rhythmic similarities occur in siciliennes from two collections of juvenalia one year prior to Stravinsky's composition: Casella's *Undice pezzi infantili* and Koechlin's *Dix petites pièces faciles* (see ex. 4.4). Here Stravinsky is near to the French sensibility although the resemblance might still be fortuitous, since the composer had a recent familiarity with the sicilienne from the "Serenata" in *Pulcinella*.

Although Stravinsky's acquaintances with Casella, Debussy, and Schmitt might encourage a pursuit for similarities in their music, it is also possible that the relationships between Stravinsky's piano pieces for children and those of his contemporaries living in Paris constitute instances of inadvertent stylistic similarities that developed from a common milieu. As to models who may have consciously inspired the composer, Satie again is the most likely candidate. In October 1913, Satie wrote three sets of piano pieces whose titles (*Menus propos enfantins*, *Enfantillages pittoresques*, and *Peccadilles importunes*) emphasize their childlike qualities, and whose left and right hands are both limited to five white keys in various transpositions. The evidence that Stravinsky's earliest sketch of an easy piano piece dates from 1913, combined with the composer's recollection that Satie's piano music was the only contemporary French keyboard repertoire he remembered hearing, suggests that Satie's music provided the most immediate and possibly direct source for Stravinsky at the outset of World War I.

Example 4.3. "Easy Pieces" for Five Fingers

a. Claude Debussy, *Douze études*, "Pour les 'cinq doigts' d'après Monsieur Czerny"

b. Alfredo Casella, *Undice pezzi infantili*, "Omaggio a Clementi"

c. Igor Stravinsky, *The Five Fingers*, "Allegro"

Stravinsky's awareness of Satie's music, as well as his friendship with the French composer, stimulated a sympathy for the aesthetic of childlike simplicity which Cocteau was to make famous in *Le coq et l'arlequin* and which coincided with Stravinsky's anti-impressionist interview of 1915. In taking his stance, Stravinsky might well have been drawing a distinction between Satie and his musical contemporaries: unlike the works of other French composers, those of Satie which evoke a childlike aesthetic are not only typical of him, they constitute virtually his entire *oeuvre*. Similar works by other musicians in Paris were hardly their most famous or familiar utterances. If the image of Satie as a solitary figure in French music before World War I was established as a truism by Cocteau in 1918, Stravinsky in 1915 was canny enough to realize that the post-war era would not treat kindly compositions like *Le martyre de Saint Sébastien* or *La tragédie de Salomé*. He could have found it convenient to divorce himself from the impressionism of the composers of these works, and ally himself with the Satie aesthetic of childlike simplicity while overlooking the fact that the realization of this aesthetic was not the exclusive preserve of just this one composer.

Objectivity

Stravinsky's statement against impressionist and academic methods is his most quoted prose before his frequently repeated words on "expression" in his autobiography. Aside from the composer's music, the 1915 interview is probably responsible for his post-war defenders' frequent essays on the objective and absolute nature of his recent works. Scarcely one month after Stravinsky's interview with Van Vechten, there appeared in the *Music Courier*, an American weekly periodical, an article by Ernest Ansermet on the composer's recently premiered the *Three Pieces for String Quartet*. Ansermet had met the composer in 1911, and during the next twenty years he became one of Stravinsky's most intimate friends and trusted advocates. Ansermet was appointed principal conductor of the *Ballets russes* at Stravinsky's urging, and the *Three Pieces* is dedicated to him.

In his essay, Ansermet expanded upon the composer's interview, which eschewed academic and impressionist procedures. He concluded thus: "This music is absolute music in the true sense of the word, that is to say, music innocent of any and all suspicion of a literary or philosophic program."[27] The American patrons to whom this article may have been directed—who were likely to attend performances by the Flonzaley Quartet who had commissioned the work and toured with it during 1915—might well have accepted Ansermet's claim that the *Three Pieces* departed from pre-war tendencies toward programmatic expression. Stravinsky encouraged that view himself, inasmuch as a lecture by Ansermet on February 13, 1919, preceding a performance of the *Three*

Example 4.4. Twentieth-Century Interpretations of the Sicilienne

a.   Charles Koechlin, *Dix petites pièces faciles*, "Sicilienne"

b.   Alfredo Casella, *Undice pezzi infantili*, "Siciliana"

Pieces in London, stated that the composer "has affixed no programme or titles
to his pieces, and wishes them to be listened to abstractly."[28] The claim for
complete autonomy of musical construction in the *Three Pieces for String Quartet* was an act of subtle dissembling. Although Ansermet made it clear to his
readers that the work was the first composition since those of Stravinsky's
student years to appear without accompanying text or dramatic argument, he
failed to mention that the second movement was inspired by a performance of the
clown Little Tich in London, an event of which he was presumably aware.[29]

Yet if it is not true that the inspiration for the *Three Pieces* was exclusively
nonprogrammatic, Stravinsky certainly trusted Ansermet as a canny advocate of

c.   Igor Stravinsky, *The Five Fingers*, "Larghetto"

his works. Two months after the performance of the *Three Pieces* in London in
1919, the composer wrote to Ansermet on April 12, thanking him for his
"*general comprehension of contemporary music.*"[30] When Ansermet again conducted pieces by Stravinsky in London the following year, the composer wrote
the day after the performance: "I embrace you with all my heart for this concert,
and for your love of my music. After such presentations of my music, and with a
friend like you, one can do the most unbelievable things. You cannot imagine the
degree of joy that you have given me."[31] Two years later, in 1922, Stravinsky
recommended Ansermet to be the author of an article on him for the German
periodical *Melos* and the latter responded by reiterating the same sentiments that
he had stated in his 1915 article on the *Three Pieces*: "Stravinsky is simplifying
his style more and more, reducing it to the most common, direct, and frank
elements, recalling the most exceptional forms without losing any of the
new-found freshness in his manner of expression. He is beginning to use instruments as groups (*Pulcinella, Symphonies of Wind Instruments*) without returning
to the orchestral system."[32] In his earlier 1915 article, Ansermet likewise described the *Three Pieces* as "working out the acoustic possibilities of a certain
family of musical instruments." Stravinsky similarly stated in an interview with
The Observer on 21 July, 1921: "We have wind instruments, stringed
instruments, percussion instruments, and the human voice—there is our

material. From the actual use of these materials the form should arise."[33] Clearly composer and critic were espousing the same aesthetic positions for their American and English audiences.

The performance of Stravinsky's music in London in 1919 and 1920 also provided English critics with the opportunity to build upon the notion that Stravinsky was the standard-bearer of a new musical objectivity. Leigh Henry, a frequent supporter of the composer after the war, quoted the 1915 interview and concluded:

> He has methods, but no mannerisms—unless, indeed, an impatience with everything prolix and a persistant striving towards brevity, conciseness, and directness of musical expression, achieved by a ruthless repudiation of everything liable to obscure the central purport of his conceptions, may be termed such. All Stravinsky's musical characteristics are consequent upon his objective consciousness, which is concerned only with vital actualities and their adequate and precise incorporation into musical expression.[34]

Eugene Goossens, who conducted early performances in London of *Le sacre du printemps* and *Symphonies of Wind Instruments*, reiterated the composer's statement in a lecture on November 27, 1919, and characterized Stravinsky's recent music in much the same terms as did Henry.

> The main features of this newest path in musical expression, of which we cite Stravinsky as the shining example, are firstly, a forcible directness of both color and form; secondly, a rigid economy of means which eliminates all but essentials; and thirdly, a concise and intense objectiveness of emotion which relegates traditional practice and dull introspection to the background.[35]

Here were descriptions of Stravinsky which fit smoothly into the post-war artist's view of himself as a champion against the pernicious and characteristic utterances of nineteenth-century romanticism.

A performance of Stravinsky's chamber music under Ansermet's direction in London's Wigmore Hall on July 20, 1920, furnished Henry with another opportunity to wax rhapsodically over the composer's recent works.

> Among the many influences combining to produce the novel aspects of contemporary music, none has been greater than that exercised by the creative attitude apparent in the works of Igor Stravinsky. These works, in their earliest phase marked by the originality of personal idiom, have in their later development given this originality an unprecedented direction, conveying music into regions where entirely new musical possibilities are apparent, the perception of which has given rise to a new conception of both spiritual function and technical artifice in creative musical art. This may be said to be the objective conception of sound as an intrinsically expressive medium, apart from supplementary exploration, and approached without any pre-fixed theories or associations or abstract intellectual concepts. His mature work derives all its musical values and characteristics from a direct investigation of the *aural* nature of sound, as distinct from the mathematical, extramusical ideas. . . . Technically Stravinsky has effec-

tive personal methods, but conforms to no hard-and-fast system. His work comes as a sanitary infusion into an art which for generations has suffered from a species of theoretical red-tape-worm. The music of Stravinsky owes nothing to pedantic clichés of modulation or the ordinarily-accepted creeds of diatonic harmony and key-relationships. His treatment of harmonic succession, correspondence, and contrast, is based solely upon the affinity of chords, i.e. the aural relationship, or relativity of effect existing betwen any given combination of notes, enunciated together as compared with any other given combination; the academic classifications of chords, abstractly-mathematical and extra-musical, are negated by him.

In all essentials, however, his work is constructional, not refutal.

Stravinsky writes without metaphysical pre-occupations; he will never be guilty of the netal confusion which produces the "ballets philosophiques" so exciting to aspiring spinsters. No pseudo-intellectual effusion, no emotional hysteria, is ever discernible in his work. Clarity is its paramount feature: musical redundance and earnest platitudes of certain German classics has [*sic*] no part in it. The clarity and sanity of his objective mentality, source of that sense of humor so patent in much of his work, preserves him from the absurdities of unctuousness, of sententiousness, and the mystical *Schwämmerei* and pot-pourri cult of vogue-ideas which intrigue the suburban intelligensia.[36]

It is difficult to imagine that the author did not have his tongue in his cheek when denying any "pseudo-intellectual effusion," since that is an accurate description of his own prose. It also seems ironic that he should claim his idol's mentality as remote from the "vogue-ideas of the suburban intelligensia," since that audience constituted at least part of the group to which this essay was directed.

Not every critic was willing to make such impressive claims for Stravinsky's works. Ernest Newman, never the composer's ardent supporter, did not take kindly to the weighty language accorded to the performance:

We do not in the least mind little people taking little things very seriously. All we ask is that they shall do really well whatever it is they have themselves to do. Now the trouble with a good deal of this later Stravinsky music is that it is *not* particularly well done. There is nothing very difficult in all this; and to speak of it as if it were a revelation that only the chosen could understand is to rate the intelligence of the rest of us uncomplimentarily low.[37]

Stravinsky's advocates were quick to respond to Newman's challenge against the composer's recent works. Edwin Evans was especially prominent in the debate.

Nearly all the meanings, noble and other, which listeners read into a musical performance, are meanings with which the idiom had become charged, not by any individual composer, but by cumulative associations. Not until this crust is broken will it be possible to make music again as Scarlatti made it. That is the problem which confronts all these alleged musical iconoclasts.

Now, Stravinsky is the soul of clarity, and of artistic sanity. In fact he is one of the sanest people at present associated with music. His evolution has been consistently logical from the beginning.[38]

Ernest Newman was, in general, unsympathetic to contemporary music. For the vast majority of intellectuals and musicians who were advocates of modern composition, the rhetoric of Ansermet, Evans, and Henry was readily acceptable. Stravinsky himself also believed in his public image as the embodiment of objectivity or, at least, he was astute enough to encourage the notion. If Evans could claim in February 1921, that his evolution toward an abstract basis of composition was present as early as *Petrushka*,[39] Stravinsky could be confident five months later that his constituency would accept this notion for *The Firebird*.

> I have never tried, in my stage works, to make music illustrate the action, or the action the music; I have always endeavoured to find an architectural basis of connection. I produce 'music itself.' Whenever 'music itself' is not the aim, music suffers. . . . Understand that this idea which I have just expressed is not one which underlies merely my most recent music. I have always felt the same. I have never made 'applied music' of any kind. Even in the early days, in the 'Firebird,' I was concerned with a purely *musical* construction.[40]

Stravinsky's early ballets are not "purely musical constructions," being intimately bound up with the stage action. Yet the fact that Stravinsky should make this assertion at all suggests his confidence in the public's perception of him as the leading exponent of contemporary music. Too, his frequent repetition of this notion elsewhere suggests that he believed his development as a composer had proceeded without spasmodic change and that what his advocates said about him was warranted. Thus he could write to Ansermet on August 15, 1922, that he willingly believed statements that placed him at the forefront of modern music.[41] Further, a comparison of these contemporary reviews with modern analyses reveals a cogent analogy: just as the vocabulary used by critics to describe Stravinsky's music during the war would be appropriated wholesale into the definition of the term neoclassicism after 1923, so too would certain compositional features of these works presage the style of the pieces that would be considered typically neoclassic.

As one example, consider the first movement of the *Three Pieces for String Quartet*, described previously by Ansermet as "absolute music in the true sense of the word." In the first movement the initial interval of a minor ninth in the viola, C# –D, is given acoustic resonance by different instruments of the quartet (see ex. 4.5). The D is simultaneously held and plucked in the viola and is reinforced by its implication as the fifth degree following the diatonic tetrachord G–A–B–C in the melody line of the first violin. The C#, which moves to D# at measure three, becomes part of the bass ostinato Eb(D#)–Db (C#)–C in the cello and part of the descending modal (transposed dorian) tetrachord F#–E–D#–C# in the second violin. Thus two separate segments, one diatonic (G–A–B–C–D) and one octatonic (C–C#–D#–E–F#), vie for prominence. Each motive is repeated without any intervallic change. Because of their varying phrase lengths, however, a climax is achieved only six measures from the end when, for the first time, the initial pitch of the first violin melody begins along with the descending

Example 4.5. Igor Stravinsky, *Three Pieces for String Quartet,* First Movement, mm. 1–11, 42–48

figure of the second violin. These two pitches, along with those of the ostinati, form interlocking perfect fourths separated by a semitone: C#–D–F#–G. This confluence emphasizes the semitone C#–D which begins and ends the movement. Neither pitch anchors a stable harmonic element, yet from a purely acoustic sense, it is the C that achieves primacy, sounding as the highest and lowest pitch in the polyphonic strata and the only pitch common to both the octatonic and diatonic segments.[42]

Ansermet described the "severity" of Stravinsky's style in the *Three Pieces* in the following fashion:

> His harmonies are based on the affinity of chords, and constructed along the lines of what might be termed "chord polyphony." In the same manner his work shows a process of evolution as regards the element of tone color, disregarding established customs regulating the fusion of different tonal qualities, and seeking the true character and tone relationships of each individual timbre.[43]

This passage might be Ansermet's attempt to characterize the shifting priority between octatonic and diatonic collections. Credit must be given to him, however, for discerning the *Three Pieces* as a novel departure in Stravinsky's music, for the composer's use of confrontational diatonic and octatonic elements as structural determinants, especially in a very lean texture and with limited timbres, was not common in his music before World War I, but was a characteristic feature of his works in the 1920s. Too, just as Ansermet's description of Stravinsky's aesthetic as severe and absolute would be appropriated into descriptions of his neoclassic pieces, the conflict between octatonic and diatonic elements is also typical of those works, as in the opening "Waltz" from the Octet.

In like manner, Henry's description of the "relativity of effect existing between any given combination of notes, enunciated together as compared with any other given combination" could serve as the critic's flowery attempt to describe a stylistic feature such as that cited above, or one caused by the conflation of octatonic melody and diatonic harmony as in the "Polka" from the *Three Easy Pieces*. Stravinsky's pitch collection for the *piano prima* of the "Polka" is A–Bb–B–C–C#–Eb–E–F#–G. The collection has the interesting feature that, if the B natural is removed, the sequence now becomes a segment of the octatonic scale. This aspect suggests that the B♮ is a "foreign" element within the collection. Yet in the *piano prima*, the Bb , appearing only on the off-beat in measures 3 and 28 in relation to the rest of the melodic line consisting of E–G–A–B, is the "foreign" member, insofar as it is a dissonant tritone in relation to E (see ex. 4.6). The confusion of the priority of Bb–B is given another meaning by the ostinato of the *piano seconda* in Bb-major. But while the Bb and F on beats one and three give priority to the Bb of the melody, the interval D–F on beats two and four, though consistent with Bb-major, uses two pitches which

Example 4.6. Igor Stravinsky, *Three Easy Pieces*, "Polka"

do not appear at all in the original octatonic collection of the *piano prima*. Hence the collision of octatonic melody and diatonic harmony again foreshadows the opening measures of the "Waltz" from the Octet.

Henry's "relativity of effect" may also apply to another feature of Stravinsky's style which became frequent in works considered to be neoclassic in the twenties: the sense of imperiled tonality arising from interlocking major and minor thirds. In the "Waltz" from the *Three Easy Pieces,* the composer's choice of pitch collection in the *piano prima* is: (G)–A–Bb–B–C–D–E–F–F#–G–(A) (see ex. 4.1). When this collection is divided equally, with D common to both halves, each part becomes a diatonic collection, the two separated at the interval of a perfect fifth, with both the major and minor third: G–A–Bb–B–C–D/D–E–F–F#–G–A. The paradigm of interlocking major thirds, for example G–Bb–B–D, is one that becomes increasingly important for Stravinsky. The "Waltz" from *Histoire du soldat* utilizes a similar pattern transposed up a perfect fifth, and the harmonic structure of the *Symphony of Psalms* is based upon chords rooted on the pitches C–Eb–E–G.[44]

The collection in the *piano prima* would appear to assert G–D as the prime interval of stability. Yet the harmonic direction toward this interval is deflected by C major in the *piano seconda* in the pattern of I–vii–vii–I. Against this ostinato, the pitches B♭ and F♯ become dissonant members, yet their strategic placement as subdominant and leading tone alternately support F and G as stable points in the melody. Thus at the double bar, C exerts a simultaneous pull as both tonic and dominant, while at other points the cojoining sonorities of *prima* and *seconda* produce D–F–F♯, a chord with both minor and major thirds (measure 7). Although this sonority appeared occasionally in the composer's works before World War I (notably at points in *Le sacre du printemps*), its occurrence in such a lean textural context was a novelty in his harmonic language in 1915, and grew in importance during the 1920s and 1930s.[45] Compositional features such as the conflation of octatonic and diatonic elements, of major and minor thirds, and the intrusion of non-diatonic pitches into otherwise diatonic groups distinguished the music of Stravinsky's neoclassic period from his pre-war compositions.[46] The early appearances of these traits were attended by critical responses which characterized the music as objective, absolute, concise, and economic. These descriptions may have been often ineloquent, but they were also remarkably persistent. Just as these stylistic characteristics became commonplace in Stravinsky's music of the 1920s—the music that was dubbed neoclassic—so too did the rhetoric become standard for the aesthetic that was termed neoclassicism.

We may summarize by recalling that several of Stravinsky's works written shortly after *Le sacre du printemps*—the *Three Pieces for String Quartet* and the *Three Easy Pieces*—employed a musical vocabulary that foreshadowed his compositions of the 1920s, and the prose used by Stravinsky and his advocates to describe this music was appropriated a decade later to characterize, in part, the aesthetic of neoclassicism. There remained, however, an important difference between the instrumental works of 1914–15 and the neoclassic works of the 1920s. The latter employed the surface features of eighteenth-century forms, such as the sonata's tri-partite structure, or certain melodic or rhythmic clichés common to eighteenth-century dance types, whereas the former did not do so. The absence of such formal or gestural devices may account for the reason why neither *néoclassicisme* nor *nouveau classicisme* was associated with Stravinsky's works before the Octet. At the outset of World War I, these terms connoted some relationship with the music of the pre-nineteenth-century past. Even if that connection was evoked in arguably surface structural designs, the fact that they were lacking in the composer's works of the war years may have been sufficient reason for the inappropriateness of the expression neoclassicism.

The metaphors chosen by Stravinsky and his supporters to describe his post-*Sacre* style—simple, straightforward, objective, pure, and concise—might well have been for them the most understandable language they could offer the public. Whereas this vocabulary was appropriated to the term neoclassicism in the 1920s, that expression was anchored to a distant cultural tradition as well. This rhetoric was, however, also a commonplace in descriptions of avant-garde art immediately before and during the war years but which bore no relationship to the remote past. Cocteau's vision of Satie falls into this category as do descriptions of artists associated with cubism—Picasso, Braque, and Delaunay—and the poetry of Apollinaire and Cendrars. In *L'intérmediaire des chercheurs et des curieux*, 10 October 1912, Apollinaire characterized the paintings of Picasso and Braque as rendering "an essential reality with great purity, and that the accidental or anecdotal aspects of the subject had been eliminated." Delaunay was quoted by Apollinaire in a review of his one-man show that was published concurrently in *Der Sturm* and *Les soirées de Paris*, December 1912, that he was striving for "purity of means in painting, the clearest expression of beauty." In "La jolie russe" of 1918, the last of the *Calligrammes*, Apollinaire gave this self-evaluation: "Je juge cette longue querelle de la tradition et de l'invention/De l'Ordre et de l'Aventure."[47]

Roger Shattuck has described the French avant-garde at the war's outset in the following fashion:

> Whatever the virtues and vices, whatever the value may be of dream logic and abruptness and humor, a significant segment of the modern arts has been constructed by juxtaposition of mutually reacting units. They do not observe smooth transition through unified development. Conflict, as opposed to connection, produced a different strain of expression. . . . Painters, writers, and musicians learned how to arrange fragments of experience, how to "cut" in montage style, how to vivisect consciousness in order to reconstruct our "inner speech. . . . " The term juxtaposition, which has served till now, finally breaks down. The "nextness" which it connotes reveals itself as an inaccurate description of the structure of the arts. Juxtaposition implies succession, even if it is at random or provoked by conflict. Exactly here one can go astray. Had the montage form of art been concerned with a real succession of events, transitions would have been included rather than suppressed, for transitions supply the guided tour, an order of events. But since instead of transition we have contrast and conflict, the successive nature of these compositions cannot sustain itself. Ultimately it becomes apparent that the mutually conflicting elements of montage—be it movie or poem or painting—are to be conceived not successively but *simultaneously*, to converge in our minds as contemporaneous events. The conflict between them prevents us from fitting them smoothly end to end; what appeared an arbitrary juxtaposition of parts can now take its true shape of enforced *superposition*. . . . Simultanism evolved as both a logic (or an a-logic) and an artistic technique. It found a childlike directness of expression free of any conventional order. It reproduced the compression and condensation of mental processes. It maintained an immediacy of relationship between conscious and subconscious thought.[48]

"A childlike directness of expression free of any conventional order:" how close this statement sounds to Stravinsky's 1915 interview. Concision, simplicity, and purity constituted the critical baggage that accompanied the Parisian avant-garde but, as Shattuck points out, the new poetry and paintings deliberately avoided the transitions and connectives common to earlier classical art. Thus the paintings of Delaunay and Léger were built up from contrasts of blocks of color; the *papiers collés* of Braque and Picasso produced analogous contrasts using planes, lines, and textures; Cendrars composed stripped-down verse without metaphors; and

Picabia's art was replete with surprising word-games. Apollinaire quoted Delaunay's definition of simultaneity for his preface to the artist's Berlin exhibit: "contrasts of complementary colors used as a means of construction in order to arrive at pure expression." After viewing Delaunay's work, Paul Klee considered it "a type of picture which is sufficient unto itself and which, without borrowing from nature, uses planes and forms which lead an absolutely *abstract* existence." Likewise Léger wrote that "a painting should be built up from a series of deliberate contrasts of color and form."[49] *Titres* (July 1914), the sixteenth verse of Cendrars' *Dix-neuf poèmes élastiques* (1913–19), reads "Dépouillé/Premier poème sans métaphores/Sans images/Nouvelles/L'esprit nouveau." The title of a 1913 painting by Picabia, *Edtaonisl*, is a conflation of "étoile" and "dans." As though to sum up this post-war avant-garde aesthetic in 1918, the poet Pierre Reverdy wrote that

> the image is a pure creation of the mind. It is not born from a comparison but from a juxtaposition of two more or less distant realities. The more distant and true the relationship between the two realities, the stronger the image will be—the more emotional power and poetic reality it will have. The emotion thus provoked is poetically pure because it is born outside of all imitation, all evocation, all comparison. It is the surprise and the joy of finding oneself before a new thing. One can create . . . a powerful image, new to the mind, by bringing together two distant realities whose relationship the mind alone has grasped.[50]

Shattuck's description of the "enforced superposition" of elements and Reverdy's statement on "juxtaposition of distant realities" accurately characterize Stravinsky's treatment of diatonic and octatonic fragments in the analyses given previously. Was Stravinsky at all aware of the French avant-garde tendencies at the outset of the war? That he knew and was influenced by Satie has been established. Stravinsky attended simultanist functions with Ricciotto Canudo in 1912. In 1914 Canudo wrote of the composer that "he partakes of our aesthetic, of cubism, of synchronism, of the simultaneity of some and the nervous, matter of fact onyrhythm of others." Reviewing *Le rossignol* in 1914, Canudo related the composition to simultanism: "Just as a simultanist conceives for us the entire painting as a coloration of surface planes, and not as a visually pure and simple harmonization, so too does Stravinsky seem, in *Le rossignol*, to conceive of music as no longer the expression of a subject, as the aural evocation of a psychic or atmospheric state."[51] In 1914, Albert Gleizes painted a cubist portrait of the composer. Cendrars' admiration for Stravinsky dates from the premiere of *Le sacre*, and the two became good friends shortly after the war.[52]

Stravinsky's compositional style in the *Three Pieces for String Quartet* and the *Three Easy Pieces* of 1914–15 may well have arisen out of largely musical associations, but his budding awareness of the French avant-garde may provide the only explanation for the visual games he used to bring this music to score. In the *Three Pieces for String Quartet* he divided the viola into two staffs, creating a quartet that reads as five instruments even though it is easier to play the viola part from one line. In the *Three Easy Pieces*, he limited the *piano seconda* to one staff, making a duet for piano four hands that visually consisted of three lines, even though from the standpoint of technique it is more likely for the performer to use two hands. The visual puns of these examples have aesthetic premises in common with Apollinaire's verse which is shaped into real objects, Cendrars incorporation of newspaper headlines into his poetry, and Picabia's use of Latin dictionary phrases as titles for his watercolors. The effect is comparable to the introduction of fragments of newspaper and other objects in the *papiers collés* of Picasso and Braque. For the performer of these compositions by Stravinsky, the scores are fragmented or telescoped, suggesting more or fewer players than are actually heard. In contemporary collages, similar techniques of splintering or compression of an image or poetic line force the viewer to make multiple inter-pretations of the object.[53]

Our survey of contemporary appraisals of Stravinsky's music after *Le sacre du printemps* has demonstrated that the rhetoric of simplicity, childhood, and objectivity was a shared affinity with French modernist trends in music, literature, and the visual arts. We may, however, recognize another concurrent tendency which was also characterized by similar language of purity, concision, and naiveté: the influence of non-Western primitive cultures on the European avant-garde. In 1916, when Egon Wellesz observed that "the sudden and wide-spread interest in primitive music, in folk-music, and in the music of savage races seems to indicate that this new tendency has already received its theoretical foundation," he was stating an already obvious cliché. Virtually every French writer and artist already discussed here can also be mentioned in the context of "primitivism."[54]

Stravinsky, of course, had been party to the welding of folkorist and avant-garde tendencies in Russian art from the time he entered Diaghilev's circle. To retill familiar ground in detailing how Stravinsky's integration of these two traditions culminated in the unprecedented series of masterpieces of *Le sacre*, *Renard*, and *Les noces* would take us too far afield from our study.[55] We have introduced the importance of primitivist tendencies among avant-garde artists in order to show that, regardless of whether a French or Russian was making modernist noises during the war years, the rhetoric was strikingly similar. For example, the painter Mikhail Larionov, the soon-to-be designer of *Renard*, had been brought to Paris by Diaghilev for the opening night of *Le coq d'or* on May 14, 1914. One year earlier, Larionov had stated in his "rayonnist" manifesto that "the essence of painting is indicated in this—combination of colour, its saturation, the relationships of coloured masses, the intensity of surface working. . . . From here begins the creation of new forms, whose mean-ing and expression depend entirely on the degree of saturation of a colour-tone and the position in which it is placed in relation to other tones."[56] How similar this sounds to Stravinsky's admission to Romain Rolland on September 24, 1914: "[I like] to make sudden contrasts in music between the portrayal of one subject and another completely different and unexpected subject."[57] We have returned to the avant-garde language of juxtaposition and simultaneity so common in French modernist art circles. Indeed, it is not difficult to locate a nearly identical assertion from 1913 by a French artist, in this case Gleizes, who had painted the composer's portrait in 1914. As co-author with Jean Metzinger of *Cubism*, Gleizes defined modern painting in familiar terms:

> Form appears endowed with properties identical with those of color. It is tempered or augmented by contact with another form; it is destroyed or emphasized; it is multiplied or it disappears. . . . Some, and they are not the least intelligent, see the aim of our technique in the exclusive study of volumes. If they were to add that it suffices, surfaces being the limits of volumes and lines those of surfaces, to imitate a contour in order to represent a volume, we might agree with them. . . . The cubist painters. . . . achieve that superior disequilibrium without which we cannot conceive lyrical art.[58]

We may conclude from the above evidence that aspects of Stravinsky's musical style from the beginning of the war in part looked toward his works of the 1920s, and that the rhetoric used to describe some of his compositions from the war years was appropriated into the term neoclassicism in connection with those later pieces of the 1920s. That style, however, also echoed a great deal of avant-garde arts and letters around 1914. This art—often called *l'esprit nouveau*—had little or nothing to do with the nostalgia for the past, accounting for the absence of either *nouveau classicisme* or *néoclassicisme* in reference to Stravinsky's works of the war years.[59] Only when the composer's music took on obvious melodic, rhythmic, or structural gestures which evoked a pre-nineteenth-century tradition did it occur to critics to consider his music neoclassic.

In this light, it might appear puzzling that *Pulcinella*—which does not merely use eighteenth-century clichés but actually relies on music by Pergolesi and others—should not have been called neoclassic. Yet Stravinsky himself was probably responsible for this; rather than emphasizing that *Pulcinella* evoked a grand tradition or restored a great heritage—essential ingredients for the new classicism—he chose to emphasize its novelty. In one of his first attempts at a pseudo-technical explanation of his music, he made the following statement the day before the ballet's premiere:

> I told you several months ago that I was preparing a work 'in collaboration' with Pergolesi, which is *Pulcinella*. In Italian libraries, principally in Naples, I rediscovered pieces considered by Giambattista Pergolesi, and these are the themes which served as the frame for the score of my ballet. This is a new genre of music, a simple music with an orchestral conception different from my other works.

And this novelty consists of the following: musical 'effects' are ordinarily obtained by the juxtaposition of different degrees; a soft one succeeding a loud one produces an 'effect'. But this is the conventional and banal method.

I have tried to arrive at an even dynamic in the juxtaposition of instrumental timbres which have similar sounding levels. A color has value only by the relationship to other colors juxtaposed with it. A red has no value by itself, it acquires it only by its proximity to another red or a green, for example. This is what I wanted to do in music and which I try to obtain above all else; this is the quality of sound.

I also try to obtain verity in the disequilibrium of instruments against the grain of that which one does in what is called chamber music where the basis itself is a conventional equilibrium of different instruments.

And this is completely new; no one has ever attempted it in music. These are innovations which occasionally surprise. But little by little the ear becomes used to these effects which at first shock it. All this is a musical education to be undertaken.[60]

The composer's visual metaphor is worth noting. Surprise, disequilibrium, and juxtaposition—Stravinsky's description of *Pulcinella*—had been the central direction in French avant-garde arts and letters throughout the war. By 1920 the pattern of Stravinsky's friendships had changed from the pre-war years: instead of composers, he was now acquainted with painters and poets, including the elite of the Paris avant-garde such as Picasso, Braque, Delaunay, Cendrars, and Gleizes. The "colored volumes" defined by Delaunay or the stippling effects in Picasso's collages may have furnished Stravinsky with a cue for characterizing his use of timbres in *Pulcinella* in visual terms.[61]

An instance of the disequilibrium of timbre described by the composer occurs in the "Vivo" at rehearsal number 170 in the duet between trombone and double bass where, despite the fortissimo marking for both instruments, the latter is almost inaudible.[62] Similar effects involve the combination of wind and string harmonics. In the "Serenata" at rehearsal number 3 the solo flute's high C harmonic is to be fingered on the low F hole. The solo string quartet and the orchestral violas and celli have pizzicati harmonics, and the orchestral violins are marked *flautando*. On stage, Florindo and Coviello mime the playing of mandolin and guitar, while a tenor in the pit supplies the lyrics. In the "Andantino" at rehearsal number 35 solo flute and orchestral celli both have lines which alternate natural pitches with harmonics, but the alternation is staggered so that one line of harmonics and one line of natural pitches are formed from two instruments. The placement of voices in the orchestra pit made the juxtapositions visual as well as musical. In one sense the repositioning was made more logical acoustically because both voices and instruments emanated from the same source; on the other hand, the words were not coming from the on-stage characters who were supposed to be uttering them, thus causing the text to retain an independence from the action.

Stravinsky's emphasis in *Pulcinella* was not to use borrowed tunes to express his connection to a noble heritage or a great tradition, and in this respect it should not be surprising that no critic saw fit to call the ballet an example of *nouveau classicisme*. Favorable reviews of the ballet rather expressed delight in the surprise caused by the novel instrumental effects.

> In hearing *Pulcinella*, the public at the Opéra was able to ask itself, like the good Marinoni, whether Igor Stravinsky or Giambattista Pergolesi was more the author of its pleasure. I doubt that there exist in music better examples of so singular a collaboration, so fine a transmutation and, in a word, so perfectly successful a legerdemain. With the announcement of a ballet made from a series of variations on motives of Pergolesi, the most faithful admirers of M. Stravinsky were a little distressed, and many a dilettante, dissatisified by the astonishing *Chant du rossignol*, announced, in the language common to amateurs of art and to highwaymen, that he "expected M. Stravinsky's turn around."
>
> The dilettante can put away his blunderbuss and confess that he has had to deal with too powerful an opponent. The young master of *Renard* this time knew how to lead each one astray and to charm with ease even the most retarded of the opposition. It would be misrecognizing this marvelous acrobat in thinking that he could be satisfied by a gentle pastiche or, judging from his roguish grin at present, by too comfortable an anachronism. Be assured that Pergolesi has not been chosen by chance nor so paradoxically as that. Over a century of music, that is to say over the thick hedge of romanticism, the composer of *Le rossignol* could spread a brotherly and a little helpful hand to the composer of *Serva padrona* who, with less genius, possessed nevertheless an equal sense of concise musical expression stripped of parasitic ornaments. "I am the fiancé of Italian melody" Stravinsky confided to us one day; prophetic words: now the wedding is going to be celebrated.
>
> With an affectionate tyranny, our enchanter has seized the Italian nightingale and has enclosed it in a little box: he opens the door for it at times: without the mixture of a tenor, a bassoon or a contrabass emerges from it deliciously. Such freshness cannot be translated into words. The orchestra, reduced by several timbres, speaks with a luminous freedom, in a language as pure as one could wish for. One becomes astonished before the effects of the obliging magician who presides over the fusion of these two arts; doubtless Pergolesi had employed these instrumental sonorities and these limpid harmonies, but it is impossible to discover the moment where, by an imperceptible gradient—Marinoni, deliver me!—they bring us back to Stravinsky, and the dialogue begins again.[63]

Negative responses generally were prompted by the feeling that the old music had been vandalized by precisely these novel timbral effects and that, if a contemporary composer were to use such works, it should be in a straightforward orchestration in the manner of Tommasini's arrangement of *Les femmes de bonne humeur*.[64] The cry of sacrilege was answered by several critics who pointed out that, in 1920, such material could only be treated successfully with a degree of irony.

> M. de Diaghilef [*sic*] has already offered us *La boutique fantasque* based on little tunes of Rossini and *Les femmes de bonne humeur* based on the piano music of Scarlatti, orchestrated according to circumstance by a more modest arranger. According to the advice of Nietzsche, one may observe the ballet russe becoming a little mediterrianized. It had perhaps more flavour when it was more native. But this cosmopolitan *Pulcinella* is an entirely charming little thing. . . . The themes of the score are hence less from Pergolesi than by M. Stravinsky amusing himself by making a pastiche of the melodic style of the creator of comic opera. I do

not have the documents necessary to examine this question of authenticity, which after all matters rather little. One imagines indeed that M. Stravinsky would be capable of making a pastiche if he wanted to do so. In any case, the tragi-comic scene of the fake death of Pulcinella is of an eminently Pergolesian character.

One would not have to say so much about the major part of the orchestration, which is on the contrary essentially modernist and Stravinskian, filled with dissonances and amusing timbral games, which the author of *Serva padrona* never imagined and which would have dumb-founded him. Here we are a little better prepared, and the author of *Le sacre du printemps* has sometimes astonished us more: but we have taken a lively pleasure in this joyous and ingenious fantasy.

There is indeed not a good reason to be shocked by a lack of respect toward Pergolesi, who is not taboo, and who knew how to take a joke as a rule, if it is true that this without doubt would have disconcerted him at first: and the funny thing about the affair is precisely having him so modernized by dressing him up in so audacious a mask. We disguise ourselves, at a carnival, in the persons of old times: why not sometimes clothe the old masters in modern costume? It is the same procedure, and this little work of M. Stravinsky is exactly a masquerade, and one of the most witty.[65]

Indeed, the criteria for choosing the music, argued these critics, ought to lie in the success of the result and not in strict adherence to the model. Stravinsky's frequently quoted defense of his choice of Pergolesi—"you respect, but I love"—could have been lifted from an exchange between Diaghilev and a scandalized patron reported by the composer Reynaldo Hahn:

Refined men have always had the taste to discover in art the mysterious genealogies of concealed but evident relationships between the most contrary personalities, the most opposed by their tendencies, by their education, and which, as is common among mortals, do not seem to be united by any bond. In this little game, "intermediaries" are neglected, transitions are not recognized, two points widely distant from each other are indicated, and one exclaims: they are contiguous! Moreover, "advanced" artists of an epoch favor this innocent divertissement by professing it, usually (and this for very humanitarian reasons) a pure and unique love for those artists of the past who resemble them the least; immediately their admirers adhere to demonstrating that these innovators and these representatives of a remote time are born from the same source and animated by the same spirit. Thus it is that Debussy, having many times manifested his affection for Rameau, is decreed to have descended from him in a straight line. Similarly, Ravel is the immediate extension of the *clavecinistes!*

Now, behold that Stravinsky has composed a gracefully strange and seductive paraphrase on motives of Pergolesi. You will see that before long it will be established by ingenious arguments that *Petrushka* and *Amor fa l'uomo ceco* are the same things, that nothing is more reconciled than *Adriano in Seira* and *Chant du rossignol*, and that lastly *Oiseau de feu* is only a modern transposition of *Il prigionero superbo*. But we are still not at the stage of exegesis; it is only a question of admiration. I was seated here next to a very beautiful young woman who said all the time: "This is delightful!" She had never heard the music of Stravinsky, she ignored the name of Pergolesi, she was seeing the *Ballets russes* for the first time; and, in front of the knowingly unusual spectacle which unfolded before her, she swooned with ecstasy. Simple spirits and intact minds are lacking in very complicated artistic contrivances. As soon as one is no longer "completely new," as soon as one has memories, elements of comparison, points of trust, bases of appreciation, bewildered enthusiasm becomes more difficult. And, then, one becomes spoiled. In witnessing the charming ballet which M. Léonide Massine has taken from a Neapolitan comedy of the eighteenth century, and where one sees Polichinelles ridiculed by malicious young women and an amusing magician performing in a cubist decor by M. Picasso that one agrees to find very beautiful, but which appeared to have no relation with the very traditional costumes of the dancers, and which it is without doubt in the music where the skeleton is by Pergolesi and the covering by M. Stravinsky (unless this might be the contrary), I felt somewhat confused. But as I let myself become astonished how M. Stravinsky had changed, in the Stravinskian sense, and orchestrated the little melodies of Pergolesi with the inspired devilry of which he alone is capable, an eminent and charming woman reproached me to "respect" the old things instead of "loving" them, and my friend Diaghilev retorted that without *Pulcinella* all the pages of Pergolesi which had served M. Stravinsky would have remained unknown. I would have been able to respond to the former that there was a unique way of "loving" old things by changing the view of them, and to the latter that the first condition of observing in order to reveal unknown pages does not consist of presenting them inside out. But I said nothing at all, because we are alive to wishing that the atmosphere permits ever so little logic, and where "feeling" is everything. This being so, I hasten to say that M. Stravinsky has never shown more talent than in *Pulcinella*, nor a more certain taste for audacity. The genius of labor which he has delivered is indescribable: there is sometimes a dissection of chords where the natural and dissonant resonances of the fundamentals are emphasized; sometimes there is a false and savory harmonization, sometimes an arbitrary pedal whose tenacity ends by staggering the thing refused instinctively by the ear; what more can I say? a whole ensemble of artifice and *passez-musicale* whose secret he has. I cannot approve of the idea of M. Stravinsky. But it is impossible for me not to admire the manner in which he has realized it, and for me it is a true joy to declare passionately this new success, here, by this great musician.[66]

Six days later the anecdote had slipped into the parlance of Louis Laloy in his support of Stravinsky's treatment of his models.

The music calls for several observations. M. Stravinsky has in fact written this score after the melodies of Pergolesi which he has arranged as freely as if the matter were popular songs. One might ask oneself if he had the right to do so. Assuredly so. It is important not to impose upon the artist the obligations of the historian. That one would perpetrate a fraud and would be a forger, if he insinuated, into the text which he edits, a single word or note which was not by the author. The savants from beyond the Rhine, before the war, were rather inclined toward this deceit, and the most monumental of their editions are frequently false. But when it is a matter of performing an old work, an adaptation is always necessary, because the composition of the orchestra has changed and because our feelings toward the music are not the same. I am no more aware of what musician proposed to reorchestrate the symphonies of Beethoven. One cried sacrilege; however it will certainly come to this, in several years perhaps, in a half-century surely, in order to save them from discredit and oblivion. In art, there is no virtue, no obligation, no morality. The end justifies the means, and all attempts are legitimate, if they result in an interesting work.

Such is the case, without any doubt, with the music of *Pulcinella*, where a restricted orchestra bandies from solo to solo the melodies of Pergolesi, accompanied sometimes by chords reduced to their most simple expression or even indicated by allusion only, sometimes by obstinate rhythms which freely slip in dissonances underneath. Recognizable despite all their suave radiance, they are taken for themes of a burlesque symphony, and the irreverent ingenuity of the musician who utilizes them brings out the most poignant effects from them. To love, not to respect, such is the motto of the *Ballets russes*. A Frenchman could not disapprove of it.[67]

Given these responses, *néoclassicisme* and *nouveau classicisme* were inappropriate terms to characterize *Pulcinella*. For Stravinsky, the manipulation of borrowed tunes had more in common with contemporary avant-garde arts and letters than with the remote past. For critics, the effect of the composer's treatment was ironic, not nostalgic. An exact regurgitation of the music might be respectful, but it was also creatively barren. Pergolesi was Diaghilev's choice at any rate and the connectives to tradition were made by the impresario. For Stravinsky the old melodies were treated rather as "found objects" or as musical "facts" in the manner that Picasso and Braque manipulated the "real" objects—fragments of newspaper or music score—in their *papiers collés*. Indeed the numerous condensations, truncations, and interpolations of material in the ballet make it clear that Stravinsky was intent upon a complete "recomposition" of the borrowed music.[68]

Cultural Elitism

Stravinsky's anecdote that Diaghilev was nonplussed when he saw the composer's treatment of borrowed material in *Pulcinella* is acceptable to the extent that their statements at the time of the premiere corroborate different attitudes toward publicizing the event. Stravinsky's stress lay upon the novelty of the music whereas Diaghilev emphasized the ties to the past. The latter was responsible for directing Massine to the subject, for recognizing its appeal to both Stravinsky and Picasso, and for supplying the stimulating environment in which the collaboration took place. Too, Diaghilev, more so than the others, possessed the cultural sophistication that might connect a contemporary use of a commedia dell'arte subject with its rich historical legacy.[69] As has been already cited, the possibility of using eighteenth-century music for balletic treatment had been brought to Diaghilev's attention by Benois after the latter had heard a performance by the *Nouvelle société des instruments anciens* in 1909 (see pp. 22–23). A ballet based on the keyboard sonatas of Scarlatti had appealed to Diaghilev as early as 1913, and Massine recalled that in 1914 the impresario "mentioned several eighteenth-century Italian composers whose works he wanted to adapt for ballets."[70] By September 1919, Diaghilev's initiative had already realized productions with musical and textual sources similar to *Pulcinella*: *Les femmes de bonne humeur*, based on a play by Goldoni with Scarlatti's sonatas arranged by Tommasini; *La boutique fantasque*, suggested by the German ballet *Puppenfee* with music of Rossini orchestrated by Respighi; and a revival of Cimarosa's *opéra-bouffe*, *Le astuzie femminili*.

The point of contact that could assure the impresario that Stravinsky would be attracted to the *Pulcinella* project was that Pergolesi fit in with the cultural elitist notions that looked upon Germans as corrupt and decadent and Latin races as embodiments of sane artistic tendencies. As has been detailed earlier, France was the European country particularly rife with German musical xenophobia in the two decades preceding *Pulcinella*. Debussy accounted for perhaps the most notorious pre-war polemics, while Cocteau and Satie continued the rhetoric during the war. The futurists made anti-Teutonic nationalism part of the avant-garde artistic program in Italy as well. Marinetti's shout, "Down with Wagner, long live Stravinsky," was often reproduced after 1914.[71] Diaghilev seduced some of the press into believing that *Pulcinella* was a reaction against German music, and that the mixture of off-stage singing and ballet stemmed from the eighteenth-century French tradition.

> The singing will be mixed: from songs offstage, from distant choruses responding to gestures and dance steps, sometimes out of ridicule, sometimes on the contrary to oppose a sad compassion to it, for a more striking effect. Ballet with song was the predilection of our French eighteenth century. In fact, is there not in mute pantomime the double advantage of a more intelligible action and a more direct emotion? It is, by the most modern means, a return to this excellent tradition which happens to inspire Diaghilev's curiosity, always seeking unknown beauties, so well served by the clever fantasy and artistic invention of Massine.
>
> The composer is Pergolesi. The score has been taken almost entirely from an unpublished manuscript, conserved in Naples, by this master. Stravinsky, the magician of color and rhythm, has orchestrated or rather has interpreted the melodies of Pergolesi for a modern orchestra, in a manner which still shows a national and popular flavor. And this will be Pulcinella in a long smock and battered hat, a scintillating evocation of this Italy, mocking and passionate, of which the author of *Serva padrona* was the immortal poet.[72]

In addition to these elements—the connection of the ballet with the French eighteenth century and the "popular" nature of the musical and textual sources—a second press release the day before the premiere emphasized that *Pulcinella* marked a departure from the conventional romanticism of German music.

> The indefatigable curiosity of Diaghilev and the clever fantasy of Massine have arranged for us a new surprise: *Pulcinella*, which the *Ballets russes* will present on Saturday at the Opéra, is still a ballet, but a ballet mixed with song, according to the excellent tradition of the French eighteenth century which always associated singers and dancers.
>
> The composer is Pergolesi, the same Pergolesi whose *Serva padrona* presented at the same Opéra in 1752, provoked, after an unprecedented success, passionate debates. These were by the Philosophes who were then attempting to give life to dramatic music bloated by conventions, like a ray of light or a dazzling revelation.
>
> Today, it is against other conventions that one revolts on all sides, conventions no longer of nobility or grandeur, but the symbolism and metaphysics from the other side of the Rhine. Pergolesi, the pure musician, lays claim, counter to the one and the other, the sacred rights of the most independent melody. Stravinsky, one of the boldest liberators of modern music, has become his eloquent interpreter.
>
> The music of Pergolesi, gathered principally from a manuscript at Naples, has been transposed to a modern orchestra with care; the contemporary master of color and rhythm, hearing the ancient master of beautiful song, wanted to reveal still all that which he recognized in its tunes of a profound nationalism, representing as far as its popular source, without resorting however to other means than those of a voluntarily reduced orchestra or wind instruments playing frequent solos, from where are excluded—according to the exigency of style and to historic truth—romantic clarinets.[73]

This material suggests that Diaghilev sensed the aesthetic climate of post-war Paris in a manner that was not identical in all respects to that of Stravinsky. The combination of anti-romantic and anti-German rhetoric with an emphasis on the melodic tradition of Latin races was undoubtedly calculated to appeal to the French critics who were to review the premiere, and several did indeed accept Diaghilev's press accounts that the use of offstage voices was a conscious extension of an eighteenth-century French tradition.[74] Although the impresario was fond of the music of the nineteenth century, including Wagner, his personal taste was not about to interfere with the practical exigencies of promoting new works favorable to audiences in Paris and London. After 1910, no *Ballets russes* production utilized nineteenth-century German music. Too, during May and June of 1919, Diaghilev carried on a public debate with Ernest Newman in the pages of the London *Observer* in which the former attacked the music of Beethoven and Brahms and the latter rose to their defense.[75]

Stravinsky's taste in German music was considerably less catholic than that of Diaghilev. The composer had been bored by *Parsifal* on August 20, 1912, when he saw it at Bayreuth with Diaghilev. He loathed Mahler's Eighth Symphony when he heard it in Zurich in 1913 and gave his reaction in a letter to Maurice Delage on December 15. Conversely, after he heard *Pierrot lunaire* on December 8, 1912, in Berlin with its composer, he reported his fondness for the work to V. G. Karatygin on December 13 and to Florent Schmitt on January 22. He heard *Elektra* on February 7, 1913, in London and wrote with enthusiasm about it to M. O. Steinberg on March 2.[76] With the declaration of war in August 1914, however, Stravinsky's opinion toward Germany atrophied considerably. He wrote to Léon Bakst on September 20, "My hatred of Germans grows not by the day but by the hour." On October 11, 1915, he wrote to Debussy that the Germans were cold-bloodedly aiming at the destruction of the morale of the Allies. While in Rome in 1917 with Diaghilev and Picasso, he was quoted as criticizing Beethoven and Wagner.[77] About May of the same year, he wrote in a sketchbook:

> The soul of Latins is closer to us Slavs than the soul of Anglo-Saxons, not to mention the Germans, those human caricatures. The Germans are *wunderkind*, but they were never young. The Germans are *überwunderkind*, since they will never be old either. This is not true of Spain. She is very moving in her old age. And will France really be deprived of the twilight *she* deserves, and deserves more than any other country?[78]

The desire to stitch together diverse cultures into a single nationalist fabric was a common ploy in anti-German rhetoric; even before World War I it had been a popular theme attending the appearance of the term *nouveau classicisme*. Stravinsky merely stretched an already questionable analogy further so that it could include his own background. In this light we might view the question of ethnic priority of Stravinsky's allegiances during the war years as secondary; the musical politics of avant-garde France and neoprimitivist Russia could accommodate one another to the extent that they were cultural light years re-moved from the German tradition. Too, the resilience of the bonds which Stra-vinsky found between his sources remained subject to circumstance. A trip to Spain during May and June 1916, stimulated his flirtation with that country's dance types in the "Española" from the *Five Easy Pieces* and the "Marche royale" in *Histoire du soldat*. Four years after he equated Spain with Russia in his 1917 sketchbook, a performance of *Cuadro flamenco* by the *Ballets russes* supplied the opportunity for him to contribute a *feuilleton* in which he made the same comparison:

> Spain in the *Ballets russes*? Why? I am asked this question, and it is easy for me to answer that for a long time we have studied and admired so many of the original manifestations of Spain's national life. It is therefore entirely natural that we look to it for inspiration and to carry away with us, I might say, a piece of Spain. The thing is to choose that which is transportable. There are certain wines which must be consumed on the spot and others which bear up under travel.
>
> It is not solely a matter of curiosity. Between the popular music of Spain, especially Andalusian music, and that of Russia, I perceive a profound affinity which is, without a doubt, related to their common eastern origins. Certain Andalusian songs remind me of the melodies from our Russian provinces, awakening atavistic memories in me. The Andalusians have nothing Latin in their music. They owe their sense of rhythm to their eastern heritage.
>
> Rhythm is very different from meter. With meter, 4 is always equal to 4. Rhythm poses still another question: what is the number 4, that which results from $3 + 1$, or that which results from $2 + 2$.
>
> Another characteristic of this popular art is the extreme precision, even in details which appear accidental: a quarter note is always the same quarter note; a rhythm which seems to sag does not, however, it resumes its steadiness at the same moment when we believe it to have vanished.
>
> There is nothing of that passionate improvisation which, for example, we ascribe to whirling dervishes. Never improvisation: but an art that is very contrived, very minute, very logical in its manner and coldly calculated. I would say almost a classic art, whose dogmas are different from our schools but no less rigorous. In a word, an art of composition.[79]

Stravinsky's characterization of rhythm is arguably applicable to those instances of rhythmic elision in his works of the war years. Too, the vocabulary that accompanies the composer's juxtaposition of Spain and Russia is familiar: rigor, logic, and precision. This rhetoric, however, is carried to almost absurd lengths: in 1917 Stravinsky could claim brotherhood between his native country and "the soul of Latins." In 1921, Russia and Spain were compatible owing to their "having nothing Latin in their music." Stravinsky's comparisons of Spain with Russia make sense in the context of his strong anti-German feelings.[80] Indeed, if the composer opened himself to a bewildering variety of musical influences during the war, the German heritage remained virtually the only one kept at a constant and remote distance.

Having passed part of the spring of 1917 in Italy with Diaghilev, Picasso, and Massine, and being preoccupied with "the soul of Latins" in the sketchbook of May of that same year, it seems natural that, in 1919, Stravinsky should be enthusiastic about collaborating with these artists on a ballet based on the music of Pergolesi. The choice of Picasso as a collaborator brought a reinforcement to the Russian-Spanish connection. Setting the ballet in Naples—the most Spanish-oriented city in Italy with a Spanish viceroy of long standing—further strengthened this bond. The composer's new attachment to the eighteenth-century Neapolitan was strong enough for him to fabricate the story that his fondness had driven him to unearth the music himself.

> I am preparing, for the month of May, another ballet which will be staged at the Opéra during the next *saison russe*: *Pulcinella*, a work in collaboration with Massine and Picasso. The music will be by "Stravinsky-Pergolesi." I composed this score, in fact, on unpublished themes of Pergolesi. It is more than an adaptation, it is entirely a musical recomposition. When I was in Italy, I searched the libraries with Diaghilev and we discovered many unpublished and unknown themes that were very interesting. I used these for my new score.[81]

This tale, however, was not repeated in the pre-performance news releases to the press, where Diaghilev's "curiosity" received credit for the discovery of the Neapolitan manuscripts.

For Paris and London audiences, the stimuli for Stravinsky's work through 1920 accommodated every country save Germany. Diaghilev's staging of *Sleeping Beauty* provided the opportunity for Stravinsky to add Tchaikovsky to his pantheon. In an open letter to the impresario on October 1, 1921, the composer reworked almost every element of what could be termed the party line of the post-war Parisian avant-garde: simplicity, spontaneity, naiveté, melody, and the "Latin-slavic" cultural *snobisme* that could accommodate Couperin, Glinka, Bizet, and Tchaikovsky.[82] Similar themes run through Stravinsky's correspondence at the time. In a letter to Ramuz, October 30, 1921, the composer wrote that the performance of *Sleeping Beauty* gave him "great pleasure, as did the music, which is extraordinarily fresh." Bakst recalled a recent visit to Stravinsky's studio where, amidst a bizarre collection of sirens, gongs, drums, and pipes, the composer played *Sleeping Beauty* in its entirety and then cried out: "There, by god, there is good music! . . . Listen to this adagio—ha, ha! . . . and those pauses, pauses dictated by the ear of a musician and not by the head of a ham!"[83] Stravinsky had recourse to again invoke Tchaikovsky at the expense of German music scarcely a year after his first open letter to Diaghilev, this time in anticipation of the premiere of *Mavra*:

> Tchaikovsky has been reproached for being German. What rot! Is he being confused perchance with the great pianist Anton Rubinstein? Is not Tchaikovsky above all a melodist, which is not the case with the Germans, who confuse melody with theme? And is his melody not essentially more Russian than the waltzes from *Sadko* or *Shéhérazade*? He has been reproached for being vulgar. It seems to me that vulgarity has no place in him. Now the art of Tchaikovsky, being without pretense, cannot fall into this defect.[84]

Critical response to *Mavra* was in fact divided precisely over whether or not there was any "melody" in the opera. Emile Vuillermoz's review may have had particular resonance for Stravinsky, because Darius Milhaud recalled that the composer pasted it on the cover of the manuscript.[85]

> Are these not strange times that we live in? What ironic fate compels us to judge Wagner on the same day that we are obliged to deplore the present orientation of Stravinsky? Why this malicious "back-step" to explore the times? As in *Renard*, Stravinsky wanted be amusing. *Mavra* is a parody of the lyric ideal of the second Empire, of *bel canto*, of duets, of roulades and of cavatinas. The esteemed author of *Le sacre du printemps* pours forth humor. In my humble opinion, he takes a false route.
>
> This man of genuis is not merry. He has nothing of the entertainer in him. His caricature is clumsy and forced. The libretto to *Mavra*, in which a hussar of chromolithography disguises himself as a cook in order to woo his beloved, is lackluster. And the music is of a weight and volume that carries the "burden" of all the ironic charm. An interminable and monotonous rag-time accompaniment blackens the whole score without gaiety. And this dangerous venture is made to appear as some singularly instructive truths in the most unexpected manner. One notices, at first, that Italian music cannot be parodied as easily as one might think. And then it proves that Stravinsky, whose rhythmic genius is prodigious, is terribly lacking in melodic invention. His preceding works gave us presentiments of him, but this does not leave us in any more doubt. When will this great musician cease giving himself up to useless jokes too? He still has such lovely things to say to us! We have clowns for "laughter and social amusement." They are sufficient and *Mavra*, which is assuredly not a masterpiece of old Russian gaiety, is certainly not one of old French gaiety![86]

Satie, Poulenc, and Auric quickly came to the composer's defense. Ansermet's review was typical of Stravinsky's advocates who declared *Mavra* to have a melodic and harmonic clarity that was unlike the composer's pre-war music.

> Further on, as if driven by the need of presenting more clearly the spirit of his music, Stravinsky simplifies his style more and more, reduces it to the most common, direct and frank elements, applies the least exceptional forms, without however losing in any way the freshness of his means of expression. And he returns to tonality, or rather he is no more in need of being atonal, his tonality no longer impeding the free play of polyphony. From all sides he cuts down his means, because he finds a new wealth in poverty. In the opera *Mavra*, the starting point of a new period, the music has made itself free from all hindrances, from everything which could cause deception, and here a musical nature manifests its character in naked truth.[87]

To the cultural melange of Spanish popular music, Pergolesi, and Tchaikovsky, the composer added Mozart, tying all these sources together under the elusive rubric of "melody." Stravinsky contrasted Mozart as the eighteenth-century Catholic Austrian with Wagner as the nineteenth-century German romantic.

> There is no musical form in Wagner: he reduces such form to the servitude of the text, whereas this ought to be the other way around. By his continual concessions to myth, he is led to have recourse to eternally modulating machinery, by which his form stays together.

Wagner understood admirably all the wind instruments, and knew how to command these ensembles with a mastery worthy of our best conductors of military fanfares. In order to attain the sublime, the need for which was created by his arrogance and vanity, he associated with the winds and brass, an army of strings which he thus detoured from their true tonal destination. It is so true that Mozart, the one whom I consider as the greatest musician of the world, as the most harmonious orchestrator that we have ever had, always avoided stumbling into this error, because he prevented bad effects.

In sum, Wagner was only a bluffer. His "divine inspiration" was only an assemblage of rather overused tricks familiar to initiates.[88]

Just as Stravinsky could find it easy to portray Wagner as the German composer burdened by bloated orchestras and philosophical pretensions to his Paris audiences, so too could he accuse Beethoven of similar faults in comparison with Mozart for London readers.

This brings us to the question of extra-musical emotion. For instance, Beethoven's works are never purely musical in their construction; his form is always dialectic, influenced by the philosophical constructions of Hegel. Wagner commits the same sin, influenced for his part by Schopenhauer, and so with all the Germans. . . . Mozart was not a German. We are talking of Bonn, Berlin, and Hamburg—not of Vienna.[89]

In 1917, at a dinner conversation with Picasso and Diaghilev, Stravinsky was purported to have said of Beethoven: "He remains German, without spontaneity. We on the whole still exalt above all Mozart and the first Italian composers because they are spontaneous like the primitives in painting. Spontaneity, there is the only truth in art. And for myself, I invent anew and am only spontaneous in my unconscious."[90] Stravinsky included Mozart in his list of great melodists in his first open letter to Diaghilev. At the Salzburg International Festival in 1922, when Stravinsky's *Piano-Rag Music* was added at the last minute only owing to the insistence of Jean Wiéner and Poulenc, the composer wrote to Ansermet on August 22: "Here I am, forty years old, and ignored in the grand prizes of the 'Great International Congress' of Salzburg—the capital of Mozart, who is for me what Raphael was for Ingres and is for Picasso."[91]

To split geographical hairs between Austria and Germany leads one to wonder how these statements could be taken seriously. Yet such rankings of German composers were nothing new to Paris. The one ingredient that made these divisions appear believable was that nineteenth-century German romantics had absolutely no place in the health of post-war French aesthetics. This concept cannot be dismissed lightly, for the essential anti-nineteenth-century German posture of neoclassicism in the 1920s was fundamental to the perception of a wrenching dichotomy in modern music. Just as Stravinsky was presenting Mozart and Tchaikovsky as his idols in 1921 and 1922, the music of Schoenberg was being heard in Paris for the first time. Invariably critics placed him as the most extreme of *fin-de-siècle* German romantics and, at the same time, provided that key bias that the term neoclassicism would have one year later: France vs. Germany, classic vs. romantic, Stravinsky vs. Schoenberg.

Darius Milhaud was one of the more dispassionate observers of the contemporary scene; he conducted the Paris premiere of *Pierrot lunaire* in 1922. In 1923, the year in which the term neoclassicism was first linked to Stravinsky, Milhaud gave the following assessment of modern music:

> There has always been, I could almost say a physiological difference determining, in art, conflicts or rather parallel ways in which one is necessarily thrown, which is no more a matter of choice than to be fair or dark, or to have blue or black eyes. This difference has always been a historic fact between the Latins and the Teutons. . . . We in Europe are actually in front of two absolutely opposed currents. The two currents I am alluding to are the school of Paris and the school of Vienna. The musicians of France and those of Austria have been isolated by the Great War; six years without any possible contact, during which the new tendencies of music have taken root on both sides. When the barrier was removed, new powers stood opposed, each ignorant of the other, or, at best, of slight acquaintance with that for which the other stood. . . . For the line of French musicians of which I am a member, or a disciple (I mean Rameau, Berlioz, Bizet, Chabrier, Satie) who really represent, I believe the purer heart of our national modern tradition, melody is the element that binds together these names. Diatonicism and chromaticism are the two poles of musical expression. One can say that the Latins are diatonic and the Teutons chromatic. Here are to be found two different points; they are entirely opposed and their consequences are verified by history.[92]

History hardly verifies such pure categories as Milhaud allowed. In a milieu in which such essays were typical, however, Stravinsky was often the beneficiary of descriptions which juxtaposed "diatonic Latins" and "chromatic Teutons." The composer's own taste in music of the post-war period suggests that he shared contemporary French attitudes of cultural elitism. On November 17, 1922, he wrote to Georges Auric:

> I've seen Satie and Poulenc in Paris on several occasions. The latter has composed two sonatas. One for horn, trumpet, and trombone and the other for clarinet and bassoon. Both are very well written and seem to me very significant in the sense that both are visibly free from those "modern prejudices" of which you tell me. I greatly loved the music of these two sonatas, very fresh music in which Poulenc's originality manifests itself like nothing else in his other compositions. In sum this music is very, very French. . . .[93]

Several months earlier, on August 14, Stravinsky made clear to Ansermet that the music of the Schoenberg circle was not at all to his liking.

> I was unable to go to Salzburg, due to expenses and work. I have an enormous amount of work, fall programs, solos, etc. I have received a score from a young gentile German, full of talent, named Paul Hindemith. It is curious to see "atonality" so prevalent. In the main, it duplicates Honegger. But justly, these people continue to put old music into another harmonic system and with a somewhat trimmed orchestra. Why do you wish that they understand *Mavra*, which has

everything which they do not even suspect exists, and which has nothing of that which they seek—or at least that which is fitting for them to take in. This Hindemith is a sort of German Prokofiev, infinitely more sympathetic than all the others under Schoenberg.[94]

When the composer journeyed to Weimar in 1923 to see the staging of *Histoire du soldat* at the Bauhaus, he also heard Hindemith's *Das Marienleben* and Busoni's *Fünf kurze Stücke zur Pflege des polyphonischen Spiels*, and considered the former boring and liked the latter. On September 1, he confessed to Ansermet: "I saw with my own eyes the enormous abyss that separates me from this country and from the inhabitants of the whole of Middle Europe. The *Kubismus* there is stronger than ever and, absurdly, it moves arm in arm with the *Impressionismus* of Schoenberg." Stravinsky told Ramuz on December 22, 1923: "In short, I do not give a damn about Berlin or other cities in the Reich, the Empire, the Kaiserthum. I care as little about the Germans in their misery as in their prosperity; what pleased me is not this single triumph [*Histoire du soldat*] but the continuing series of triumphs of which this last is only one further confirmation."[95]

When Stravinsky wrote these letters, he had heard only *Pierrot lunaire* in 1912 at its Berlin premiere. Ten years had considerably cooled his esteem for the work inasmuch as he associated it with impressionism, a derogatory term for him by 1924. It is possible that, given his very limited first-hand knowledge of music of the Schoenberg circle, his private opinion was equally due to post-war anti-German sentiment. Too, given the large amount of publicity that heralded the Paris premieres of several works by Schoenberg at this time, Stravinsky may have begun to perceive that here was a composer whose work might rival his own in public attention.[96] With these first French performances of Schoenberg's music, critical opinion began to place the Austrian's name in tandem with Stravinsky. Invariably *Pierrot lunaire* was viewed as the legatee of the German romantic tradition to which the Russian's compositions were totally foreign:

Other musicians in their respective countries have followed a path parallel to that which Schoenberg indicated. Stravinsky has even benefited from a popularity greater than that of the Austrian composer, at the moment when *Le sacre du printemps* designated him as the symbol of the new aesthetic. Certainly Stravinsky showed us the marvels of a sparkling musical vocabulary. However, the spirit of his music, the great popular breath which animates it, maintained the composer gloriously in the tradition of the "Five" from which he strayed by the greatest of harmonic and rhythmic liberties. Stravinsky is perhaps more profoundly original in *Petrushka*, a marvelous equilibrium between thought and style, than in *Le sacre* where the musical neologisms seem sometimes out of his element and do not always appear to accord with the object which they envelop.

This slight contradiction is not to be found in the most recent works of Schoenberg, notably in *Pierrot lunaire*. Here the music, ruled by a sensibility and a spirit which lend mutual support to each other, reflects a strong and lively unity. The musical language is justly appropriate to the impression the composer wishes to suggest and to evoke for the listener. The novelties of style, the bold confusions of melodic lines which, by their collisions, provoke redoubtable conflicts of pitches, incorporate themselves magisterially into the whole. The astonishing variety of procedures at work in *Pierrot lunaire*, the art of opposing them, the general romantic sentiment of the work, all contribute to letting in the spirit of that which one hears, the impression of a perfect equilibrium and of a striking harmony.[97]

French contributors to German periodicals generally echoed this view: the subjective, romantic Schoenberg was placed in contrast to the post-war objective, classic Stravinsky:

> Moreover we know here in France very little of the music of Schoenberg up until now, here the majority of his works were never performed in Paris; some few were introduced publicly under pretty bad conditions, so that the critic was obliged in most cases to restrain himself from reading the unknown works. I admit frankly that under these conditions many pages of Schoenberg's method have remained thoroughly impenetrable to me. Unquestionably it seems to me in any case that Schoenberg is of enduring importance to German music, above all through his expression and his intensified lyricism. He is just as romantic as Beethoven, Wagner or Brahms and reveals in his works in innermost soul.
>
> Therein he stands in absolute contrast to artists like Stravinsky or Prokofiev, who disavow every sentimentality, every possibility of expression, who do not want music to be a confession, but "objective" art, as they say, or as one says for them.
>
> Schoenberg is a romantic; our young composers are classic.[98]

Schoenberg's music was known in England shortly before these Paris performances, and there judgment of Stravinsky and Schoenberg was made on the basis of the critics' sympathy for the former. Ernest Newman, hardly a Stravinskyan, found him to be "in comparison with such a man as Schoenberg, almost comically simple. Schoenberg does at all events vary his expression, and keeps working his harmonies out with a sort of dogged logic over several pages at a time. The latest Stravinsky thinks only in snippets, and repeats the same childish devices till we are weary of them." By contrast, Edwin Evans wrote that "already people are discovering that what was wrong with Schoenberg was only the Teutonic lack of clarity, which persisted into his newer mode of expression. Now, Stravinsky is the soul of clarity, and of artistic sanity. In fact he is one of the sanest people at present associated with music. His evolution has been consistently logical from the beginning, and, though it has been rapid, it had included no leaps such as that taken by Schoenberg."[99]

So much attention was paid to Schoenberg's music that, shortly before the premiere of *Mavra* on June 3, one critic referred to the sometimes caustic debate over the Austrian as "le cas Schoenberg." Even so staunch a Stravinsky advocate as Ansermet suggested that the Russian composer, although now embarked upon a path different from that of Schoenberg, may have been inspired by his older predecessor.[100] Given the increased attention paid to Schoenberg in the French press, and given Stravinsky's increased preoccupation with his own position of leadership in avant-garde musical circles, he might well have begun to view Schoenberg as a competitor. This attitude in turn may have exacerbated his distaste for German music in general and that of the Schoenberg circle in particular. The composer's anti-German posture may even have induced his uncharacteristically tight-lipped and patently untrue response about his music to the German periodical *Musikblätter des Anbruch*:

> I have always refused to pronounce publicly to everybody either about the music of others or of myself. Putting aside the question of the music of others, which does not interest me at the moment, I'll give you the reasons for my refusal to speak about my own music. I have always thought that the only thing by which a composer can viably satisfy his public is indeed by his music and not by his music accompanied by explanations, however useful they may seem to him; and if he does not succeed in it today, then he is not excluded from succeeding in it later. The history of music (and of art in general) teaches this to us with particular eloquence. I have even had occasion to prove the truth of this affirmation several times and by my own works. I can cite as an example the well-known case of *Le sacre du printemps*.[101]

Stravinsky had, of course, been giving lengthy interviews about his music to English and French journals since *Le sacre*.

5

Neoclassicism and Stravinsky: 1923–1927

Critical Responses: Octet, Piano Concerto, and Sonata

The decade of the 1920s, during which the term neoclassicism and Stravinsky were united, encouraged a view of artistic creativity that was underlaid by a strident nationalism. Neoclassicism was easiest to identify when it was expressed in cultural values: simplicity, objectivity, purity, and clarity were transformed from vague rhetoric to quantifiable attributes. Whatever pejorative meaning the term may have had before World War I, it was lost in post-war polemics which sought to knit an arguably elusive terminology and individual works of Stravinsky into a single, unified aesthetic fabric.

In February 1923 Boris de Schloezer introduced the term neoclassicism in connection with Stravinsky for the first time. His essay reinforced the idea that had surfaced the previous year: the composer's music was diametrically opposed to that of Schoenberg.

The concerts organized by Jean Wiéner and which are entering into the second year of their existence, are certainly in the avant-garde of the Parisian musical movement. The latest performances to which we were invited by M. Wiéner, an intelligent and energetic organizer, an enthusiastic artist, and a precise and refined pianist, have caused us to notice once more the diversity and opposition of new tendencies in the presence of which each one aspires to reign alone to the exclusion of all others. Art is always in a condition of motion, a condition of becoming, its equilibrium is unstable, but in the case of music, such instability, such a *complexio oppositorum* is never lasting. I envy those critics, those aestheticians who succeed in unraveling the dominant tendency, who foresee the direction to be taken, and who proclaim that we move undeniably toward a denuded, stripped-down style, whereas others announce to us no less categorically that we march toward a greater complexity. M. Wiéner is personally inclined toward Stravinsky and that which one would be able to call neoclassicism, if this term had not been distorted from its original meaning; but the programs of these concerts reflect a very eclectic choice within the limits of modern art. Thus it is that we have heard in the interval of two weeks Schoenberg and Webern on the one hand, and Stravinsky, Satie, and Poulenc on the other hand. Arnold Schoenberg and Igor Stravinsky! These two names incarnate, it seems to me, the two poles of modern music (this adjective taken in the most highly precise sense). A third name perhaps will surface which will come to decide between them; but acutally it is their combined and *diverging* action which determines the character and the general development of modern music. I certainly simplify things and schematicize somewhat in leaving out the very powerful activity of Ravel and, in Russia, preponderantly that of Scriabin, but I venture to believe, however, that the activity of the majority of young composers is actually the result of these two forces—Schoenberg-Stravinsky—acting in an inverse sense. I have heard *Pierrot lunaire* again for the fourth time, admirably interpreted by Mme. Marya Freund and the orchestra under the direction of Darius Milhaud, and I have been newly turned upside down by the novelty of musical means, by the strength of expression of this work, totally repellant in its expressionist aesthetic, in its infra- or ultra-musical conception. *Pierrot lunaire* realizes musically a conception, a group of ideas, of images which are outside of music.

Schoenberg retains on one of these sides Mahler, more distantly Brahms; but his art is in its essence Tristanesque, romantic (the same as that of Scriabin). This Wagnerian spirit also is clear through the exquisite *Five Pieces for String Quartet* of Webern (a pupil of Schoenberg). The same has been said of these *Five Pieces* as that of the pieces for piano of Schoenberg; that these were only sound experiences, laboratory experiments. Experiences, perhaps, but psychological experiences, not sound experiences. It is a matter of forging a new musical implement, perfecting the sound language which sets about pouring out emotions, transporting feelings. The music of Schoenberg, a direct function of his psychology, never attains absolute autonomy; moreover it does not even tend there.

With Stravinsky, we are at the antipode of this expressionist aesthetic. Stravinsky is the most anti-Wagnerian of musicians; he realizes the most forceful reaction against "Tristan" which has ever been accomplished. His *Symphonies for Wind Instruments* (dedicated to the memory of Debussy), which Ansermet came to direct at the Concerts Wiéner, is convincing on this account; this genial work is only a system of sounds, which follow one another and group themselves according to purely musical affinities; the thought of the artist places itself only in the musical plan without ever setting foot in the domain of psychology. Emotions, feelings, desires, aspirations—this is the terrain from which he has pushed his work. The art of Stravinsky is nevertheless strongly expressive; he moves us profoundly and his perception is never formularized; but there is one specific emotion, a musical emotion. This art does not pursue feeling or emotion; but it attains grace infallibly by its force and by its perfection.

In the face of the neo-romanticism of Schoenberg, Stravinsky reestablishes the ancient classical, pre-Beethovenian tradition. It is this tradition also to which Poulenc tries to attach himself, the charming art of whom is full of promise (we have heard from Wiéner the two sonatas for winds).[1]

Schloezer's attitude toward Stravinsky was not always so euphoric; as noted earlier he was disappointed by *Mavra*.[2] In no previous article, however, was the idea of two irreconcilably different composers so categorically stated: Schoenberg the expressionist, whose works sprang from a deeply personal and not altogether healthy emotion; and Stravinsky, the neoclassicist, whose anti-Wagnerian music was pure, graceful, and even sanitary by comparison. Too, Schloezer's essay soon attracted attention. André Coeuroy reproduced a portion of it under the heading "Le couple Schoenberg-Stravinsky" in *La revue musicale*.[3] Auric, in specific reference to it, affirmed that "it would be truly foolish to have set aside Wagner in order to embrace the romantic Schoenberg. The good lesson of Stravinsky, for those who know how to listen to him, is that he impels us, more strongly than any other, toward a path which, at all times, was our own."[4]

Schloezer took up the theme of neoclassicism and Stravinsky again in August in connection with the composer's influence on Milhaud, Poulenc, Auric, and Tailleferre.

> [In Milhaud's *Etudes symphoniques*] there are pages which take up Bach and also Stravinsky, and which realize that conception of music which one could call "neoclassic" and which is certainly one of the dominant forces of the moment as much in music as in poetry. Pure music, stripped of all psychological meaning; the sentiments, emotions, and desires, which are at the root of all artistic creation and which try to exteriorize themselves and to manifest themselves freely, are here enclosed in a rigorous form which subdues them, purifies them, and gives them an exclusively resonant existence. This ideal of pure musicality is more difficult to attain in a lyric and dramatic work such as the cantata *L'enfant prodigue* (at the Concerts Wiéner). Milhaud was not successful there; but this failure presents more interest from the musical point of view; it is more fecund than many successes obtained according to formulas already experimented and consecrated.
>
> The two sonatas for clarinet and for bassoon of Poulenc are also connected to this neoclassic aesthetic; but I prefer by far to these pleasing pastiches seasoned by unexpected harmonic and rhythmic effects, the delicious *Promenades* for piano which was performed brilliantly at one of the last concerts of *La revue musicale* by Arthur Rubinstein. With Georges Auric (*Sonatine* for piano) we are witness to the search for a melodically simple and naive style where Igor Stravinsky and the masters of the eighteenth century or indeed even the sentimental romantics of the past century are incorporated as in the majority of neoclassic works or those which claim to be so. This proclaims to us probably the approaching renaissance of Italian and French melodists: Bellini, Verdi, Gounod. . . . who knows, perhaps even Massenet, if fashion and snobbism have a hand in it. The same process, because it is already unfortunately a process, is very cleverly employed in the *Marchand d'oiseaux* of Germaine Tailleferre (by the *Ballets suédois*), which presents to us the rhythmic and melodic style of Scarlatti charmingly in the style of today, according to the model given by Stravinsky in his *Pulcinella* (Pergolesi).[5]

Schloezer's definition of neoclassicism was nothing new: a rigor, simplicity, and purity that was foreign to the nineteenth-century German tradition. It was also common to portray Stravinsky as the most important influence on young French composers, so much so that it occasionally worried critics preoccupied with a specifically French identity.[6]

The premiere of the Octet on October 18, 1923, confirmed for its listeners the main tendency in modern music in general and in that by Stravinsky in particular. Whereas *classique* and *le nouveau classicisme* appeared often in reviews of the work, the term *néoclassicisme* was absent. Despite the connection of neoclassicism with Stravinsky just months before the premiere of the Octet, and despite the nearly identical description of both the term and the work, the expression neoclassicism in 1923 still had not acquired the specific lingering resonance which made its association with Stravinsky lasting. It was only one of many code words circulating in French intellectual circles that sought to define post-war avant-garde tendencies. By 1923 *néoclassicisme* was one of a half dozen slogans—including *nouveau classicisme*, *classique*, *objectivisme*, *réalisme*, and *style dépouillé*—that were characterized by the same familiar terminology.

Schloezer was perhaps the most likely candidate to use the term neoclassicism in connection with the Octet inasmuch as it was part of his rhetoric in 1923. When he wrote his review of the Octet his description of Stravinsky's aesthetic had not changed, but the terms he choose to define it were different.

> After *Pulcinella*, which is only a game, a pastiche, but a pastiche of genius, which could only be realized with success by the one who wrote *Le sacre*; after *Histoire du soldat*, this instrumental tour-de-force which is also and justly so a poignant drama, we have the *Concertino*, the *Symphonies of Wind Instruments*, and the Octet, all works which appear to us as an organic, natural synthesis of many different elements, such as Bach and the eighteenth-century masters, sentimental or playful romance of the past era, and the rhythmic frenzy of negro-american music. This synthesis, this is our new classic style, otherwise called objective.
>
> In designating this particularity or this tendency of modern music which I call objectivism, Ernest Ansermet employed the term, "realism." But it seems to me that this word lends itself to equivocating and suggests, in any case, the idea, evidently false, but difficult to make clear, of a certain reproduction or representation of objective reality. Now when we oppose romanticism to classicism, we oppose two methods of creation or of different aesthetic organization; one, subjective, which consists of the artist constructing his work in a direct function of his state of consciousness which this work is destined to express; the other, objective, which consists of attributing to a work of art an absolute and completely autonomous existence in only causing to intervene in its structure purely formal considerations.[7]

For Schloezer, any number of expressions could serve as the rubric under which he might describe the Octet. Other listeners chose different terms; *nouveau classicisme* satisfied Roland-Manuel:

> In the course of the last few years we have seen Stravinsky detach himself little by little from the ballet. Eliminating anecdotal and picturesque elements from his sources of inspiration, he reached *Les noces*—which indeed proceeds from the cantata—beyond which there is no possibility other than pure music, denuded of all the illusions of poetry, all plays of color. Without a balance, on the tightrope of the new classicism, Stravinsky pursues his perilous path under the expressionless eye of the critic, despite the adjurations of several frightened old friends.
>
> The Octet for wind instruments is assuredly the most precious fruit that this discipline has given him up to the present. The Octet consists of three parts: "Sinfonia," "Theme and Variations," and "Finale." Flute, clarinet, two bassoons, two trumpets and two trombones are the instruments of this marvel. The mere choice of these instruments indicates the difficulty of the attempt. The acrobat must juggle on his rope with ball, chair and iron. He lacks nothing, and the prowess shows so little effort that we soon cease to pay attention to it. Something else attracts us. This is the same structure of the work of art which affirms an evolution whose origins one might discover in *Pulcinella*, the little ballet which appeared in 1920 under the false semblance of a pastiche, a valuable lesson which young French musicians have not turned to mediocre account; far from it. After the formidable juxtapositions of *Le sacre* and the subtle mosaic of *Le rossignol*, Stravinsky's evolution is brought back to linear construction and to thematic development. But the game which was played not long ago under the aegis of Pergolesi, now is pursed by the invocation of Bach. It could no longer be a question of a pastiche in kind. No whim, no arbitrariness has dictated this new devotion: a musician who has

no longer any concern other than technique, and who accords to metier alone the right to resolve all difficulties of the aesthetic, must certainly encounter old Bach on his route, the old Bach for whom inspiration was always to align a robust set of counterpoints.[8]

Although the specific "isms" chosen by reviewers of the Octet appear random, words such as "contrapuntal" and "linear" surfaced with relative consistency. For Roland-Manuel, Stravinsky's polyphony was simple because it was not chromatic. Counterpoint resulted from the unexpected superimposition of "wrong" pitches, intervals, or chords.[9] Nadia Boulanger had much the same response:

> Under the attentive and willful direction of the composer, the Octet was given its premiere. In this work, Stravinsky appears in the light of the constructivist, of geometry; all of his thought is translated into precise, simple, and classic lines; and the sovereign certainty of his writing, always renewed, here takes on in its dryness and precision an authority without artifice.
>
> No transpositions, all is pure music, and one thought is disengaged from the work born through the unfolding of the lines and their design. Values are brought into equilibrium, plans are disentangled, sonorities opposed and blended; this is what a reading will make most easily understandable. The score of the Octet is among those which furnish the satisfaction of the spirit and the eyes which recognize the passions of counterpoint, for those who love to reread the old masters of the Renaissance and Johann Sebastian Bach.[10]

Boulanger's opinion was generally shared by French composers like Auric and Milhaud, although the Octet also came in for its share of negative criticism.[11] Reviews of the Octet were not the first ones to dub Stravinsky's music as objective, constructivist, architectural, and so on. The Octet rather furnished critics with an easy confirmation of the central direction in modern music. All that the rhetoric lacked was a single term whose appearance would symbolize that tendency. In 1923, neoclassicism was one of several expressions that served this function.

Stravinsky seemed be sympathetic to this view of his music to judge by his contemporary public pronouncements. In the December 1923 issue of *La revue musicale*, devoted entirely to the composer, he was quoted as saying: "My work is architectonic and not anecdotal; an objective, not a descriptive construction." One month later he told a Belgian interviewer of his passion for counterpoint: "It is the architectural base of all music, regulating and guiding all composition. Without counterpoint, melody loses its consistency and rhythm." That same month there appeared in *The Arts* Stravinsky's essay, "Some Ideas about my Octuor." This frequently reproduced article need not be quoted here in its entirety.[12] It is sufficient to observe that the composer's observations about his most recent work shared a common vocabulary with those critics who might be considered his advocates. Thus, for example, Stravinsky's statement—"My Octuor is not an 'emotive' work but a musical composition based on objective elements which are sufficient in themselves"—essentially repeats Schloezer's conclusion that the Octet led "an absolute and completely autonomous existence in only causing purely formal considerations to intervene in its structure." Critic and composer had met in May 1923, and had conversed shortly thereafter.[13] It is unlikely, however, that the former could have been an enlightening force, because such pronouncements by Stravinsky had already appeared. The composer rather may have realized the benefit of using literary acquaintances as conduits to the public. A symbiotic relationship seems to have been reached between Stravinsky and several sympathetic critics; advocates could enjoy an intimacy with a musician of vast creative and intellectual gifts while he could rely on their conveying his thoughts and keeping his name in the vanguard of contemporary art. Too, inasmuch as Stravinsky appears to have been receptive to a large variety of creative stimuli, the critical writings of his friends may have served to help bring his attitudes into clear focus.

The correspondence between Stravinsky and critical reception of his music can be gleaned by returning to another idea in the essay on the Octet. Wind instruments, the composer tells us, were chosen because the difference in their volumes "renders the musical architecture" more evident (than string instruments). A contrapuntal play of these volumes determines the form. This concept had surfaced as the radical element in *Pulcinella* when Stravinsky discussed the ballet in 1920. In 1921 Edwin Evans, whose writings were approved by the composer, described him as follows:

> His employment of instrumental timbres is essentially contrapuntal. When, for instance, he associates for a brief moment in "Pulcinella" the double bass and the trombone, it is not that he wants to mix these two sounds into a blended timbre, which would correspond with harmonic method. He takes a soft and fatty, penetrable sound, and sets against it a hard, penetrating one, and if they are of unequal intensity, they possess in another way equal strength. But their respective characters differ so widely that their identities are in no danger of being sacrificed. They exist as independently of each other as any two parts in a piece of counterpoint.
>
> I recently committed myself to the statement that Stravinsky was identifying himself more and more as a successor to Bach, that he was in fact becoming the Bach of today. . . . In impulse and incentive there is quite a remarkable affinity between Bach and Stravinsky, and I feel that it will become more apparent as time goes on.[14]

The identification of the relationship of volumes appears very much like that by the composer, and the example of trombone and double bass is one for which Stravinsky had a particular fondness. The appearance of Bach's name, however, is without precedent. If Bach hovered in the background of the composer's aesthetic, he mentioned him only in passing in July 1921, five months after the article by Evans appeared: "Bach belongs to the earlier half of the eighteenth century, and, moreover, properly speaking, he is not a representative of secular music."[15] In one instance Evans was even given credit for establishing the notion of a Stravinsky-Bach connection.[16] Stravinsky only invoked Bach's name with any frequency after critical response to the Octet and the Concerto for Piano and Winds had established the connection as a cliché. Both Roland-Manuel and Boulanger introduced Bach in their reviews of the Octet in October and November 1923. In January 1924, the composer told an interviewer for *Le matin*: "I consider [Bach] the imperishable model for us all."[17] The music of Stravinsky was thus perceived in language that was an elected affinity for both the composer and his supporters, one which solidified the identification of the central direction in modern music and shaped the rhetoric that was used to explain it.

That both *néoclassicisme* and *nouveau classicisme* were associated with Stravinsky in 1923 reinforces the impression that the terms defined similar aesthetic premises in contemporary music. The latter term appears to have been the one that most often informed critical response to the Concerto for Piano and Winds in 1924. Roland-Manuel chose *nouveau classicisme*, the term he had introduced in regard to the Octet:

> Charm is the dominant quality of this new Concerto for piano and wind instruments with the addition of contrabasses. Classic in plan, classic in certain respects of style, which ally themselves nicely to the style of Bach, the Concerto of Stravinsky is also and above all sustained by a serenity which becomes particularly evident during the "larghetto," the second part which is joined to the finale. Such charm and such serenity assures us, after *Pulcinella*, the Concertino, and the Octet, that this new classicism is not a vain attitude, but that it responds to a strong need in Stravinsky.[18]

By 1924 the language Roland-Manuel used to define *nouveau classicisme* had been been in the province of French and English prose about Stravinsky's works for almost a decade in which, for André Schaffner, "the words anti-romanticism and classical discipline have been ceaselessly on one's lips," and in which, for Jean Bloch, "universal consent has already agreed on the man who symbolizes . . . the degermanization of music: Stravinsky."[19] Schloezer was a typical voice in asserting that the Concerto, "as in all true classical compositions . . . is conditioned exclusively by a certain specific, formal logic, which alone assures it reality and authenticity." For this critic there also appeared to be a spiritual kinship between the composer's sensibility and that of the pre-nineteenth-century epoch, an affinity which also informed *Les biches* and *Les fâcheux*.[20] The author of the latter could easily have agreed with such an analogy, because he found the Concerto to be an ideal opportunity to contrast Stravinsky and Schoenberg in extreme terms characteristic for the French avant-garde.

> From *Petrushka* to the Octet to the first performance of the marvelous Piano Concerto, one observes an inspired and self-conscious artist, more lyric than one ever knew him (think of *Le sacre!*) and incredibly lucid, sure of himself and his resources. This is my master, I avow it, he stirs me without troubling me, enchants me without impairing me, excites me without shatter-

ing me. Yes, I know he is Russian, and have I not been reproached elsewhere for my musical "nationalism"? . . . But study the work of this Russian and you will see everything that a Frenchman can gain by practicing and cherishing it.

As for Schoenberg, in order to complete the review of "our masters" I resolutely detest him, and I will wish that all musicians of my country close their hearts to such an art. *Pierrot lunaire* is decadent romanticism, the morass which desires to be taken for the ocean, Rollinat at the Caribbean. With this, a superb mastery, an ape-like address, which bounds and rebounds ceaselessly beneath the conjugal rockets of flute and clarinet, the bundles of chords dispersed among the quartet and piano. Ominous and disquieting music which was necessary to know, and which is odious to me because it subverts everything I love and opposes its irritating assertion to the cheerful spirit of Igor Stravinsky.[21]

Ansermet too succumbed to the fashion of using *nouveau classicisme* as the catchall term to define Stravinsky's aesthetic.[22] By 1924 the composer himself recognized the developing stages of a cliché: writing to Ramuz on July 23 (in the wake of reviews of the Concerto) he could take for granted that the poet would know what he meant by his "so-called classical works."[23]

Critical response to the composer's European tour at the end of 1924, particularly his appearances in Berlin, only seems to have encouraged comparison of Schoenberg and Stravinsky. Adolf Weissmann seems to have been the German critic most responsible for bringing the two names together, to judge by the frequency of the subject in his prose.

One can therefore not understand Stravinsky, if one considers him from the point of view of German culture. And only from the strong revolt against this, which was stirred up through the world war, does his ruling power declare itself. Again a composer's reputation has flourished outside of Germany, but his durability cannot be determined without Germany's participation. This should now happen. Stravinsky's seed has so plentifully sprung up, because the course of German music produced standards which subsequently were considered as being no longer beneficial, since, one admits, that one can no longer compose fruitfully according to the German system. And while Arnold Schoenberg draws out of German music culture the last, most audacious conclusions, Stravinsky is placed opposite him, not as an enemy to be sure, but Schoenberg perceives nevertheless himself as his opposite. . . . The war against the romantic began a decade ago, but the unromantic produced its first positive achievement with Stravinsky. . . . Gradually the Russian folk song or its imitation was abandoned one piece at a time, and the way to the new classicism was sought with the example of the eighteenth century. The Piano Concerto, with wonderful terseness of form, is a model of this prevailing latest phase.[24]

Although it is apparent from contemporary critical assessments of the Octet and the Concerto that the terms *nouveau classicisme* and *neue Klassizismus* had become commonplace in describing Stravinsky with praiseworthy intent, during the same period one can still find occasional attempts to isolate neoclassicism as a derogatory expression. One observer had this retrogressive aspect of the term in mind when writing about recent trends:

If at the present moment the current of imitation is tending diversely toward Stravinsky or Schoenberg, the tending of musical thought in the immediate past is so inclined toward the assimilation of French methods as to present irrefutable testimony to the vitality of the movement as a whole and its permanent contribution to the musical literature of the world. . . . Moreover, advancement in artistic development invariably coexists with the survivals of the classic, or at best of a questionable neoclassicism, so that no period exclusively presents a clear-cut adherence to one style.[25]

Similarly, when the German periodical *Das Kunstblatt* quoted from the French newspaper *Sélection*, it translated the pejorative *néoclassicisme* as *Neoklassizismus*.[26] Too, Schloezer, who had introduced *néoclassicisme* to Stravinsky's name in 1923, pronounced this scathing indictment of the term two years later:

First of all, does this expression neoclassicism, which today is used so much, have a precise meaning? I strongly doubt it. There is a classical art, a classic spirit on the one hand and an academic art and academic spirit on the other hand. What the concept "neoclassicism" relates to, is therefore self-contradictory. If one wants to establish again the forms of the old masters, which were taught and learned in well-known schools by formulae and prescriptions, one becomes academic. If one strives for the model of this master, in order to create some form in a classical spirit (that is, antipsychological), if one endeavors to lay clear the singular logic of this particular art and to establish complete autonomy, then one is classical. Between the two arts there is not room for neoclassicism. On closer observation those who are called neoclassic instead appear always as academics and decadents. . . . If one puts oneself in this point of view, then one sees Stravinsky as classic, not in the sense that he copies certain qualities of Bach or Scarlatti, but in his highest, personal art, which just like those of the great masters is capable of creating an independent and objective art, which affects us with an urgency of a phenomenon of nature.[27]

Schloezer's cautionary words were irrelevant at mid-decade because by that time the meanings of *néoclassicisme* and *nouveau classicisme* were simply not distinguishable nor did they invariably appear with every article on Stravinsky. The Prague journal of modern music, *Der Auftakt*, in its special Stravinsky number for 1924, devoted five separate articles to the composer without once mentioning the term.

Critics found the Sonata of 1925 to be still further confirmation of Stravinsky's tendency toward "linear construction," "contrapuntal development," and veneration for Bach without need to dub it neoclassic. Arthur Lourie, who was to become one of the composer's closest friends during the 1920s, used the term rather in a way closer to its pre-war meaning.

The Sonata for piano is the latest work by Stravinsky, resulting directly from the Octet and the Concerto. I say resulting, and yet a solid recognition of the two preceding works does not eschew a surprise for the listener, a surprise caused at first by a return to original musical forms. This return is not contradictory to the preceding technique of the composer, but rather is in contradiction to the appearances of customary contemporary technique. This is a first impression and it seems that Stravinsky goes to the limit of reactionary ideas. But this return is not an abandonment of acquired experience. The original classical forms catalyze in themselves new ideas, totally comprised in new forms—but the deceptive appearance is that of obsolete idea and form—and the finished work constitutes an organism in itself. In writing the Sonata, Stravinsky voluntarily forgets the evolution sustained by this form from Beethoven through the nineteenth century toward the German pseudo-classic tradition. The neoclassic sonata, of which the last sonatas of Beethoven are at once the point of departure and the summit, is essentially constituted by dramatic action. This is the struggle between the principle of individual emotion and the principle of the foundations of a sonority in itself.[28]

For Lourie nineteenth-century Germany was the provenance of the neoclassic sonata. Stravinsky, to him, "poses anew the principle of the instrumental problem and of the organic form of the sonata. Such is the nature of this return to the original tradition of the eighteenth century. It logically determines the birth of a form-type."[29] Lourie may have been familiar with Stravinsky's Octet essay of 1924 and possibly his interviews from his American tour in 1925 as well, because description of the Sonata frequently echoes the composer: the work as an "object" that occupies space, its linear construction, its suggestion of Bach, and its simplicity and purity.

The anti-German and anti-romantic bias which Lourie among others expressed had been the one constant feature in the history of the term neoclassicism. Yet by 1925 even this characteristic was becoming obscured. Reviews of the Sonata, while still keeping Bach's name prominent, sometimes suggested that the work was related to Beethoven and Liszt. The appearance of the former's name may seem surprising, given Stravinsky's negative comments about Beethoven several years earlier. Even if the composer's stance mellowed after the war, his confirmation of an affinity with Beethoven in his autobiography must be viewed with skepticism, since any analogy between the Sonata and that composer can also be made with works of others. Two of the most frequently repeated relationships between the Sonata and Beethoven's work are the major third key relationship between sections of the second movement and the purported reference of the first movement's unison opening to the "Appassionata" Sonata. The former is hardly exclusive to Beethoven, however, and an equally justifiable model for the latter is the finale of Chopin's Sonata in Bb minor. Too, Bach's F minor two-voice Fugue of the first book of *The Well-Tempered Clavier* and Beethoven's F-Major Sonata, op. 54 have both been cited as models for the final movement of Stravinsky's Sonata.[30] Liszt seems an even less likely source for Stravinsky. Richard Taruskin has suggested recently, however, that the composer's octatonicism may have derived indirectly in part from Liszt through Rimsky-Korsakov and other nineteenth-century Russians.[31] Stravinsky made two laudatory references to Liszt at the time of the Sonata, and so the latter was not an unreasonable name for contemporary critics to cite. To an interviewer for

Comoedia on January 15, 1924, Stravinsky indicated cryptically that Liszt, not Pergolesi, had "provided the example," and two years later he asserted that he had a higher admiration for Liszt's underrated talent than he had for Chopin.[32]

Whether a relationship to either Beethoven or Liszt is fortuitous or deliberate, or, if the latter, whether it occurs as superficial melodic quotation or structural modeling, for neoclassicism to be associated with Stravinsky after 1925, a further revision of meaning was needed: composer and term had to be poised against a post-Beethovenian, exclusively German *fin-de-siècle* aesthetic.[33] This variation on the term neoclassicism became general after 1925, because a series of events in that year brought the names Schoenberg and Stravinsky together and indirectly helped to secure the term neoclassicism to the latter.

Critical Responses: Schoenberg's Polemics

The post-war milieu significantly altered the opinions of Stravinsky and Schoenberg toward each other. Stravinsky's change in attitude toward Schoenberg within a ten-year span, chronicled on pages 124–27, is explicable only in that context, given that he heard no new works by Schoenberg in the decade after the premiere of *Pierrot lunaire*.[34] Schoenberg appears to have undergone a nearly identical *volte-face* during the same time: he privately admired *Petrushka,* which he heard in 1912, and in 1923 he derogatorily classified Stravinsky as one of many *Polytonalisten,* who included Milhaud, Casella, and Bartók.[35] Several works by Stravinsky were performed immediately after World War I by the Society for Private Musical Performances, which was founded by Schoenberg in 1918. Although the choice of compositions was not made according to Schoenberg's personal preferences, he might have been aware that Stravinsky's works made deep impressions on even his most dedicated disciples. The Society gave *Berceuses du chat* and *Pribaoutki* on June 6, 1919, and on June 9 Webern reported to Berg his ecstatic reaction to them. On June 9, 1921, Berg described the previous evening's performance of *Ragtime* by the Society as "something very fine!"[36] Too, Stravinsky's music was often performed in Berlin and Vienna during the 1920s, and was frequently cited as the most important influence on German composers of the generation after Berg and Webern.

In the past few years, however, and especially after the first performance of his *Le sacre du printemps* by the German section of the International Society for Contemporary Music, he has exerted a strong influence over German composers, among them Paul Hindemith and Ernst Krenek. It cannot be denied that the Concerto is in some respects the solution of the problem with which most composers of the younger generation are absorbed. We live, however, in a country where the influence of Schoenberg overshadows that of any other composer. Schoenberg has undoubtedly enriched music theory. Never contenting himself with the surface of things, he probes to the very heart of music. He seems, however, to be prostrated by his own theory, whereas Stravinsky, who is, apparently, much more superficial in theory, wields a creative force enabling him to solve all the problems of his inspiration. Now we are on the way to a realization of the potentialities of this modern art; we feel its effects in the great and never-ceasing efforts of our young composers.[37]

It is perhaps not coincidental that Schoenberg often wrote about the misdirection of young composers at this time. He later identified 1924, the time of Stravinsky's first European tour, as the year in which the public became hostile toward him, and indicated the period between 1922 and 1930 as "the first time in my career that I lost, for a short time, my influence on youth."[38]

Unlike Stravinsky, Schoenberg endured widespread and sometimes vicious negative criticism outside his immediate circle during 1923 and 1924 when his first twelve-tone compositions were introduced.[39] Contemporary reviews of works by Schoenberg and Stravinsky heard in Germany even suggest that a growing competition between their advocates was being played out during the performances. One observer at the public premiere of Schoenberg's Serenade on July 20, 1924, reported: "We do not claim that no one understood or enjoyed the music, but we gravely doubt it, and doubt it not less for the extraodinary demonstration made by the Schoenberg clique at the end of the performance. They clapped and stamped and howled. The others made for the door and out into the summer's day."[40] A witness to the premiere of the Concerto in Berlin reported that the public "relieved themselves in a combat between acceptance and refusal that one could have believed was a question of nothing less than the future of music," and that its "utter success" came despite "isolated whistling from the futurist provocateurs."[41] Against the widespread negative response to Schoenberg by the conservative German press one can juxtapose the support of those in the composer's immediate circle of friends and former students. Like Stravinsky's advocates, those of Schoenberg often reiterated their leader's thoughts. Schoenberg's obsession with establishing himself as the legatee of the German tradition via serial composition is replicated by his supporters' avowal that his recent works were the true representatives of the structural and thematic clarity inherited from the eighteenth century. While recognizing that contemporary audiences used to tonal gestures would require patient study to comprehend these new scores, Schoenberg's adherents insisted that he was the only living composer who deserved the accolade of "classic."[42] Even their advocacy, however, was sometimes made difficult by Schoenberg's expectation of absolute and unswerving loyalty that broached no questioning. Letters to Paul Stefan on April 24, 1923, and Paul Bekker, August 1, 1924, reveal Schoenberg's intolerance of criticism, and on November 11, 1925, Berg wrote to his wife that Schoenberg made faithfulness really hard.[43]

By 1925 Schoenberg was surely aware of the great attention that Stravinsky's music was receiving, and contemporary negative reception of his own music may have encouraged a combative mood. It is likely that when Stravinsky made some widely publicized comments at the outset of his American tour against "modern music," Schoenberg interpreted them as referring to him. The *bons mots* reported by the press were arguably calculated more to attract considerable publicity than to state an aesthetic position. Discussion of the Concerto prompted the following exchange between Stravinsky and his American interviewers.

> "It is only eight months old," said he. "The idea is sort of a great passacaglia or toccata. It is full of counterpoint—piano counterpoint, as I call it. It is quite in the style of the Seventeenth Century; that is, the style of the Seventeenth Century viewed from the angle of today. You know I detest modern music."
>
> He dropped that last sentence quite incidentally, but the interviewers fairly whooped with joy. There was the headline.
>
> "But," objected someone at once, "you say you detest modern music and yet you are generally looked on as the foremost of the modernists."
>
> "No, no," protested Stravinsky. "My music is not modern music nor is it music of the future. It is the music of today. One can't live in yesterday nor tomorrow."
>
> "But who are the modernists then?"
>
> Stravinsky smiled. "I shan't mention any names," said he, "but they are the gentlemen who work with formulas instead of ideas. They have done that so much they have badly compromised that word 'modern.' I don't like it. They started out by trying to write so as to shock the Bourgeoisie and finished up by pleasing the Bolsheviki."[44]

Another witness reported the interview in a slightly altered version.

> "I detest modernist music," he says. "I am not modernist. I do not pretend to write the music of the future any more than I attempt to copy the music of the past. I am of today and I hope I am writing the music of today. Many of my friends among the new composers spend their time either inventing the music of tomorrow or repeating that of yesterday. Modernism is too pretentious for me. *C'est un mot compromis.* There is no sincerity left in it. The modernists set out to shock the bourgeoisie, sometimes they succeed only in pleasing the Bolshevists. I am not interested in either the bourgeoisie or the Bolshevists. My object is not to shock the world with stock phrases and theories, which, like 'futurism,' have turned into mere formulas. My music, I suppose, occasionally shocks the world, but that is only because people are always shocked by what they do not understand. It is the easiest way out."[45]

A question about quarter-tones prompted an indictment of the String Quartet of Alois Hába and provided the composer with a suitable pretext for introducing his allegiance to Bach.

> Igor Stravinsky is not a modernist he repeats. He does not experiment in the isms and alities. He does not write in quarter-tones. "I was born under the 'Wohltemperiertes Clavier' and I write in the well-tempered scale" he says. "I have heard some of these experiments, Alois Hába and the rest. It sounds to me like ordinary music just a little off. *Es klingt falsch.* That's all. They try to write the music of the future, strange unheard of combinations and all they succeed

in writing is quarter-tone Brahms. No, I go back to Bach, not Bach as we know him today, but Bach as he really is. You know now they play Bach with a Wagner orchestra and make him sound very pleasant, so people will like him. That isn't the real Bach. I heard the real Bach once at Basel, the St. Matthew Passion as it was written, for organ, wind instruments and Männerchor. That was the real Bach, but a modern audience wouldn't have liked it any more than his contemporaries did."[46]

Little from these interviews illuminates our understanding of the composer's aesthetics at the time, and the few relevant comments that can be separated from his verbal sparring—the contrapuntal nature of his recent music and his abhorrence of Wagnerian orchestrations of Bach—are not new. Yet it was precisely the statements "I go back to Bach" and "I detest modern music" that were frequently reproduced in Europe. The critic for *Der Auftakt*, perhaps exasperated with the carnival atmosphere of the interview, satirically portrayed it as a two-act farce.[47] Schoenberg may have assumed Stravinsky's criticism of "music of the future" referred to him because he preserved a copy of an interview that appeared in a German-language newspaper and wrote brief criticisms of his own in the margin. The title of the article is "Igor Stravinsky über seine Musik," and is authored by N. Roerig. With the exception of several sentences which bear no date, all of Schoenberg's marginal notes are dated 1932. One paragraph has the following words emphasized: "*Aside from Jazz however I detest all modern music!* I myself by no means compose modern music, I also never write music of the future, I write for today. I will *cite no names* in this regard, but I could tell you composers who spend all their time for the purpose of *inventing music of the future*; that is still really very presumptuous. Where is the sincerity in that?" It was certainly this article which prompted Schoenberg to write his essay, "Igor Stravinsky: *Der Restaurateur*," dated July 24, 1926. Its first line is: "Stravinsky pokes fun at musicians who are anxious (unlike himself—he wants simply to write the *music of today*) to write the *music of the future*."[48] Schoenberg's testiness is somewhat ironic because, although he believed that Stravinsky meant to criticize him even though he was not mentioned by name, Stravinsky did refer to him in a subsequent interview with Paul Rosenfeld, although this was not known to Schoenberg. Rosenfeld quoted the composer: "But in their very effort to escape from romanticism, people are committing the most grotesque errors. Take Schoenberg, for example. Schoenberg is really a romantic at heart who would like to get away from romanticism. He admires Aubrey Beardsley! Just think—he considers Aubrey Beardsley wonderful! It's unbelievable, isn't it?"[49]

It is hardly surprising then that, when the two composers attended the International Society for Contemporary Music Festival in Venice in September 3–8, 1925 (Stravinsky played his Sonata and Schoenberg conducted his Serenade), they did not meet. Stravinsky did not attend the performance of the Serenade and Schoenberg walked out on the Sonata.[50] To judge from contemporary reviews, which tended to treat the event as "a genuine sensation from the encounter between the two leading masters of new music," English and French critics were enthusiastic for the former and reserved about the latter. Evans reported that the Serenade was "of course hailed with delight by the faithful," but that "the general view outside the Schoenberg circle was that the Serenade was clever but depressing." Similarly for one French critic the Serenade had "a lack of variety and clarity, a grimacing side, hateful, sardonic, a scarcely sympathetic dryness," whereas for another the Sonata had qualities of clarity and simplicity in returning to the style of Bach and Mozart. Even German advocates of Schoenberg like Paul Stefan who admired the Serenade reported an enthusiastic reception for Stravinsky and that his "classical transformation" was an "incontestable triumph."[51]

The general perceptions in 1925—Stravinsky and Schoenberg as the indisputable leaders of contemporary music; Stravinsky as the heir of Bach, the greatest German composer; Stravinsky as the composer to be emulated by young musicians throughout Europe, including Germany; and Schoenberg as an almost insidious radical—combined to incite Schoenberg to compose *Three Satires*, op. 28, at the end of 1925. The reception of the two composers' works in Venice undoubtedly supplied the immediate catalyst. On September 25 Webern wrote to Berg that their teacher told him "about the disaster of 'modern Music' including Stravinsky, of whom he said that he had had his hair cropped close; he 'bachelts' (Bach Imitation)."[52] Even as Schoenberg began the work in November, Stravinsky's music was enjoying its warmest reception in Germany with a festival in Frankfurt on the 24th and 25th.

> The fact the festival not only finally established Stravinsky's fame in Germany, but also proved representative of his actual standard of creative development, was due to the judicious inclusion on the program of past works and those of his most recent neoclassic period. Of the latter, Stravinsky played his Concerto, already performed last season at Berlin, the Sonata (first performance since the Venice Festival) and his newest work, the "Serenade" for piano. There are critics who see in the first two of these three works something of the Parisian snob. Such a point of view is naturally out of the question for anybody who understands Stravinsky's constructive methods and independence. With a composer of his creative genius, the adoption of several modes of construction as elementary as some of those of the Bach period, is merely a means to an end, just as is the adoption of national melodies or rhythms. His combination of marvelous rhythmic and harmonic invention with his typically Russian romanticism results in a highly interesting group of pieces. It is obvious, however, that the question of importance of this new creative perspective of Stravinsky's, as well as of the general development of music, can be solved only by the future; but there are some that predict already the birth of a new and imposing form of musical Europeanism.[53]

Three Satires cannot be considered merely as a polemical footnote to Schoenberg's works, in the manner of Wagner's satire of Hanslick in *Die Meistersinger*. Schoenberg took its composition very seriously: he interrupted work on the Suite, op. 29 in order to write it, and the many letters to his publisher record the care with which he wished them printed.[54] *Three Satires* represents an important milestone in the composer's output: it is the only composition by

Schoenberg to include a lengthy Foreword that seeks to explain its inspiration, and it is the first completed work to exploit certain aspects of the row that would become regular features of his later style. The Foreword* is worth quoting in its entirety:

> The greatest danger seems to me that many, at whom I have aimed these Satires, might be in doubt about whether they have felt themselves attacked.
>
> Where text and music appear obscure enough that one, who fears the light, thinks he could hide, so then let unclarity be accounted for by a little veiled language.
>
> 1. I wanted to attack all who seek their personal salvation upon the middle road, because the middle road is the only one which does not lead to Rome. But those who nibble at dissonances, wanting thus to pass as modern, profit by it, but are too cautious to draw conclusions from it. Conclusions do not result just from dissonances but, even more so, result from consonances. It is the case just as with those who find a tasteful selection of dissonances without being able to account thereon why their discords should be allowed and why others should be forbidden; they "don't go so far" without stating why they go as far as they do. Also the quasi-tonalists who propose to allow themselves everything that convulses tonality if only they render an acknowledgment of tradition by a tonal triad, whether appropriate or not. Who believes it of them, when they hear it. And who, endowed with the knowledge and conscience of form, can overlook that their yearning for "form" and "architecture" to such a degree cannot be fulfilled.
>
> 2. I take aim at those who allege to aspire to "a return to. . . . " Such a one should not try to make believe it lies in his hands to determine how far back he deems far enough; and even that he comes close to one of the great masters (who has "taken pains to aspire"), although he is always talking about him, he really only insults him! This backward-living man, hardly born again, already has missed a lot in school and therefore newly experiences, just now, tonics and dominants. One would like to help him by means of a round-trip ticket to style. But to divulge to him the "rules of the game" (as one droll mediocrity puts it) is unnecessary, because his mastery of the "lust for lucre" endures and offers security so that he will help himself as always, while he peeps at the cards of an involuntary partner. Moreover, since many already allow themselves to attribute the so loudly extolled "Renaissance," after a short time, to a discreet *fausse couche*, it would confirm that such a one voluntarily composes so shabbily, like a poor music student is forced to compose.
>
> 3. With delight, I also attack the folklorists, who want to apply to the natural, primitive concepts of folk music a technique which is suitable only for a complex way of thinking—obliged so to like it (since to them proper themes are not at their disposal) or not (although an existing musical culture and tradition could even still ultimately sustain them).
>
> 4. Finally all " . . . ists," in whom I can see only mannerists, whose music is the most pleasant to those who, by it, consider *continuous* to be a slogan which is given out to exclude any other thoughts.
>
> I cannot judge if it is fair of me (it certainly will not be more fair than anything else of mine) to make fun of the many seriously-minded, often gifted and, in part, estimable, when I know that one can make fun of everything—of very sad things and very merry things. In any case, forgive me that I have done it, as always, as well as I am able. Others may be able to laugh more than I about that which I also am able to take seriously!
>
> Perhaps I also wanted to hint at that?[55]

Stravinsky is clearly the target of most of this prose. Schoenberg ridiculed those who yearn for "form and architecture" and those who aspire to "a return"; statements borrowed from Stravinsky's American interview in the German translation, which Schoenberg knew. Too, that the "ists" might refer most notably to "new classicists" in the person of Stravinsky is suggested by the texts of the second and third movements of *Three Satires*. Although their titles went through some revision, their content makes clear that the contemporary method which Schoenberg so disliked was "the new classicism" and that its leading exponent was Stravinsky.[56] For Schoenberg, Stravinsky was the greatest offender among the *Scheintonalisten* though by no means the only one.[57] To consider Stravinsky as only the most notorious among the "polytonalists" is, if course, inaccurate; as he told Ansermet in 1922, his music was quite unlike that of his contemporaries.[58] Yet Schoenberg's judgment was scarcely based on his acquaintance with Stravinsky's scores. Like that of Stravinsky, Schoenberg's assessment of his contemporary was gleaned from what he read, not from what he heard: contemporary reviews and essays of their music made up the evidence upon which the composers made their aesthetic conclusions.[59]

The un-Schoenbergian moments in "Der Neue Klassizismus," the final movement of *Three Satires,* suggest the composer's satire of certain gestures which he considered to be fingerprints of the new classicism. The cadences that end the four sections (mm. 11–13, 52–57, 78–79, 179–81) in particular suggest Schoenberg's dismay over a style which he perceived allowed dissonances to appear in an arbitrary fashion as long as the parts resolved to a stable harmony. The construction of the row itself appears to have been devised to permit the composer to allude to certain tonal functions and at the same time to develop certain methods of comprehensibility which would increasingly occupy him. The row is: C–B–C#–A–Eb G–Bb–Ab–D–F#–E–F. The first five pitches are a retrograde of the last five pitches. The disruption of this order in pitches six and seven does, however, give a "tonal" sense to the row because of their V–I relationships to pitches one and twelve.

The ordering of the first hexachord affords Schoenberg an opportunity for satire: he extracts pitches one, two, four, and six to create a descending white-note tetrachord, and to them he sets the text "Siehe Riemann." The gibe is intended for historians like Hugo Riemann, the German musicologist in whose *Musik-Lexikon* Schoenberg found not only what he considered to be a fatuous definition of classicism, but an explanation of the legacy of German music which contradicted the composer's own professed lineage.[60]

When the inversion is transposed a fourth (F–F#–E–Ab–D–Bb– G–A–Eb–B–C#–C) the hexachords become combinatorial with those of the original row, that is, the pitch content of the first hexachord of the original row is the same as the second hexachord of the transposition. Combinatoriality became one of Schoenberg's chief means of creating coherence among the row and its transpositional levels. Although he had earlier constructed such a row for the Suite, op. 29, *Three Satires* is the first completed work by the composer to exploit this structural property.[61] The formation of the row thus provided Schoenberg with a two-edged sword: it permitted him to replicate the surface appearance of certain tonal functions without their serving as unifying elements of the entire work (his satire of their use in the new classicism), while in the structure of the whole the combinatorial properties of the row and its chosen transpositions imparted a comprehensibility that did not require superficial effects of tonal harmony. One might even hazard an intepretation that "Der Neue Klassizismus" is at once the satire of neoclassicism and also the presentation of what is properly to be considered classic.

Three Satires was by no means an isolated phenomenon in its composer's creative activity at this time. In many statements, especially from mid-decade, "polytonalists" or "pseudo-tonalists" were, for Schoenberg, composers whose style was marked by simple melodies harmonized in unnaturally complex ways, by frequent reptition of meager ideas, and by chords in C major with added F♯.[62] An unpublished aphorism entitled "Ostinato," dated May 13, 1922, is characteristic:

> For me, what needs to be true for nobody else is what I first expect from a work of art: *richness!* This insufficiency in Latins and their Russian, Hungarian, English, and American imitators for me, although it should be comical, is always more ridiculous and painful. This method—variation of the harmonies once in a while produces something "clever," or until this asinine repetition itself turns out "witty," since it at least cannot possibly be taken seriously—recalls as much the humor of drunks, clowns, and blockheads (above all ones that are offensive, falling down, fighting, mocking) as much as I am able to extract from it. One certainly smiles to a degree every time from the novelty, but always one does so with little sympathy and especially always with little respect! On the other hand there is a growing displeasure: the feeling of annoyance turning to disgust![63]

Schoenberg was perhaps more concerned with the aesthetic premises of the music of the "polytonalists" than he was with the specific gestures used by them. For the composer, one's means of creativity was bound by one's cultural heritage: only a German composer was capable of comprehending the artistic truths of the past which, for him, were essentially German. An unpublished essay, "Polytonalisten," from November 29, 1923, emphasizes this point.

> An important difference between me and the polytonalists and folklorists and all the others who manufacture folk melodies, dances, and so on in a homophonic manner—Stravinsky, Milhaud, the English, Americans, and everyone else—is that they seek the solution by means of a historical parallel, while I have found it from within, in which I merely obeyed the subject and followed the imagination and the feeling for form.
>
> They know, as I, that just now the old model of harmony could not be taken further. (I have even said so in my book; they know it well even from there!) They now obviously look upon the present to be a phenomenon parallel to Palestrina's time, which Pfitzner wanted to bring to life.[64]

The use of the old harmony—tonality and its functional relationships—could not survive merely leavened by a more cavalier attitude toward the placement of dissonances. In another contemporary essay, Schoenberg stated that such a tendency was the attempt by foreign countries to free themselves from the hegemony of German music. *Three Satires* might appear droll in its ridicule of this attempt, but also, according to the composer, it was created in earnest to demonstrate that twelve-tone composition was the only method capable of sustaining comprehensibility while making use of the structural procedures of the past. Writing music "in the ancient style" was not in itself a sin, but it could hardly serve as the basis for a contemporary method of composition.[65]

Except for the derision in which he held the term, Schoenberg's perception of the new classicism corresponded to contemporary usage. That use did not indicate which composers or what techniques were to be included in the concept of the term, but rather who was to be left out. Certain musical details might be invoked, but neoclassicism affronted Vienna because its use interpreted the history of music in terms other than that of German dominance. Schoenberg understood the polemical nature of the term in the context of national traditions, and he concluded that the rhetoric of the new classicism denied him as the legatee of that history and posited Stravinsky as its heir. For both composers and their advocates, musical creativity was bound by culture; for Schoenberg neoclassicism signified a crossing of the boundaries.

It is unclear to what extent *Three Satires* fueled the controversy between the advocates of Schoenberg and Stravinsky. Both Berg and Webern admired it, but rather than dwelling upon its satiric elements, members of the composer's circle treated it as the most recent evidence that the twelve-tone method was the logical evolution following the breakdown of tonality, and that Schoenberg was the true beneficiary of the great German tradition.[66] Only in 1929 did an article address itself to the circumstances which had inspired the composer to write it.

Music which displays polyphonic techniques to the extreme extent of *Three Satires*, when it is played, can only have an effect to a limited degree. It remains predominantly a visual and intellectual affair. It is perhaps no accident that Schoenberg noted the choral theme in the technically simple key of C. Evidently he wanted to show here that one is only entitled to a consummate technical compositional mastery from above, to use to such an extent as a critic of the times. So we stand before a paradoxical phenomenon, that classicism becomes ridiculed in a hyperclassic style, whose objective attitude was freely possible only at the cost of any direct relation to the text.

Schoenberg's *Satires* is important, whether as a work in itself or from the point of view of his evolution. But it may also be taken as constituting a symptom. After all, this personal statement of someone creatively set apart and whose development as an artist was established with the currents of the time, whose method could be astonishing, can indeed be understood not only from a lofty standpoint of inherent safety. . . . The more dispassionate observer sees this conflict in a broader perspective. He sees in it Schoenberg's resistance against a development which now threatens to progress away from him, and to which he himself showed the way.[67]

Such nonpolemical articles were uncommon in the 1920s, and even fewer critics observed that the burgeoning controversy was largely a result of noncompositional, cultural differences that had been fomenting for decades.[68]

Stravinsky does not appear to have known of the relationship of *Three Satires* to him at the time he wrote his well-known 1927 essay on neoclassicism. He was apparently prompted by his despairing of comments on his music like the one below, which suggested that his "classicism" lay in his choice of gestures borrowed from the eighteenth century. The composer's own statement appeared two months later and responds so specifically to this article that one is tempted to conclude that it incited him to write.

> By his objectivity the art of Stravinsky allies itself narrowly with classical art toward which a movement of reversion currently takes shape. This reaction against romanticism can be discernible a bit in every domain of artistic activity. . . . Two factors influence our actions: our reason and our feelings. Classicism is the principal role for reason, conceiving things only in this faculty which seems equally common to all. From then the interest will be to reproduce in a harmonious and proportional form things in themselves, and to manifest them in the greatest objectivity. . . . The art of Stravinsky is obliged to become classical. His elements are always objectively chosen. The art resides in the intelligence for discovering them and in the exquisite taste for uniting them.[69]

The composer declared that the choice of "the thing in itself" was not sufficient to imitate classicism. The term neoclassicism was acceptable to him only if it meant an affinity with an earlier period's conception of form, "the quality of the interrelation between the constituent parts," rather than with the imitation of stylistic gestures.[70] For Schoenberg, however, the new classicism misplaced the functions proper to tonality, while to Stravinsky, "atonality" was merely the husk of a technical procedure.[71]

By the end of the decade the link was secure: neoclassicism was invoked invariably for Stravinsky's music when it was contrasted with that of Schoenberg.[72] If Robert Craft's assertion of the signficance of Arthur Lourie's article "Neogothic and Neoclassic" is perhaps overstated, Lourie did voice a characteristic feeling of the decade.

> A material change is taking place in the esthetic approach of artists who are lending this period its vital significance. The stimulus of the emotional is being obviously replaced by the stimulus of the intellect. A new style is coming to life in the clash of two tendencies. Of these one may be termed neogothic, by which I do not mean a return to the style of the middle ages but a movement toward the expressive in art, a tendency which finally becomes an end in itself. Here, slightly transformed, is the same strain of individualism which belongs to the nineteenth century and whose natural consequence was expressionism in its extreme form. . . . To put it exactly, neo-romantic emotionalism is giving way to classical intellectualism. . . . Concretely speaking, the controversy concerns itself chiefly with the work of Schoenberg and Stravinsky. The art of these two composers, who are at opposite poles in the world of contemporary music, exactly expresses the dualism I have been describing. . . . Whatever their activity, it is quite

certain that Schoenberg will continue to create neo-gothic music, while Stravinsky will try to strengthen the creation of an objective style. Schoenberg's case is particularly delicate. He will probably not be able to continue his atonal system much longer, even though he is developing it along scientific lines. The reason is that his work is essentially "monomethodic." In all his music the essential point of departure, the procedure remains the same. He has occasionally changed only its form.[73]

To be sure, not every article on Stravinsky used the word neoclassicism. Yet where the names of Stravinsky and Schoenberg were juxtaposed, the term lay just beneath the surface.

The catchword is no doubt fatal to the evolution of art, if it persists too long. But after all, it means the petrification of what has a good and fruitful germ in itself. It ceases to be dangerous as soon as we have recognized what is good in the germ and are capable of canceling what has lost its right of existence. . . . From all this it may be gathered that Stravinsky had acted for a long time as an antidote to Schoenberg in Germany, whose influence he had evidently undergone for some short moments of his creative career. The directness of his music, the unemotional, unsentimental side of his work attracted the young musicians, who had got tired of the eternal problematic character of Schoenberg's work. It was the satirical and the grotesque part of Stravinsky's compositions that most strongly appealed to the young composers, who thought it possible to shake off the fetters of the problematic and to take the mask of buffoons. They thought, like the musical world around them, of making jazz part of their work. Most happily they understood very soon that the reality of life and the lightheartedness of it all, are not the only goal of art. When they were conscious of this fact, they had a great chance of discovering another Stravinsky, resolved to follow the ideals of the seventeenth and eighteenth centuries.[74]

Stravinsky approved of the term neoclassicism in 1927 only insofar as it reflected an affinity with formal procedures of early music. Only through the critics' employment of neoclassicism in terms of culture as well as style, however, did it to become permanently grafted to him during the 1920s. The composer's scores subsequent to the *Sonata* may have seemed too bewilderingly varied for even his advocates to discern them as a musical unity. As long as they could be juxtaposed against the language of Schoenberg, however, there remained a common ground upon which the term neoclassicism could thrive.

Conclusion

The preceding study of the genesis of the word neoclassicism, from its first appearance at the turn of the century to its widespread usage at the end of the 1920s, has revealed two contexts for the term. From its birth, neoclassicism was reckoned as an aesthetic idea. In this guise its meaning leapfrogged from a derogatory term before World War I to one of approbation in the 1920s. Its use as an indicator of style was, by contrast, a relatively late development. Only after World War I did it begin to be defined in terms of specific musical gestures within a given composition, and only when a group of works by one composer, Stravinsky, was juxtaposed with those of another, Schoenberg.

The origin of the word neoclassicism has its explanation in the nineteenth century's attitude toward music history. It is arguable that the nineteenth century invented a particular kind of history of music in which great works of the past were not merely accorded respect or subject to quotation, and were not just worthy of study or of assimilation into contemporary composition. The homogenous and uniform past created by the nineteenth century demanded that artists confront and relate themselves to this hitherto insular tradition.[1] For the first generation of romantic composers, those creative liaisons were made by Germans of Germans. Bach was a revelation for Schumann and Mendelssohn, but a subject of near ridicule for Berlioz.[2]

By the end of the century, a look back brought with it the realization that the history of music was a history of *German* music. That awareness was particularly keen in France, a country which boasted of its rich nineteenth-century traditions in literature and the *beaux arts*. Living in a European milieu which cast its most cherished musical icons of the recent past in Germanic terms, and in which political tensions and nationalist insecurities tended to skew attitudes toward culture, French composers and musicians at century's end were keen to devise a terminology that might buttress their notions of artistic parity (at first) and (later) of superiority. The invention of *le néoclassicisme* and *le nouveau classicisme* supplied a convenient code by which French composers could put forward aesthetic ideas based upon a nostalgic evocation of a moribund style.

If the term neoclassicism arose in part from the coalescence of music historicism and nationalism generated by composers in the nineteenth century, their artistic progeny in the twentieth century inherited the perception that they were obliged to relate themselves to the history created by their forebears. Not a single composer after World War I was indifferent toward the past. (The surrealists, the only group to make self-conscious denial of the European cultural heritage a centerpiece of their polemic, significantly counted no composers among their number.) By the twentieth century, however, the sense of a uniform tradition had begun to disintegrate and vary widely, as did the extent of its presence, whether overt or disguised, in individual works, and only the greatest artists were able to mediate between the lure of the past and their own personal styles.

If only few composers were able to effect a reconciliation between order and freedom, there were others who recognized that the nineteenth century had bequeathed both the aesthetic of an authoritative history of music and the slogans to define it. The most adept advocates among the French avant-garde recognized that the critical baggage of the *fin de siècle* could be tailored to their own ends. Catch phrases like *nouveau simplicité* and *style dépouillé* incorporated much of the old terminology, but without its sentimental or nostalgic attachments to remote traditions. The decidedly ironic cast given to the uses of the past by Parisian artistic circles helps explain why Cocteau's polemics could appear so radical in 1917, when in fact the language of *Le coq et l'arlequin* had been common in France for decades. Too, not every observer of the artistic scene had Cocteau's facility at manipulating public perceptions of radical culture. Schloezer described the word neoclassicism approvingly in 1923 in connection with Stravinsky, knowing its disreputable history. His call to ignore the term only two years later suggests that, in an era in which novelty and tradition vied for attention, any semblance of a clear terminology was impossible to maintain.

Stravinsky's concern for entering the mainstream of European music was nourished by his awareness of French avant-garde artistic tendencies. His superimposition of blocks of sonorities mirrored contemporary efforts at juxtaposition of language, shapes, and colors in poetry and art. Yet the similarities went beyond those of musical gesture. By the premiere of *Pulcinella*, Stravinsky was a composer who was canny at observing trends in musical aesthetics and skilled at stage-managing his own publicity. Stravinsky at the very least tolerated the word neoclassicism in the 1920s because he recognized that this otherwise innocuous catchword carried a familiar resonance: it could accommodate his position in a music history of his own invention to suit his own compositional and personal needs. Stravinsky knew that the "great tradition" of the nineteenth century excluded him, and he was compelled to devise his own, and to constantly reinvent it; with Pergolesi, with Tchaikovsky, later with the Second Viennese School, and finally, in old age, with his own early work (a trait he shared with Picasso).

Robert Craft recently found it difficult to answer the rhetorical question of what the composer felt was his place in the history of music, and his own query of Stravinsky had brought the answer: "That is for history to decide."[3] The recompositions of *The Five Fingers* as *Eight Instrumental Miniatures* (1962) and of the theme of the finale of *The Firebird* as the *Canon on a Russian Popular Tune* (1965) suggest that Stravinsky had come to believe that he had finally placed himself in history's musical mainstream.

Had Stravinsky known the original meaning of the word neoclassicism, he might have been amused at the irony of having a term originally intended to derogate the nineteenth-century German lineage serve to describe his own aesthetic in approving terms. His tolerance of the term, however, was marginal in the 1920s, and in later years he treated it with withering contempt, introducing it into his conversation books only when it served his purpose to do so.[4] Yet to suggest that the term neoclassicism had no more value than that of a well-turned "buzz word" might lead one to conclude that, to Stravinsky, everyone who used it, including trusted advocates like Ansermet and Lourie, marked themselves as musically illiterate.[5] To be sure, there was a healthy dose of self-promotion in Stravinsky's public pronouncements of the 1920s. Yet the concern for aesthetics and the search for the *mot juste* to articulate one's artistic position was still fundamental for Stravinsky's generation and the artistic milieu in which he worked. The word neoclassicism indeed furnished a wary public with an easy access for coming to terms with the composer's music of the 1920s. It likewise supplied a symbol which represented for Stravinsky's supporters a cultural value system whose vocabulary elucidated for them the central direction of post-war composition.

That vocabulary—sobriety, purity, monumentality, and so on—appeared tailor-made for Schoenberg, who was equally devoted to the reconsideration of his place in the continuum of music history. His response to the polemic of neoclassicism was only secondarily judged in terms of music, since his knowledge of Stravinsky's works was sketchy at best. His reaction was gauged in terms of culture: the terminology of neoclassicism rightly suited him as the heir to the German line. To deny him, Schoenberg, as its legatee was to misconstrue totally the history of music. When, in 1931, he asserted that his originality consisted of the imitation of "everything I saw that was good," he took pains to list only German composers: "My teachers were primarily Bach and Mozart, and secondarily Beethoven, Brahms, and Wagner . . . I also learned much from Schubert and Mahler, Strauss and Reger too. I shut myself off from no one."[6]

The gradual disrepute into which the word neoclassicism fell is parallel to the rise in literature on Stravinsky and Schoenberg which has devised increasingly elegant methods for analyzing their music. As scholars furnished evidence that neither composer's music of the 1920s was so radically different from his pre-war work as once thought, the vagueness that had attended the word neoclassicism only served to lend credence for supporting its interment. In 1933, Roger Sessions made one of the earliest calls for the abandonment of the term as a consequence of suggesting that there was a point of contiguity between the styles of the two composers:

> A curious parallel with the beginnings of so-called "neo-classicism" may be seen in the definite formulation by Schoenberg of the constructive principles of his school—the well-known "twelve-tone system." The need for a fresh formal principle in contemporary music was felt, in other words, at very much the same moment by the leading spirits in the musical world and by composers of widely different feeling and background.[7]

More than four decades later, Charles Rosen made virtually the same observation:

> Neoclassicism and serialism (or twelve-tone music) are often considered polar opposites. The enmity between Vienna and Paris, between the school of Schoenberg and the school of Stravinsky, is a fact of history. . . . This opposition has long since broken down: not only have the two "schools" drawn closer together, but their differences—even at the height of the crossfire in the late 1920s—no longer seem significant.[8]

Rosen concludes that "the invention of serialism was specifically a move to resurrect an old classicism as well as to make a new one possible."[9] If the theoretical apparatuses that have illuminated the styles of the two composers have encouraged us to hold the term neoclassicism in contempt because of its ambiguity, it must be realized that that same frustrating lack of clarity in the word was the source of its attraction and the reason for its survival. Neoclassicism was the sign that accommodated both innovation and tradition in composition in the 1920s. Contemporary focus may indeed have little use for the word, but an understanding of the music of the first quarter of this century is incomplete without an awareness of the meaning that neoclassicism had for its protagonists.

Notes

Preface

1. René Wellek, *Discriminations: Further Concepts of Criticism* (New Haven: Yale University Press, 1970), 56.

2. See, for example, Ron Manheim, "Expressionismus—Zur Entstehung eines kunsthistorischen Stil- und Periodbegriffes," *Zeitschrift für Kunstgeschichte*, 49.1 (1986): 73–91; and Ronald L. Byrnside, "Musical Impressionism—The Early History of the Term," *The Musical Quarterly*, 66.4 (1980): 522–37.

3. Joseph Kerman, "Theories of Late Eighteenth-Century Music," *Studies in Eighteenth-Century British Art and Aesthetics*, ed. Ralph Cohen (Berkeley: University of California Press, 1985), 217.

4. William Austin, *Music in the 20th Century* (New York: Norton, 1966), 32; and Eric Salzman, *Twentieth-Century Music: An Introduction*, 2nd ed. (Englewood Cliffs: Prentice-Hall, 1974), 44.

5. Keith W. Daniel, *Francis Poulenc: His Artistic Development and Musical Style* (Ann Arbor: UMI Research Press, 1982), 96; Antony Beaumont, *Busoni the Composer* (Bloomington: Indiana University Press, 1985), 24–25; Larry Sitsky, *Busoni and the Piano* (New York: Greenwood Press, 1986), 244; and David Neumeyer, *The Music of Paul Hindemith* (New Haven: Yale University Press, 1986), 1–2.

6. On the contribution of nineteenth-century historians to the formulation of unified style periods in the arts, see Harry Elmer Barnes, *A History of Historical Writing*, 2nd ed. (New York: Dover, 1962), 239–56, 310–29; Peter Allan Dale, *The Victorian Critic and the Idea of History* (Cambridge: Harvard University Press, 1977), 1–12, 236–45; Stephen Kern, *The Culture of Time and Space 1880–1918* (Cambridge: Harvard University Press, 1983), 36–64; and Wellek, 55–89.

7. C. B. von Miltitz, "Was heisst klassisch in der Musik?," *Allgemeine Musikalische Zeitung*, December, 1835: 838–43; and Gustav Schilling, *Encyclopädie der gesammten musikalischen Wissenshcaften oder Universal-Lexikon der Tonkunst*, 2nd ed., 6 vols. (Stuttgart, 1841), 4: 131.

8. Heinrich Adolf Kostlin, *Geschichte der Musik im Umriss* (Berlin, 1899), 481.

Chapter 1

1. Barbara W. Tuchman, *The Proud Tower* (New York: Macmillan, 1966), xvii.

2. Carl E. Schorske, *Fin-de-siècle Vienna* (New York: Knopf, 1980), xix.

3. Peter Gay, *The Bourgeois Experience, Victoria to Freud* (New York: Oxford University Press, 1984), 60. See also Koenraad W. Swart, *The Sense of Decadence in Nineteenth-century France* (The Hague: M. Nijhoff, 1964), 187; and Claude Digeon, *La crise allemande de la pensée française* (Paris: Presses universitaires de France, 1959), 353–54.

4. Roger Shattuck, *The Banquet Years* (New York: Vintage Books, 1968), 4.

5. Frederic Morton, *A Nervous Splendor* (Boston: Little, Brown, 1979), vii; John Rewald, *Post-Impressionism from Van Gogh to Gaugin* (New York: Museum of Modern Art, 1978), 133; and Raymond Rudorff, *The Belle Epoque, Paris in the Nineties* (London: Hamilton, 1972).

6. Joris-Karl Huysmans, *Oeuvres complètes*, 18 vols. (Paris: G. Cres et Cie., 1926), 2: 303.

7. Camille Saint-Saëns, *Harmonie et mélodie* (Paris, 1885), 189–90; and E.-M. E. Deldevez, *La société des concerts, 1860 à 1885* (Paris, 1887).

8. After the Lamoureux performance of *Tristan und Isolde*, the list includes: *Lohengrin* on May 3, 1887, at the Théâtre Eden, and on September 16, 1891, at the Opéra; *Das Rheingold* in fragments on May 6, 1893, at the Opéra in concert form on January 13, 1901, and staged completely on November 17, 1909; *Tannhäuser* on May 13, 1895, at the Opéra (the hundredth performance reached on November 26, 1900); *Der fliegende Holländer* on May 17, 1897, at the Opéra comique; *Die Meistersinger* on November 10, 1897, at the Opéra; *Tristan und Isolde* staged on October 28, 1899, at the Nouveau Théâtre; *Siegfried* on January 3, 1902, at the Opéra; and *Götterdämmerung* on May 17, 1902, at the Château d'eau.

9. Richard Wagner, "An das deutsche Heer vor Paris," and "Eine Kapitulation," *Gesammelte Schriften und Dichtungen*, 3rd ed., 10 vols. (Leipzig, 1897), 9: 1–41.

10. Charles Baudelaire, "Richard Wagner et *Tannhäuser* en Paris," *Revue européenne*, 1 April 1861. See Lois Boe Hyslop and Francis E. Hyslop Jr., trans. and ed., *Baudelaire as a Literary Critic* (University Park: Pennsylvania State University Press, 1964), 194–231.

11. Paul Cézanne, *Letters*, trans. Marguerite Kay, ed. John Rewald (Oxford: B. Cassirer, 1976), 103. Renoir's early infatuation with Wagner was recounted to Ambroise Vollard, *Renoir, an Intimate Record*, trans. Harold L. van Doren and Randolph T. Weaver (New York: Knopf, 1925), 107. See also Edward Lockspeiser, "The Renoir Portraits of Wagner," *Music and Letters*, 28.3 (1937): 18.

12. *Selected Writings of Jules Laforgue*, trans. and ed. William Jay Smith (Westport, Conn.: Greenwood Press, 1956), 192–93. The article, entitled "Impressionism," was unpublished during his lifetime.

13. *The Complete Letters of Vincent van Gogh*, 3 vols. (London: Thames and Hudson, 1958), 3: 431.

14. Stephane Mallarmé, "Averses au critique," *La revue blanche*, 1 September 1895. Reprinted as "Crisis in Poetry," *Stephane Mallarmé: Selected Prose, Poems, Essays and Letters*, trans. and ed. Bradford Cook (Baltimore: Johns Hopkins Press, 1956), 39. Tristan utters these words in the final scene after he hears Isolde's off-stage voice.

15. Compare Baudelaire, 190–200: "Soon I experienced the sensation of a brighter *light, of an intensity of light* increasing so quickly that none of the nuances furnished by the dictionary would suffice to express *this always renascent increase of brilliance and whiteness,*" (Baudelaire's italics) with Mallarmé, "Lecture in Oxford and Cambridge," *La revue blanche,* October 1894: "And when, a moment ago, I was sketching those winding and mobile variations of the Idea which are the prerogative of the written word, some of you may have been reminded of certain orchestral phrasings in which we hear, first, a withdrawal to the shades, swirls and uneasy hesitation, and then suddenly the bursting, leaping, multiple ecstasy of Brilliance, like the approaching radiance of a sunrise." Mallarmé, *Selected Prose,* 49.

16. The most familiar are Houston Stewart Chamberlain, *Le drame wagnérien* (Paris, 1894) and *Richard Wagner, sa vie et ses oeuvres* (Paris, 1896); Judith Gautier, *Richard Wagner et son oeuvre poétique* (Paris, 1882); Adolphe Jullien, *Richard Wagner, sa vie et ses oeuvres* (Paris, 1886, with fourteen original lithographs by Henri Fantin-Latour); Maurice Kufferath, *Le théâtre de Richard Wagner,* 6 vols. (Paris, 1887–98); Lionel La Laurencie, *La légende de Parsifal* (Paris, 1888–94); Albert Lavignac, *Le voyage artistique à Bayreuth* (Paris, 1897); Charles Malherbe, *Mélanges sur Richard Wagner* (Paris, 1892) and *L'oeuvre dramatique de Richard Wagner* (Paris, 1886); Catulle Mendès, *Richard Wagner* (Paris, 1895); and Joséphin Péladan, *Le théâtre complet de Wagner* (Paris, 1894).

17. Dujardin's novel, *Les lauriers sont coupés,* published serially in *Revue indépendante,* May–August, 1887, was the first effort, albeit primitive, to employ interior monologue in prose. In "Au XX et aux Indépendants—Le cloisonisme," *Revue indépendante,* 6 March 1888, Dujardin coined a term, cloisonism, to describe a technique which he discerned in the art of Gaugin, van Gogh, Bernard, and Anquetin.

18. Edouard Dujardin, *Mallarmé par un des siens* (Paris: A. Messein, 1936), 201. See also Dujardin, "La revue wagnérienne," *La revue musicale, Wagner et la France,* numéro spécial, 1 October 1923: 144.

19. Edouard Dujardin, "Chronique (Les wagnéristes)," *Revue wagnérienne,* 8 April 1885: 57–58; Dujardin, "Chronique: fin de saison; M. Lamoureux; M. d'Indy et Chabrier," *Revue wagnérienne,* 8 April, 1886: 97–99; Catulle Mendès, "Le jeune prix de Rome et le vieux wagnériste," *Revue wagnérienne,* 8 June 1885: 131–35; and Téodore de Wyzewa, "La musique descriptive," *Revue wagnérienne,* 8 April 1885: 74–76.

20. Léon Vallas, *Claude Debussy: His Life and Works* (London: Oxford University Press, 1933), 76; and Yvonne Tienot, *Chabrier par lui-même et par ses intimes* (Paris: H. Lemoine, 1965), 35. For a list of the French composers attending Bayreuth between 1876 and 1896 see Lavignac, *Le voyage,* 549–617.

21. Claude Debussy, "Correspondence Ernest Chausson-Claude Debussy," *La revue musicale, Ernest Chausson,* numéro spécial, 1 December 1925: 120. A serviceable summation of other Wagnerian influences among French composers can be found in Elliot Zuckerman, *The First Hundred Years of Wagner's "Tristan"* (New York: Columbia University Press, 1964), 83–122. For an intensive analysis of Wagner's influence upon *Pelléas et Mélisande,* see Robin Holloway, *Debussy and Wagner* (London: Eulenburg, 1979), 60–78.

22. Tienot, 85. D'Indy wrote to Camille Bellaigue, in answer to the latter's review of his *Fervaal* ("Revue musicale," *Revue des deux mondes,* 15 April 1897: 925–34): "As to wagnerism, I have lived too near the orbit of the star of Wagner not to have been fatally swept along in his revolution. It is only human, it is almost a physical law." See Léon Vallas, *Vincent d'Indy,* 2 vols. (Paris: Albin Michel, 2: 297. Not suprisingly, Bellaigue described *Fervaal* and its Wagnerian traits in terms of the decadence: "symbolism, legendary coloration, mysticism, obscure poetry, passages of lethargy and ennui."

23. On the diplomatic relationship between the two countries, see Allan Mitchell, *The German Influence in France after 1870. The Formation of the Third Republic* (Chapel Hill: University of North Carolina Press, 1979), xi: "Under the psychological burden of a lost war, the French groped unsteadily toward a redefinition of their national identity. Throughout that complex process their fledgling republic was constantly and sometimes oppressively submitted to the influence of the victorious German Reich." See also Theodore Zeldin, *France, 1848–1945*, 2 vols. (Oxford: Clarendon Press, 1973), 2: 117: "The defeat—on one level—shook the whole country profoundly. Revenge and the recovery of Alsace-Lorraine became a principal object of French policy for the next forty years. That Germany was France's enemy became the basic fact of international relations. The cosmopolitan, fraternal aspect of France received a crushing blow—though the socialists revived it—and a new strident, inward-looking nationalism developed, demanding rearmament if not war. The liberal illusion appeared to have been unmasked and a return to the chauvinist, power-conscious, egocentric traditions of the old monarchy was demanded."

24. Arnaldo Bonaventura, "Progrès et nationalité en musique," *Congrès international d'histoire de la musique*, 1901: 231; Camille Mauclair, "La fin de l'impressionisme," *La revue bleue*, 14 January 1905: 5; and Charles Morice, *Paris-Journal*, April 1910, quoted by André Billy, *L'époque contemporain (1905–1930)* (Paris: Tallandier, 1956), 25. The changing fortunes of Wagner in the French press are chronicled by Ursula Eckart-Bäcker, *Frankreichs Musik zwischen Romantik und Moderne* (Regensburg: Bosse, 1965), 77–147.

25. Jeffrey Cooper, *The Rise of Instrumental Music and Concert Series in Paris, 1828–1871* (Ann Arbor: UMI Research Press, 1983), 108–10.

26. To celebrate Moréas's *Pèlerin passionné* of 1890, *La plume* devoted its January issue to "Symbolisme de Jean Moréas," featuring a wide-eyed portrait of the poet by Gauguin entitled "soyez symboliste." In February a banquet in his honor was attended by the intellectual elite of Paris.

27. *Le Figaro*, September 14, 1891. See Jean Moréas, *Cent soixante-treize lettres de Jean Moréas à Raymond de la Tailhede et divers correspondants*, ed. Robert A. Jouanny (Paris: Lettres modernes, 1968), 148–49.

28. Jean Moréas, *Les syrtes* (Paris, 1892), 53–54.

29. Jean Moréas, *Jean Moréas, écrivain français*, ed. Robert A. Jouanny (Paris: Lettres modernes, Minaud, 1969) 531–68; Charles Maurras, "Barbares et romans," *La plume*, 1 July 1891: 229–30; and Ernest Raynaud, "L'école romane française," *Mercure de France*, May 1895: 131–45. Occasionally, virulent nationalism produced absurd conclusions. Both Moréas and Maurras, for example, considered Huysmans to be foreign because his father was Dutch. Maurras classified Judith Gautier as *tartare* despite the fact that her father was one of the nineteenth century's most admired French poets. Not coincidentally, both Huysmans and Gautier had equally impressive Wagnerian and symbolist credentials.

30. Henri Clouard, *Les disciplines. Nécessité littéraire et sociale d'une renaissance classique* (Paris: M. Rivière, 1913) 32–37. Clouard's book was in part a response to the writings of André Gide and others in *Nouvelle revue française*. They felt that the orthodoxies of classical clarity and the French tradition were too narrow to satisfy their sense of the complexity of artistic creativity.

31. Vollard, 118–23.

32. Vollard, 123. See also Téodore de Wyzewa, "Pierre-Auguste Renoir," *L'art dans les deux mondes*, 6 December 1890: 27–28.

33. Albert C. Barnes and Violette de Mazia, *The Art of Renoir* (New York: Minton, Blach & Co., 1935), 199–207; and Francis Daulte, "Renoir's 'Ingres' Crisis," *Paintings by Renoir* (Chicago: Art Institute of Chicago, 1973), 13–17.

34. For Cézanne's relationship to Poussin see Katia Tsiakma, "Cézanne's and Poussin's Nudes," *Art Journal*, 37.2 (1977/1978): 120–32; Judith Wechsler, ed., *Cézanne in Perspective* (Englewood Cliffs: Prentice-Hall, 1975), 5–6; and Maurice Denis, "Cézanne," *L'Occident*, September, 1907: 118–33. A late pastel and charcoal sketch of bathers by Degas done between 1895 and 1905 may also have classical allusions in continuing the "post-impressionist bather tradition." See Richard R. Brettell and Suzanne Folds McCullagh, *Degas in the Art Institute of Chicago* (Chicago: Art Institute of Chicago, 1984), 188–91.

35. Camille Mauclair, "La fin de l'impressionisme," *La revue bleue*, 14 January 1905: 49–53; and Maurice Denis, "La peinture," *L'ermitage*, 15 May 1905: 310–20. In the case of the painter Emile Bernard the path to tradition was directed to the Italian masters of the Renaissance. During the late 1880s, Bernard had been Gauguin's colleague at Pont-Aven. After ten years in Italy and the Near East, however, Bernard's style changed and he founded the journal *La rénovation esthétique* in which he criticized almost every progressive trend in *fin-de-siècle* painting, declaring: "In comparison to Correggio or Titian, every impressionist is pale, anemic, hollow, and crude for the very simple reason that what is taken for color is only harshness." See Emile Bernard, "Sur la méthode picturale," *La rénovation esthétique*, May–September, 1905: 191–92.

36. For other sources that define classicism in this way, see Camille Mauclair, "Le classicisme et l'académisme," *La revue bleue*, 14 March 1903: 335–40; Adrien Mithouard, "Le classique occidental," *L'occident*, March, 1902: 179–87; and Mithouard, "Le classique de demain," *L'occident*, April 1902: 289–300.

37. Charles Lalo, *Esquisse d'une esthétique musicale scientifique* (Paris: F. Alcan, 1908), 308. See also Arthur Coquard, *La musique en France depuis Rameau* (Paris, 1891), 235–36, 269–70; Alfred Bruneau, *Musiques d'hier et de demain*, (Paris: Charpentier, 1900) 226–28; Bruneau, *La musique française* (Paris: E. Fasquelle, 1901) 144–51; and Camille Mauclair, *La religion de la musique* (Paris: Fischbacher, 1909), 243–44, 250–52.

38. Jacques Morland, "Enquête sur l'influence allemande: VI. Musique," *Mercure de France*, January 1903: 89–110.

39. Paul Landormy, "L'état actuel de la musique française," *La revue bleue*, 26 March and 2 April 1904: 394–97, 421–26.

40. Morland, 89.

41. Landormy, 394. Debussy's response might be viewed with some caution. On April 3, 1904, he wrote to Louis Laloy: "Have you read an article by Landormy in *La revue bleue* where he records a conversation with C. Debussy? It is extraordinary how badly this so-called musician hears." See *La revue de musicologie, Claude Debussy, textes et documents inédits*, numéro spécial, 48 (1962): 9. This observation suggests a misattribution, although the nature of the offending excerpt is unstated. Indeed, all of the article's assertions are echoed in other essays and letters of the composer.

42. Morland, 89. The answers of Gustave Robert, Pierre de Breville, Camille Chevillard, Jules Combarieu, and Maurice Kufferath are similar, as are those of Bruneau, Henri Duparc, and Paul Dukas in Landormy, 394.

43. Morland, 89. Romain Rolland's answer is similar. Suprisingly, the two responses from Germans, Arnold Schering and Hugo Riemann, while hardly hostile to their native composers, are not distant from the others. See Landormy, 394. The only point of disagreement was on Berlioz's influence. Duparc and d'Indy felt that Berlioz was outside the French tradition. Their dissent was understandable, given their intimacy with the circle of César Franck.

44. Louis Laloy, "Wagner et nos musiciens," *La grande revue*, 10 April and 10 May 1909: 558–66, 160–64.

45. Louis Bertrand, *La fin du classicisme et le retour de l'antiquité* (Paris, 1897); André Fontane, *Les doctrines d'art en France* (Paris: H. Laurens, 1909); and Louis Hautecoeur, *Rome et la renaissance de l'antiquité à la fin du xviie siècle* (Paris: Fontemoing et Cie., 1912). The term is used by Jean Locquin, *La peinture d'histoire en France de 1747 à 1785* (Paris: H. Laurens, 1912). See also Hugh Honour, "Neo-classicism," *The Age of Neo-classicism* (London: Arts Council of Great Britain, 1972), xxii; and Michel Roland, *Autour du néo-classicisme* (Paris: Galerie Cailleux, 1973), 1. Germans referred to this period as "Die antikisirende Epoche." See Hermann Hettner, *Literaturgeschichte des achzehnten Jahrhunderts*, 4 vols. (Brauenschweig: 1879), 3: 253.

46. Bertrand, *La fin*, vii-viii.

47. Louis Bertrand, preface, *Les chants séculaires*, by Joachim Gasquet (Paris: P. Ollendorff, 1903), iii-iv. Painters of the late nineteenth century like Bouguereau and Gérôme, who pandered to official taste by using subjects drawn from Greek and Roman mythology and history, were called "pompier." See James Harding, *Artistes Pompiers, French Academic Art in the 19th Century* (New York: Rizzoli, 1979).

48. Bertrand, *Chants*, xxiv-xxv.

49. *Wiener Salonblatt*, 1 January 1887. See Henry Pleasants, trans. and ed., *The Music Criticism of Hugo Wolf* (New York: Holmes & Meier, 1978), 247–48. Wolf never missed an opportunity to savage Brahms in print. For the more usual German opinion of French music in general, and of Saint-Saëns in particular, see Eduard Hanslick, *Als neuer und neuester Zeit. Der modernen Oper* (Berlin: Allgemeiner Verein für deutsche Literatur, 1900), 57–70; and Hugo Riemann, *Geschichte der Musik seit Beethoven* (Berlin and Stuttgart: W. Spemann, 1901), 690–705. The latter so upset the historian Jules Combarieu that he solicited positive responses about Saint-Saëns from such German musicians as Max Bruch and Siegfried Wagner. See Jules Combarieu, "Camille Saint-Saëns et l'opinion musicale de à l'étranger," *La revue musicale*, October, 1901: 355–63.

50. For a general account of performances, see Hughes Imbert, "Johannes Brahms," *La revue bleue*, 17 January 1903: 79–84; and Paul Landormy, "Johannes Brahms et le goût français," *La revue bleue*, 7 January 1905: 30–32.

51. Romain Rolland, "Les concerts," *La revue musicale*, November, 1902: 480–81.

52. Romain Rolland, *Musiciens d'aujourd'hui*, 1908. See Romain Rolland, *Musicians of Today*, trans. Mary Blaiklock (New York: Holt, 1915), 101–2.

53. Paul Dukas, "A propos César Franck," *La chronique des arts*, 33 (1904): 273. D'Indy admired this excerpt enough to quote it in his *César Franck* (Paris: F. Alcan, 1906), 58–59.

54. Paul Dukas, "Le nouveau lyricisme," *Minerva*, February 15, 1903; reproduced in *La revue musicale, Paul Dukas*, numéro spécial, May–June, 1936: 8–17. For earlier positive statements about Brahms, see Paul Dukas, *Chroniques musicales sur deux siécles, 1892–1932* (Paris: Stock, 1980), 128–32.

55. Vincent d'Indy, *Cours de composition musicale*, 3 vols. (Paris: Durand, 1902), 1: 427.

56. Camille Chevillard, the conductor invited to perform the French works, was shocked to learn that the festival committee, led by Ernst Münch, an Alsatian organist, had chosen Charpentier's *Impressions d'Italie* and a severely edited torso of Franck's *Les béatitudes* as the representative French compositions, sandwiching them between Weber's *Oberon* Overture and the last scene from *Die Meistersinger*. By comparison, other German works offered were Beethoven's *Coriolan* Overture, Fourth Piano Concerto, and Ninth Symphony, Mozart's "Salzburg" Violin Concerto, Brahms's *Alto Rhapsody*, and Strauss's *Sinfonia Domestica*, conducted by the composer.

57. Romain Rolland, *Richard Strauss and Romain Rolland Correspondence*, ed. Rollo Myers (Berkeley: University of California Press, 1968), 206.

58. Alma Mahler Werfel, *And the Bridge Is Love*, in collaboration with E. B. Ashton (New York: Harcourt, Brace, 1958), 50. To describe Mahler's music as "too Slavonic" seems bizarre, but to characterize his work as "too Viennese," and to choose Schubert as his likely epigon is more accurate than the French could possibly have known. Mahler's admiration for Schubert is documented in his correspondence, by the works he chose to conduct, and in a melodic reminiscence from the first movement of the Piano Sonata in E♭ major, D. 568 in the first movement of his Fourth Symphony. See Henry-Louis de La Grange, *Mahler* (Garden City: Doubleday, 1973) 817; Donald Mitchell, *Gustav Mahler, the Wunderhorn Years* (London: Faber and Faber, 1975), 29; and Miriam K. Whaples, "Mahler and Schubert's A Minor Sonata D. 784," *Music and Letters*, 65.3 (1984): 255–62. Moreover, the fondness for Schubert was rife among the avant-garde in *fin-de-siècle* Vienna. Gustav Klimt had painted his *Schubert-Idyll* in 1899 and a copy hung over Peter Altenberg's bed under which the poet had written: "One of my Gods!" Both Schoenberg and Webern orchestrated Schubert songs.

59. For opinions of Schubert, see Claude Debussy, *Debussy on Music*, trans. and ed. Richard Langham Smith, coll. and intro. François Lesure (New York, Knopf, 1977), 40, 317. Alma recalled that the French staged their walk-out "in the middle of the second movement." This observation coincides, fortuitously perhaps, with the E♭ clarinet's entry at measure 143 of a 301-measure movement. Yet Mahler's affection for the piercing tone of the instrument in his first three symphonies and its association by him with popular or bizarre elements in the programs of these works are precisely those qualities of tone color and dramatic image which would have repelled Debussy. See Mitchell, *Mahler*, 327–28 and 369–70 for the symbolism underlying Mahler's use of the instrument. The strident sonority of the E♭ clarinet was also exploited by Berlioz in the final movement of the *Symphonie fantastique* and by Strauss in *Till Eulenspiegels lustige Streiche* and *Ein Heldenleben*.

60. Several critics considered the second movement to be a minuet: Amadée Boutari, "Revue des grand concerts," *Le ménestrel*, 23 April 1910: 133; and "S.," "Concerts Colonne: La 'deuxième symphonie,' de M. Gustav Mahler," *La revue musicale*, 1 May 1910: 226–30. Mahler himself termed the movement an intermezzo, but he also suggested that he intended a self-conscious, archaic evocation in a letter to Julius Buths on March 25, 1903, in which he described the movement "as the echo of *long* past days in the life of the man borne to this grave in the first movement—'when the sun still smiled on him.'" See *Selected Letters of Gustav Mahler*, trans. Eithne Wilkins, Ernst Kaiser, and Bill Hopkins, ed. Knud Martner (New York: Farrar, Strauss, Giroux, 1979), 269. Mahler deliberately obscured the line between the more Schubertian *Ländler* and the minuet in several other compositions: the second movement of the Third Symphony and the first movement of the Fourth Symphony.

61. Edward Lockspeiser, *Debussy, his Life and Mind*, 2 vols. (London: Cassell, 1965), 2: 133.

62. The Brahms concert consisted of the *Tragic* Overture, First Symphony, Haydn Variations, and Violin Concerto. The latter work had earlier met with Debussy's disfavor. In *Gil blas* on March 16, 1903, he commented that its "finicky trivialities competed with a Tchaikovsky serenade in boredom." Ravel expressed similar reservations with regard to Brahms. See Arbie Orenstein, *Ravel. Man and Musician* (New York, Columbia University Press, 1975), 122.

63. Liliane Brion-Guerry, ed., *L'année 1913. Les formes esthétiques de l'oeuvre d'art à la veille de la première guerre mondiale* (Paris: Klincksieck, 1973), 328.

64. Friedrich Nietzsche, *Der Fall Wagner* and *Nietzsche contra Wagner*, both appearing in 1888. See also Digeon, 454–58.

65. D'Indy, *Franck*, 55; Claude Debussy, *SIM revue*, November, 1912 (in Debussy, *Debussy on Music*, 270); and Igor Stravinsky and Robert Craft, *Conversations* (Garden City: Doubleday, 1959), 84.

66. Richard Strauss, *Instrumentationslehre von Hector Berlioz*, 2 vols. (Leipzig: Peters, 1905), 1: ii. See also Gustav Mahler to Gisella Selden-Goth, February 7, 1893, in Mahler, *Letters*, 147–49. Wagner had considered Böcklin a suitable candidate to design the sets for *Parsifal*, although the painter refused. Max Reger so admired Böcklin that he wrote a suite of orchestral pieces, his op. 128, inspired by his work.

67. Louis Bourgault-Ducoudray, "Discours l'overture du congrès," *Congrès international d'histoire de la musique. Documents, mémoires et voeux*, ed. Jules Combarieu (Solesmes: Imprimerie Saint-Pierre, 1901), 8. The congress was held at the *Bibliothèque de l'Opéra* between July 23–29, 1900.

68. Works by Brenet include: *Grétry: sa vie, ses oeuvres*, 1884; *Jean de Ockeghem*, 1893; *Claude Goudimel*, 1898; and *Notes sur l'histoire du luth en France*, 1899. See note 16 above for works on Wagner by Lavignac and Malherbe. It should be pointed out that this generation of historians also evinced an interest in early music. Malherbe co-edited the *Opera omnia* of Rameau and Tiersot published monographs on Gluck (1910) and Rousseau (1912).

69. Expert's dissertation was *Les théoreticians de la musique au temps de la renaissance*, 1900. Quittard's most important work was *Les Couperins*, 1913, one of the earliest biographies of that family of musicians. Pirro's dissertation subjects were *L'esthétique de J. S. Bach* and *Descartes et la musique*, 1907. Ecorcheville's doctorates were *Vingt suites d'orchestre de xviie siècle francais* and *De Lulli à Rameau, 1690–1730*, 1907. Ecorcheville was a rarity among his colleagues in receiving some training in Germany, e.g. with Riemann in Leipzig. La Laurencie published biographies on Rameau (1908) and Lully (1919). Emmanuel's thesis from the Sorbonne was *Essai sur l'orchestrique grecque*, 1895. He also edited works of Bach and Rameau.

70. See excerpts from Rolland's diary published in Rolland, *Correspondence*, 122, 146–47. See also Rolland, *Musicians*, 202.

71. Rolland's doctorates were in music, *Les origines du théâtre lyrique moderne. Histoire de l'opéra en Europe avant Lulli et Scarlatti* and in Latin, *Cur ars picturae apud Italos xvi saeculi deciderit?*, 1895. See also David Sices, *Music and the Musician in Jean Christophe* (New Haven: Yale University Press, 1968), 8–16, 127–36. Among Rolland's students were Paul Marie Masson (1882–1954), whose thesis was *L'opéra de Rameau* (1907); Georges Cucuel (1884–1918), whose doctorates were *La Pouplinière et la musique de chambre au xviiie siècle* and *Etude sur un orchestre au xviiie siècle* (1913); and Henri Prunières (1886–1942), whose dissertations were *L'opéra italien en France avant Lulli* (1913) and *Le ballet de cour en France* (1914).

72. Vincent d'Indy, "Une école d'art répondant aux besoins modernes," *La tribune de Saint Gervais*, November, 1900: 305.

73. Charles Bordes, "Credo d'art," *La tribune de Saint Gervais*, September, 1903: 307.

74. Morland, *Enquête*, 90.

75. Bordes, *Credo*, 308. For a history of concerts, see Vincent d'Indy *et al*, *La Schola Cantorum en 1925* (Paris: Bloud & Gay, 1927) 203–11, 228–35.

76. D'Indy, *Cours*, 1: 215–18

77. Vincent d'Indy, "Jeunes musiques," *La tribune de Saint Gervais*, January, 1901: 16. See also d'Indy, "De la sophistication de l'oeuvre d'art par l'édition," *Dritter Kongress der Internationalen Musikgesellschaft, Bericht*, (Vienna, 1909), 137–41.

78. Bordes, *Credo*, 314.

79. Wanda Landowska, *Landowska on Music*, trans. and ed. Denise Restout and Robert Hawkins (New York: Stein and Day, 1964), 10.

80. Albert Schweitzer, *J. S. Bach*, trans. Charles Marie Widor (Leipzig: Breitkopf & Härtel, 1908), 308.

81. Landowska, 167–70, originally "Le clavecin ou piano dans l'exécution des oeuvres de Bach," *Bulletin de SIM*, 1910.

82. Wanda Landowska, "Bach et ses interprètes. Sur l'interprétation des oeuvres de clavecin de J.-S. Bach," *Mercure de France*, 15 November 1905: 230.

83. Amadée Boutarel and Louis Schneider, "Nouvelles diverses—concerts et soirées. Deux soirées de musique ancienne et moderne," *Le ménestrel*, 27 January and 3 February 1889: 31, 39; and E. Poulain de Corbion, "Séances de musique de chambre à l'exposition universelle de 1889," *Le guide musicale*, 9 June, 1889: 5.

84. Julien Tiersot, "Promenades musicales à l'exposition," *Le ménestrel*, 9 June 1889: 180.

85. The ensemble, in addition to Casadesus on viola d'amore, consisted of his brother Marcel (1882–1914) on viola da gamba, his sister Regina Patorni (1884–19?) on harpsichord, and Maurice Devilliers on bass viol and also boasted the partisanship of Saint-Saëns as honorary president. The *Société des instruments anciens* was made up of Diémer on harpsichord, Laurent Grillet (1851–1901) on vielle, Louis van Waefelghem (1840–1908) on viola d'amore, and Jules Delsart (1844–1900) on gamba. See Arthur Pougin, "Nouvelles diverses—Paris et departments," *Le ménestrel*, 5 May, 1895: 143; and Reyval, "Chronique de la semaine," *Le guide musicale*, 12 May, 1895: 448. The first concert took place on May 2.

86. Alexandre Benois, *Reminiscences of the Russian Ballet*, trans. Mary Britnieva (New York: Da Capo Press, 1977), 349.

87. Benois, 350. Diaghilev had intended that Nijinsky choreograph the Bach ballet but there is no evidence that he had approached a composer to arrange the pieces which he had chosen. In 1913, Diaghilev requested Ravel to arrange works of Scarlatti, but in a letter of August 28 to Stravinsky, Ravel confessed that "I should write again to Diaghilev that he cannot count on me for the Scarlatti ballet." See Eric Walter White, *Stravinsky, The Composer and his Works*, 2nd ed. (Berkeley: University of California Press, 1979), 588. In a letter to the publisher Durand on July 18, 1909, Debussy indicated that Diaghilev, perhaps with either the Scarlatti or the Montéclair music in mind, had proposed a ballet with an eighteenth-century subject. Debussy apparently accepted because he soon after wrote the livret *Masques et bergamasques*.

Debussy, more than Ravel, seems to have been drawn to the idea of adapting pices from the eighteenth century for incorporation into a ballet. In a letter to P.-J. Toulet on November 30, 1911, he wrote about *Les damées*, a new ballet [sic] by Couperin and adapted by D. S. Inghelbrecht, danced by N. Trouhanowa, "which constitutes an eminently French spectacle." See *Lettres de Claude Debussy à son editeur* (Paris: Durand, 1927) 77–78; and *Correspondence de Claude Debussy et P.-J. Toulet* (Paris: Le Divan, 1929), 67.

88. Théodore Michaelis, *Chefs-d'oeuvre de l'opéra français* (Paris, 1880), xii; and Henri Expert, ed., *Les maîtres-musiciens de la renaissance français*, 23 vols. (Paris, 1894), 1: iii. Other collections include *Les plus anciens monuments de la musique francaise* (1905) edited by Pierre Aubry (1874–1910); *Anthologie des maîtres religieux primitifs des quinzième, seizième et dix-septième siècles* (189?) edited by Bordes; *Archives des maîtres de l'orgue des xvie, xviie et xviiie siècles* (1898–1910) edited by Guilmant and Pirro; *Les maîtres-musiciens de la renaissance française* (1894–1908) edited by Expert; and *Les clavecinistes français* (c.1888–c.1912) edited by Diémer (volumes 1–3), Saint-Saëns, d'Indy, Dukas, Guilmant, and Georges Marty (1860–1908).

89. After World War I, Bartók edited Couperin's compositions in 1924 for Universal Edition. Strauss, perhaps with the example of *Pulcinella* in mind, arranged several keyboard pieces by Couperin as a suite for small orchestra in 1923.

90. Other contributors were Auguste Chapuis (*Castor et Pollux*, 1903), Georges Marty (*Platée*, 1907), Reynaldo Hahn (*Les fêtes de l'Hymen et de l'Amour*, 1910; *Naïs*, 1927), and Henri Busser (*Pygmalion, Les surprises de l'amour, Anacréon,* and *Les sybarites*, 1913).

91. Debussy, *Gil blas*, January 19, 1903. See Debussy, *Debussy on Music*, 86.

92. The *Société nationale* was co-founded by Romain Bussine and Saint-Saëns. See Saint-Saëns, *Harmonie et mélodie*, 207–16, for its early history. On November 21, 1886, d'Indy introduced a motion to admit non-French music. The vote was twenty-six to sixteen, Saint-Saëns resigned, and Franck was installed as the new president.

93. *Esquisses symphoniques* ("Prélude," "Gavotte," "Allegretto," "Retour de prélude et finale"); *Cinq airs de danse* ("Introduction et ronde," "Tempo di walzer," "Sicilienne," "Menuet," "Danse guerrière"); Suite No. 1 ("Canon," "Scherzo," "Thème et variations," "Gavotte," "Marche,"); were composed between 1870 and 1873.

94. Saint-Saëns, *Harmonie et mélodie*, xxi.

95. Saint-Saëns, *Harmonie et mélodie*, iv. "The first time I heard the celebrated Quintet of Schumann, I failed to recognize its great value to a point that astonishes me still when I think of it. Later, I acquired a taste for it and maintained for several years a furious enthusiasm."

96. Léon Vallas, *Vincent d'Indy*, 2 vols. (Paris: A. Michel, 1946), 1: 174–75.

97. The sicilienne rhythm was a very common accompaniment for pastoral scenes in Baroque opera although often not titled as such, though it appears in Gluck's *Armide*, edited by Saint-Saëns in 1873. A sicilienne appears in Castillon's *Cinq airs de danse* but was never published. Meyerbeer named the Finale to Act I of *Robert le diable* (1831) a sicilienne but he treated it as an "allegro con spirito" tempo which was foreign to the earlier type. Other composers who utilized the name and rhythm of the sicilienne minus its texture were Pierné in the fourth *double* of his *Pastorale variée* (1894); Fauré (1893); Casella in *Sicilienne et burlesque* for flute and piano (1914) and *Undice pezzi infantili* (1920); Koechlin in *Dix pièces faciles* (1921); Vierne in the Second Suite of his *Pièces de fantasie* (1926); and Poulenc in *Concert champêtre* (1927).

98. Debussy, *Gil blas,* March 30 1903. See *Debussy on Music*, 159. Dukas's *Variations, interlude et finale sur un thème de J.-Ph. Rameau* is based on a minuet "Le lardon" from *Deuxième livre de pièces de clavecin* in volume 1 of *Oeuvres complètes.*

99. James Briscoe, "The Compositions of Claude Debussy's Formative Years (1879–1887)," diss., University of North Carolina, 1979, 385.

100. Vallas, *Debussy*, 145; and Edward Lockspeiser, *Debussy* (London: Dent, 1963), 146.

101. Julien Tiersot, "Promenades musicales à l'exposition," *Le ménestrel*, 23 June 1889: 196.

102. Debussy, *Debussy on Music*, 112; originally in *Gil blas*, February 2, 1903.

103. Debussy, *Lettres à son editeur*, 8. The letter is dated February 18, 1903.

104. Debussy, *Debussy on Music*, 124; originally in *Gil blas*, February 23, 1903.

105. Debussy, *Debussy on Music*, 230–31; originally in *Le Figaro*, May 8, 1908.

106. Debussy, *Lettres inédites à André Caplet* (Paris: Editions du Rocher, 1957), 61. The letter is dated October 11, 1912. See also Debussy, *Debussy on Music*, 254–55.

107. Debussy, *Debussy on Music*, 273; originally in *Bulletin de SIM*, January 15, 1913.

108. Debussy, *Debussy on Music*, 322–23; originally in *L'intransigeant*, March 11, 1915. Varèse told François Lesure that he showed Schoenberg's opp. 11 and 16 to Debussy. See François Lesure, "Claude Debussy after his Centenary," *The Musical Quarterly*, 49.3 (1963): 268. Léon Vallas maintained that Debussy told him in December 1913, that he didn't know any music by Schoenberg.

109. Igor Stravinsky, *Selected Correspondence*, ed. Robert Craft, 3 vols. (New York: Knopf, 1985), 3: 8.

110. Debussy, *Lettres à son editeur*, 145.

111. Stravinsky, *Correspondence*, 3: 9.

112. Debussy, *Debussy on Music*, 229–30; originally in *Le Figaro*, May 8, 1908, the article on *Hippolyte et Aricie.*

113. Debussy, *Debussy on Music*, 296; originally in *Bulletin de SIM*, November 1, 1913.

114. Roland-Manuel, *Ravel* (Paris: Gallimard, 1948), 34; originally in *Bulletin de SIM*, Feburary, 1912.

115. Orenstein, 141, 150; Roger Nichols, *Ravel* (London: Dent, 1977), 7; Roland-Manuel, 34; and G. W. Hopkins, "Maurice Ravel," *The New Grove Dictionary of Music and Musicians*, gen. ed. Stanley Sadie, 20 vols. (London: Macmillan, 1980), 15: 617.

116. Maurice Ravel, "Esquisses autobiographique," *La revue musicale*, 1 December 1938: 17–23.

117. Roland-Manuel, *Ravel*, trans. Cynthia Jolly (London: B. Dobson, 1947), 75; Norman Demuth, *Ravel* (London: Dent, 1947), 143; Rollo Myers, *Ravel, Life and Works* (New York: Yoseloff, 1960), 182, 185; and H. H. Stuckenschmidt, *Maurice Ravel*, trans. Samuel R. Rosenbaum (Philadephia: Chilton, 1968), 151–52. Orenstein, 183, considers it "a Latin counterpart of the adagio cantabile in Beethoven's Sonata Opus 13, or of Schumann's *Romanze*, Opus 28, No. 2." He also suggested that the "unusually clear contouring of the melodic lines" could be traced to André Gedalge, Ravel's teacher in fugue and counterpoint at the Conservatoire, and to whom the Trio is dedicated. Ravel stated that he owed to Gedalge "the most valuable aspects of my technique." See Orenstein, 19–20. It has been suggested that

Ravel may have been Diaghilev's choice to arrange Bach's music for a ballet to be choreo-graphed by Nijinsky. See Richard Buckle, *Diaghilev* (New York: Atheneum, 1979), 259. But the *Passacaglia* was not among the works of Bach chosen by Diaghilev for this aborted project. The first half of Bach's theme is virtually identical to the "Trio en passacaille" from the Second Mass by André Raison (ca. 1650–1719) which appeared in volume 2 of *Archives des maîtres de l'orgue*, edited by Guilmant and Pirro, in 1899. However, there does not appear to be any connection between this piece and Ravel's *Trio*. The passacaglia also surfaces in Brahms, Fourth Symphony, fourth movement; Franck, Chorale in B minor (1890); Reger, opp. 16, 33, 63, 96, and 127; Schoenberg, *Pierrot lunaire*; Webern, *Passacaglia*, op. 1; and Berg, *Altenberglieder*.

118. René Chalupt, *Ravel au miroir de ses lettres* (Paris: R. Laffat, 1956), 106: "I would like to have it danced at the Vatican by Mistinguett and Colette Willy in drag." The latter refers to Henri Gauthier-Villars, Colette's husband and a music critic.

119. Ravel to Roland-Manuel, October 1, 1914: "No, it's not what you think: *La Marseillaise* won't figure into it, and there will be a forlane, a gigue; not a tango, however." See Roland-Manuel, 93. At this point, work on the *Le tombeau de Couperin* was in its infancy since no gigue appears in it. Ravel's mention of the French national anthem might be an oblique reference to Debussy's quotation of it in "Feux d'artifice" from Book II of *Préludes* (1912).

120. Ravel, *Esquisses*, 17.

121. Louis Laloy, "Exercices d'analyse," *La revue musicale*, November, 1902: 471.

122. Debussy, *Debussy on Music*, 315. The alternating sections of imitation and block chords which are common to the Parisian chanson also occur in the third of Debussy's *Trois chansons*, "Yver, vous m'estes qu'un villain." On Debussy's knowledge of sixteenth-century composers, especially Palestrina, see François Lesure, "Debussy et le xvie siècle," *Hans Albrecht in Memoriam*, ed. W. Prennecke and H. Hasse (Kassel: Bärenreiter, 1962), 242–45.

Chapter 2

1. H. H. Stuckenschmidt, *Arnold Schoenberg, his Life, World and Work*, trans. Humphrey Searle (New York: Schirmer, 1977), 37.

2. See reviews by Alfred Kalisch, *Musical Times*, 1 March, 1911: 165–67; Georg Kaiser, *Neue Zeitschrift für Musik*, 12 February, 1911: 64–66; and Edgar Istel, *Die Musik*, 10.11 (1911): 298–99. More recent writers have indicated that the music for Ochs's entrance is borrowed from the trial by fire and water in *The Magic Flute*, that his waltz music is an adumbration of Josef Strauss's *Dynamiden*, op. 173, and that character relationships have parallels to *Die Meistersinger*. See Charles Rosen, *Arnold Schoenberg* (New York: Viking, 1975), 16; William Mann, *Richard Strauss: A Critical Study of the Operas* (London: Casell, 1964), 126; and Norman Del Mar, *Richard Strauss*, 2 vols. (Philadelphia: Chilton, 1962), 1: 334–412. Hugo Hofmannsthal, Strauss's librettist, identified himself with Da Ponte in a letter to the composer on June 4, 1908.

3. Egon Wellesz, "Die jüngste Entwicklung der neufranzösisches Musik," *Der Merker*, 2.16 (1911): 665.

4. R. B. Farrell, "Classicism," *Periods in German Literature*, ed. J. M. Ritchie (London: Wolff, 1966), 99–120. Kuno Francke, *A History of German Literature as Determined by Social Forces* (New York: Holt, 1901), 178–87 uses "pseudo-classicism" as described above. Friedrich Vogt and Max Koch, *Geschichte der Deutschen Literatur von dem ältesten Zeiten* (Leipzig: Bibliographischen Instituts, 1914) substitute *Aufklärung* (Enlightenment) for the entire eighteenth century and avoid reference to any of the above terms.

5. Friedrich Krummacher, "Klassizismus als musikgeschichtliches Problem," *International Musicological Society Report*, 2 (1972): 518.

6. Thomas Mann, "Auseinandersetzung mit Richard Wagner," *Der Merker*, 2.9 (1911): 21–23; and *Neue Zeitschrift für Musik*, 3 August 1911: 476–77.

7. Mann, *Auseinandersetzung*, 21. R. Hinton Thomas, *Thomas Mann, the Meditation of Art* (Oxford: Clarendon Press, 1956), 80, translates the phrase *eine neue Klassizität* as "a new classicality." This seems too rare and peculiar a use, however, for classicality and classicism in English simply do not suggest the differences that *Klassizität* and *Klassizismus* do in German.

8. Letter to Korfiz Holm, March 20, 1911. Hans Bürgin and Hans-Otto Mayer, *Thomas Mann, a Chronicle of his Life*, trans. Eugene Dobson (University: University of Alabama Press, 1969), 28.

9. Richard Wagner, *Richard Wagner an Mathilde Wesendonck: Tagebuch-blätter und Briefe*, 1904 and 1906. An English translation by William Ashton Ellis appeared in 1905. Mann refers to a passage from the diary in a series of notes written between 1909 and 1910 for an unfinished article, "Geist und Kunst." See Paul Scherer and Hans Wysling, *Quellenkritische Studien zum Werk Thomas Manns* (Bern: Francke, 1967), 169.

10. Mann had attended the premiere of the Eighth Symphony on September 12, 1910 and sent the composer a copy of his novel, *Königliche Hoheit*, as "a very poor return" for the deep impression made upon him by the work. See Alma Mahler, *Gustav Mahler, Memories and Letters* (New York: Viking, 1969), 342.

11. There is a rich tradition for this metaphorical treatment of Venice: Hofmannsthal's *Titian's Death* (1892), d'Annunzio's *Fire* (1900), Barres's *Amori et Dolori Sacrum* (1903), Regnier's *Les vacances d'un jeune homme sage* (1903), Pound's *A Quinzaine for This Yule* (1909), and Proust's *Remembrance of Things Past* (1913–27). In music, Liszt composed the two versions of *Die Trauer-Gondel* when he visited Wagner in Venice at the end of 1882, and with the premonition that his son-in-law would soon die. These works and his "R. W.—Venetia," written the following year, have parallel chords and water imagery reminiscent of Debussy's "La cathédrale engloutie." In 1891, Fauré set five poems of Verlaine under the title, *Cinq mélodies "de Venise."* The lovely and deadly atmosphere of sunken cities and exotic gardens has a strong literary heritage: tales of the Grimm brothers, Poe's *The City in the Sea,* and Hawthorne's *Rappacini's Daughter.* Yet works that employ these symbols multiply during the *fin-de-siècle*. At this time, Venice shared its melancholy features with the Belgian city of Bruges, the inspiration for Rodenbach's novel, *Bruges-la-morte* (1892); Korngold's opera, *Die tote Stadt* (1920); and paintings by Khnopff and Degouve de Nunques. The sign of an exotic, overgrown garden as a screen from reality appears frequently around the turn of the century: *Pelléas et Mélisande* as a drama by Maeterlinck (1892) and as an opera by Debussy (1902); *The Book of the Hanging Gardens* as verse by George (1895) and as a song cycle by Schoenberg (1908–9); *Serres chaudes* as verse by Maeterlinck (1889) and as a song by Schoenberg (*Herzgewächse*, 1911); *Le jardin clos* as verse by van Lerberghe (*Entrevisions*, 1898) and as a song cycle by Fauré (1914); Leopold Andrian's novel, *The Garden of Knowledge* (1895); Kokoschka's *The Dreaming Boys* (1908); and art by Hugo, Bresdin, Moreau, Rousseau, Böcklin, and Toorop.

12. Thomas Mann, *Stories of Three Decades*, trans. H. T. Lowe-Porter (New York: Knopf, 1930), 430.

13. Mann, *Stories*, 386. The homosexual overtones of the story are mildly autobiographical, for Mann in his youth had experienced an infatuation for a schoolmate. A possible literary source for this theme is August Graf von Platen, a nineteenth-century poet with homosexual tendencies whose *Sonette aus Venedig* (1825) is reminiscent of the symbolism of Mann's novella. Coincidental in time though doubtful in influence, a gifted and beautiful boy, Maximin, had been the center of the *George-Kreis* for three years before his death in 1904, and his relationship to George undoubtedly affected the tone and subject of *Der Siebente Ring* (1907).

14. Letters to Ernst Bertram, August 3 and 11, 1911. Thomas Mann, *Die Briefe Thomas Manns, Regesten und Register*, ed. Yvonne Schmidlin, Hans Bürgin, and Hans-Otto Mayer, 3 vols. (Frankfurt am Main: S. Fischer, 1976), 1: 136. For specific parallels between Wagner's operas and Mann's novella see William H. McClain, "Wagnerian overtones in *Der Tod in Venedig*," *Modern Language Notes*, 79 (1964): 481–95.

15. Scherer, 162.

16. Scherer, 203. Mann offered his rhetorical selection in a letter to Julius Bab on September 14, 1911. See Mann, *Briefe*, 1: 137.

17. Thomas, 80. See also James Northcote-Bade, "The Background to the 'Liebestod' Plot Pattern in the Works of Thomas Mann," *The Germanic Review*, 59.1 (1984): 11–18.

18. On Goethe's influence on literary movements in Germany during the late nineteenth and early twentieth centuries, see R. Hinton Thomas, *German Perspectives: Essays on German Literature* (Cambridge: W. Heffer, 1946), 1–25.

19. This letter is located in the Special Collections of the Music Division of the Lincoln Center Library, N.Y. Although not named, the correspondent is possibly Isidore Philippe, professor of piano at the Paris Conservatoire, whose name figures prominently in other letters in the Busoni collection at Lincoln Center.

20. The fourteen works consisted of: Bach, Concerto in D minor, BWV 1052; Mozart, Concertos in D minor, K. 466, in A major, K. 488, and in C minor, K. 491; Hummel, Concerto in B minor, op. 89; Beethoven, Concerto No. 1 in C major, op. 15; Schumann, Concerto in A minor, op. 54; Mendelssohn, Concerto in G minor, op. 25; Weber, *Konzertstück*, op. 79; Liszt, *Totentanz*; Saint-Saëns, Concerto in F major, op. 103; Brahms, Concerto in D minor, op. 15; Rubinstein, Concerto in D minor, op. 70; and Busoni's own Concerto of 1903–4. For a review of the final concert, see Paul Schlesinger, "Ferruccio Busoni und Deutschland," *Vossiche Zeitung*, 15 May 1919: 2–3.

21. Ferruccio Busoni, "Gedanken zu einer 'Neuen Klassizität'," *Musica Viva*, October 1936: 27–28. The draft, originally in German, appears also in English, French, and Italian although the translators are not cited.

22. The letter is reprinted in Ferruccio Busoni, *Von der Einheit der Musik, Verstreute Aufzeichnungen* (Berlin: M. Hesse, 1922), 275–80. For an English version, see Ferruccio Busoni, *The Essence of Music and Other Essays*, trans. Rosamond Ley (London: Rockliff, 1957), 19–23. The *Frankfurter Zeitung* published three times daily at the time and this space was often set aside for articles on artistic matters: concerts, museum exhibitions, and book reviews as well as biographies and obituaries of Germany's leading musicians, writers, and painters. For other denunciations of Pfitzner's 1920 essay, see Hermann Scherchen, "Zu Hans Pfitzners Aesthetik der musikalischen Impotenz," *Melos*, 1 February 1920: 20; and Alban Berg, "Die musikalische Impotenz," *Musikblätter des Anbruch*, June 1920: 1–3. For a discussion of the polemic between Pfitzner and Bekker see Robert Cherney, "The Bekker:Pfitzner Controversy (1919–1920), Its Significance for German Music Criticism during the Weimar Republic," diss., University of Toronto, 1974.

23. Ferruccio Busoni, "'Neue Klassizität'?," *Frankfurter Zeitung, erstes Morgentun,* 9 February 1920: 1. Bekker, not Busoni, affixed the heading "Neue Klassizität?" to the newspaper version. Instead of translating *zur neuen Klassizität* as "toward a new classicism," Ley interprets the phrase as "toward Young Classicism," which gives the misapprehension that *neue Klassizität* is never used by Busoni.

24. Busoni, *Frankfurter Zeitung,* 1. Hugo Leichtentritt, Busoni's first biographer, translated this passage as "the mastery, study and exploiting of all achievements of former experiments carried over into firm and beautiful forms." See Hugo Leichtentritt, "Ferruccio Busoni," *Music Review,* November 1945: 215. Another partial translation is that of Roman Vlad, "Busoni's Destiny," *The Score,* December, 1952: 9, "the examination, the mastery and the exploitation of the results of past experience."

25. Although Busoni is the first writer to employ *junge* in relation to music, the term appears earlier. *Jugendstil,* the German name for Art Nouveau, is derived from *Die Jugend,* a Munich art magazine started in 1896. In *Studien zur Kritik der Moderne* (1894), Hermann Bahr used the terms *Das Junge Deutschland* and *Das Junge Oesterreich* to characterize contemporary literature in those countries.

26. The original letter is in the Library of Congress and reprinted in Ferruccio Busoni, *Fünfundzwanzig Busoni-Briefe,* ed. Gisella Selden-Goth (Vienna: H. Reichner, 1937): 61.

27. Emil Debusmann, *Ferruccio Busoni* (Wiesbaden: Brucknerverlag, 1949), 14.

28. In his translation of Busoni's letter, Luigi Dallapiccola recognized the importance of the composer's preference for *junge Klassizität.* He used the Italian *nuovo classicismo* instead of *giovane classicismo* because he argued that the adjective *giovane* did not possess the meaning equivalent to what Busoni intended in his choice of *junge,* and that *nuovo* was a word that was better suited to render that meaning. See Ferruccio Busoni, *Scritti e pensieri,* trans. and ed. Luigi Dallapiccola and Guido Gatti (Florence: F. Le Monnier, 1941), 68–70.

29. Ferruccio Busoni, *Busoni: Letters to his Wife,* trans. Rosamond Ley (London: E. Arnold, 1938), 40, 232.

30. The list includes: *Zwei Gedichte* for baritone and piano (1919), *Die Bekehrte* for mezzo-soprano and piano (1921), *Zigeunerlied* for baritone and orchestra (1923), *Schlechter Trost* for baritone and piano (1924), and *Lied des Brander* (no date). See H. H. Stuckenschmidt, *Ferruccio Busoni, Chronicle of a European* (New York, St. Martin's Press, 1970), 130–31, for the argument to include it in this period.

31. Johann Wolfgang Goethe, "Einfache Nachahmung der Natur, Manier, Stil," *Goethes Werke,* 36 vols. (Stuttgart: J. G. Cotta, 1866), 27: 27.

32. Ferruccio Busoni, *A Sketch of a New Esthetic of Music,* trans. Theodore Baker (New York: Schirmer, 1911) 10–11; Johann Wolfgang Goethe, "Die Metamorphose der Pflanzen," *Werke,* 27: 11–47; "Naturformen der Dichtung," *Werke,* 14: 193; and "Einleitung in die Propyläen," *Werke,* 26: 225–45.

33. Johann Wolfgang Goethe, "Diderots Versuch über die Malerei," *Werke,* 25: 311. See also René Wellek, *A History of Modern Criticism: 1750–1950,* 5 vols. (New Haven: Yale University Press, 1955), 1: 34.

34. Busoni, *Sketch,* 34.

35. Busoni, *Fünfundzwanzig Briefe,* 59. The original is in the Library of Congress.

36. The need for the distance of an unspecified amount of time as a determining factor of *Klassizität* had the influential advocacy of Hugo Riemann, *Musik-Lexikon*, trans. J. S. Shedlock, 10th ed. (London: Augener, 1922), 148: "Classical: a term applied to a work of art against which the destroying hand of time has proved powerless. Since only in the course of time a work can be shown to possess this power of resistance, there are no living classics; also every classic writer is considered romantic by his contemporaries, i.e. a mind striving to escape from ordinary routine."

37. Busoni, *Essence*, 42, 44; and Busoni, *Fünfundzwanzig Briefe*, 56–57. The letter is in the Library of Congress. Goethe's definition of "classic" was reported to his friend Eckermann on April 2, 1829. See Johann Wolfgang Goethe, *Goethes Gespräche*, 5 vols. (Leipzig: F. W. v. Biedermann, 1910), 4: 87.

38. Busoni, *Essence*, 21.

39. Eduard Hanslick, *The Beautiful in Music*, trans. Gustave Cohen (Indianapolis: Bobbs-Merrill, 1957), 14.

40. Busoni, *Sketch*, 13.

41. Arthur Schopenhauer, *Das Welt als Wille und Vorstellung*, 2 vols. (Leipzig, 1891), 1: 309; and Hanslick, 21. By further comparison, Busoni gives the example: "Is it possible to imagine how a poor, but contented man could be interpreted by music? The contentment, the soul-state, can be interpreted by music." See Busoni, *Sketch*, 13. Hanslick states thus: "These abstract notions, however, are by no means the subject matter of the pictures or musical compositions, and it is still more absurd to talk as if the feelings of 'transitoriness' or of 'youthful contentedness' could be represented by them." See Hanslick, 23–24.

42. Busoni, *Sketch*, 18.

43. The expression *Ur-pflanze* appears in a letter to Herder, May 17, 1787, during Goethe's trip to Italy. See Goethe, *Werke*, 20: 5.

44. Busoni, *Sketch*, 11. See also Goethe, *Gespräche*, 1: 479. Busoni defined *Gestalt* in his letter of February 7, 1921, to Selden-Goth. See Busoni, *Fünfundzwanzig Briefe*, 59.

45. Busoni, *Frankfurter Zeitung*, 1.

46. Busoni, *Letters*, 188. An expanded version of this letter appeared in *Zeitschrift für Musik*, 2 July 1912.

47. Paul Bekker, *Neue Musik* (Berlin: E. Reiss, 1920), 185. A measure of the general predilection for melody as the primary structural force in post-war European composition is suggested by Satie in a statement of 1919, taken from a notebook for his *La mort de Socrate*: "Do not forget that melody is the Idea, the contour just as much as it is the form and content of a work." Erik Satie, *Ecrits*, ed. Ornella Volta (Paris: Editions Champ libre, 1977), 48. See also Shattuck, 167.

48. Busoni, *Frankfurter Zeitung*, 1.

49. Busoni, *Essays*, 25. The term appeared in an article in *Melos*, 17 January, 1922. In a letter to Selden-Goth, August 4, 1920, in the Library of Congress, Busoni objected to the term expressionism to designate a specific type of composition because, since no work could slavishly copy an object, all music was fundamentally expressionist.

50. The letter is in the Library of Congress. Busoni wrote: "Have you—has anybody—read my letter in No. 100 of the *Frankfurter Zeitung*?"

51. Hermann Scherchen, "Neue Klassizität?," *Melos*, 16 July 1920: 242–43.

52. On February 28, 1920, in Berlin, Scherchen conducted the fifth orchestral performance of his *Neue Musikgesellschaft* with Bartók as soloist. The composer played one of his *Two Elegies*, op. 8b, "Ein Abend auf dem Lande" from *Ten Easy Piano Pieces*, and *Allegro barbaro*. Busoni's *Berceuse élégaique* and Concertino for clarinet were also performed. Scherchen led the Berlin revival of *Pierrot lunaire* on October 7, 1922. More than thirty years after Scherchen's gloss, it was remarked that his work as a conductor had annulled his written comments. See Willi Reich, "Hermann Scherchen und *Melos*," *Melos*, June–July 1951: 189.

53. Adolf Aber, "Wohin des Wegs," *Melos*, 16 October 1920: 378. Aber was music critic for the *Leipziger Neuesten Nachrichten*.

54. Hermann Scherchen, *Alles hörbar machen: Briefe eines Dirigenten*, ed. Eberhardt Klemm (Berlin: Henschel, 1976), 16.

55. Edwin Lendvai, "Spaziergang am Diesterweg," *Melos*, 1 November 1920: 423.

56. Philipp Jarnach, "Das stilistische Problem in der neuen Klassizität in Busonis Werk," *Musikblätter des Anbruch*, January 1921: 19. Busoni had reviewed the contents of this issue in September 1920, and was pleased by the quality. See Busoni, *Letters*, 299. He may have looked over only his own prose, however, and Jarnach's article may have been submitted after this date.

57. Edward Dent, "Italian Neo-Classicists," *The Nation and the Athenaeum*, 3 September 1921: 807.

58. Gisella Selden-Goth, *Ferruccio Busoni* (Leipzig: E. P. Tal & co., 1922), 139–41.

59. Franz Roh, *Nach-Expressionismus: Magischer Realismus* (Leipzig: Klinhardt & Biermann, 1925), 112–13; Philipp Jarnach, "Das Romanische in der Musik," *Melos*, November 1924: 191–95; Hugo Leichtentritt, "German Music of the Last Decade," *The Musical Quarterly*, 10.2 (1924): 193–218; and Raymond Petit, "Notes et documents de musique," *Mercure de France*, 1 November 1924: 816–20.

60. Heinrich Schenker, *Free Composition*, trans. and ed. Ernst Oster (New York: Longman, 1979), 5.

61. Hans and Rosaleen Moldenhauer, *Anton von Webern: A Chronicle of his Life and Work* (New York: Knopf, 1979), 276, 328, 575, 689; Anton von Webern, *Letters to Hildegarde Jone and Josef Humplik* (Bryn Mawr: T. Presser, 1967), 44, 47; Webern, *Sketches: 1926–1945* (New York: C. Fischer, 1968), 6; Webern, *The Path to the New Music*, trans. Leo Black, ed. Willi Reich (Bryn Mawr: T. Presser, 1963); Paul Klee, *Watercolors, Drawings, Writings* (New York: H. Abrams, 1969), 8; Werner Haftmann, *The Mind and Work of Paul Klee* (New York: A. Praeger, 1967), 150–61; Robert Rosenblum, *Modern Painting and the Northern Romantic Tradition* (New York: Harper & Row, 1975), 154–56; and Nancy Perloff, "Klee and Webern: Speculations on Modernist Theories," *The Musical Quarterly*, 69.2 (1983): 180–208.

62. Ernst Krenek quoted by Robert Craft, *Stravinsky, Chronicle of a Friendship, 1948–1971* (New York: Vintage Books, 1973), 69; and Edgard Varèse quoted by Louise Varèse, *Varèse, A Looking-Glass Diary* (New York: Norton, 1972), 50.

63. By marked coincidence, the line in Faust's final monlogue at which the music ends, "O beten, beten. Wo die Worte finden?," bears a striking similarity to the last line of *Moses und Aron* set to music by Schoenberg, "O Wort, du Wort, das mir fehlt," and in what are essentially identical dramatic contexts.

64. Stravinsky, *Correspondence*, 1: 171. Vladimir Vogel recalled that, after the performance of Busoni's pieces by Egon Petri, Stravinsky wrote three words on his program, "Merci, Busoni! Stravinsky." See Vladimir Vogel, *Schriften und Aufzeichungen über Musik* (Zurich: Atlantis-Verlag, 1977), 178–80. Vogel undoubtedly exaggerates when he states: "Now were the words, 'Merci, Busoni' only a conventional phrase or was he hiding a gratitude for something much more deep and important, which was like a mere compliment? In those hours neoclassicism of the Stravinsky kind might have been born or at least it took a surer and clearer form in the thoughts of the composer of *Le sacre du printemps*." But Stravinsky was already working the Concerto for Piano and Winds.

Chapter 3

1. Edwin Evans, "The Foundations of twentieth-century Music," *Musical Times*, 1 August 1917: 347; Cyril Scott, "The Genius of French Music," *The New Statesman*, 8 September 1917, and quoted in *Musical Times*, 1 October 1917: 447; Jean Huré, "The Immediate Future of French Music," *The Musical Quarterly*, 4.1 (1918): 74–77; Paul Landormy, "Reviews," *Musical Times*, 1 April 1918; and Gabriel Fauré, preface, *French Music of Today*, by Georges Jean-Aubry, trans. Edwin Evans (London: K. Paul, Trench, Trubner & Co., 1919), xxviii.

2. Ernest Newman, "The New French Recipe," *The Birmingham Post*, 20 August 1917, and reprinted in *Musical Times*, 1 October 1917: 441. See also Ernest Newman, "The Present Trend," *The Birmingham Post*, 15 May 1917, and reprinted in *Musical Times*, 1 June 1917: 249. Newman's apparent neutrality may have arisen from his awkward position as a critic writing in an allied country and who much preferred German music to that of France. Ravel was a similar solitary figure when he refused to sign the proposal for a ban against the performance of German and Austrian music made in 1916 by the National League for the Defense of French Music. See Orenstein, *Ravel*, 73–74.

3. Georges Jean-Aubry, "Claude Debussy," *The Musical Quarterly*, 4.4 (1918): 542–54; Camille Mauclair, *L'art indépendent français* (Paris: La renaissance du livre, 1919), 136; René Chalupt, "Ravel," *Les écrits nouveaux*, December 1918: 312–19; and Roland-Manuel, "Maurice Ravel," *La revue musicale*, 1 April 1921: 18.

4. Egon Wellesz, "Die jüngste Entwicklung der neufranzösischen Musik," *Der Merker*, May 1911: 657–65; Wellesz, "Die letzten Werke Claude Debussys," *Melos*, 16 May 1920: 168; and Wellesz, "Maurice Ravel," *Musikblätter des Anbruch*, October 1920: 546.

5. Leigh Henry, "London Letter," *Chesterian*, January 1921: 371.

6. Jean Cocteau, *Oeuvres complètes de Jean Cocteau*, 11 vols. (Geneva: Marguerat, 1950), 9: 24–25, 30–31. See also Jean Cocteau, *Cocteau's World*, trans. and ed. Margaret Crosland (New York: Dodd, Mead, 1972), 310–13.

7. Jean Cocteau, "Fragments d'une conférence sur Erik Satie," *La revue musicale*, 1 March 1924: 223.

8. Guillaume Apollinaire, *Oeuvres complètes*, ed. Michel Décaudin, 4 vols. (Paris: Balland and Lecat, 1965–66), 3: 900. "L'esprit nouveau et les poètes" was given as a lecture on November 26 1917, and appeared in *Mercure de France*, December 1918). Apollinaire indicated that the ideal way to mediate between freedom and order was via a synthesis of arts achievable only with the phonograph and the cinema. This idea may have prompted Cocteau to introduce non-musical sounds into *Parade*, although such procedures were common fare among the Italian futurists. Ironically, although Apollinaire admired *Parade* and even contributed an

essay for the program at the premiere, he credited only Satie, Massine, and Picasso for its creation. Francis Steegmuller, *Cocteau* (New York: MacMillan, 1970), 183, called Apollinaire's exclusion of Cocteau in the essay "one of the more famous snubs in the annals of modern art."

9. Roger Little, *Guillaume Apollinaire* (London: Athlone Press, 1976), 92–93.

10. Apollinaire had written a preface for a Derain exhibition at Paul Guillaume's gallery in October 1916. See Denys Sutton, *André Derain* (London: Phaidon Press, 1959), 32.

11. Steegmuller, 87. Cocteau's evaluation of art for its shock value may have been encouraged by Apollinaire's lecture in 1917, where the poet stated: "Surprise is the great new resource. It is by surprise, by the important place that surprise is given, that the new spirit sets itself apart from the artistic and literary movements which precede it." Apollinaire, *Oeuvres*, 3: 900.

12. Steegmuller, 95–108; and Stravinsky, *Correspondence*, 1: 74–86.

13. Jean Cocteau, "Nous voudrions vous dire un mot," *Le mot*, 27 February 1915: 1. Cocteau was among the earliest to juxtapose the names of the two composers. Ravel made a similar comparison minus Cocteau's condemnation of Schoenberg in a review of the premiere of *Le rossignol*: "Stravinsky's newest creation approaches the last manner of Arnold Schoenberg, who is harder and more austere as well as—let us use the word—more cerebral." Maurice Ravel, "Les nouveaux spectacles de la saison russe—*Le rossignol*," *Comoedia illustré*, 5 June 1914: 811–14.

14. The poet's intermediary, Valentine Gross, made certain that Satie did not know that Cocteau had recently failed to convince Stravinsky to work with him. Steegmuller, 135.

15. Cocteau, *Oeuvres*, 25, 39. Cocteau's cooler assessment of *Le sacre* may owe something to Apollinaire's rejection, in his lecture of 1917, of "the Italian and Russian futurists who have pushed the new spirit too far; for France abhors disorder."

16. Francis Steegmuller, "New York Celebrates the Genius of Jean Cocteau," *The New York Times*, 13 May 1984, sec. 2: 18.

17. Paul Landormy, "Le déclin de l'impressionisme," *La revue musicale*, 1 February 1921: 109. "Amazingly, and for a long time and perhaps today still unknown, E. Satie was, according to Jean Cocteau, a very great artist, a sort of Ingres in music, and the true father of the new school. When Debussy was enveloped in impressionism 'Satie continued his little classical route.' What does this law prescribe? We already know that it ought not to be French, not romantic, impressionist, Wagnerian, Debussyist. But what should it be? In sum, a very sober art and, as they themselves say, very stripped, which does not fear dryness and, in any case, not a preference for bloatedness and grandiloquence. A realist art, a simple art, a nude art."

18. Gino Severini, *Du cubisme au classicisme* (Paris: Povolovsky, 1921) 34–37.,

19. Maurice Brillant, "Les oeuvres et les hommes," *Le correspondent*, 25 February 1921: 744–45.

20. Giorgio de Chirico, "Une lettre de Chirico," *Littérature*, 1 March 1922: 11–13. See James Thrall Soby, *Giorgio de Chirico* (New York: Arno Press, 1966), 158–59.

21. Georges Auric, "La musique: quelques maîtres contemporains," *Les écrits nouveaux*, March 1922: 70–78. The statement was reprinted in *La revue musicale*, 1 June 1922: 185.

22. Robert Brussel, "Les concerts," *Le Figaro* 10 April 1922: 4.

23. Carlo Carrà, "Canova e il neoclassicismo," *Valori plastici*, 2.9–12 and 3.1–2 (1920–21). The first issue of *Valori plastici* appeared on November 15. It was published in Rome under the editorship of Mario Broglio.

24. Alberto Savinio, "'Anadiomenon': (Principes d'évaluation de l'art contemporain)," *Le néo-classicisme dans l'art contemporain* (Rome: Editions de "valori plastici": 1923) 5–14; Carlo Carrà, "L'état de la peinture italienne," and "Petite histoire de notre jeunesse," *Le néoclassicisme*, 49, 70.

25. Paintings by de Chirico from the war years have titles like *The Mystery and Melancholy of a Street* (1914), *The Torment of the Poet* (1914), *The Anguish of Departure* (1914), and *The Disquieting Muses* (1917). This style was known as *Pittura metafisica*, the title of a book by Carrà in 1919. As a group the *Scuola metafisica* had a short life. Carrà and de Chirico met in 1917, but the latter criticized Carrà's book in which the author appeared to take credit for initiating the style, and by 1920 their relationship had come to an end.

26. Giorgio de Chirico, "Il ritorno al mestiere," *Valori plastici*, 1.11–12 (1919); "Classicismo pittorico," *La ronda*, 2.7 (1920): 506–19; and "Considerazione sulla pittura neoclassici milanesi," *Il primato artistico*, September-October 1920.

27. Michel Georges-Michel, *Ballets russes: Histoire anecdotique* (Paris: Aux éditions du monde nouveau, 1923), 8.

28. The terms "realism" and "realist" here refer to a nonabstract, figural style. There is no connection between this usage and that intended by Apollinaire in his program note for the premiere of *Parade* in 1917, wherein he credits Cocteau for calling the work a "realistic ballet." See Guillaume Apollinaire, *Apollinaire on Art: Essays and Reviews 1902–1918*, trans. Susan Suleiman, ed. LeRoy C. Breunig (New York: Viking Press, 1972), 452–53.

29. William Rubin, Elaine L. Johnson, and Riva Castleman, *Picasso in the Collection of the Museum of Modern Art* (New York: Museum of Modern Art, 1972), 103, 107–11, 114–17, 220; Mary Mathews Gedo, *Picasso: Art as Autobiography* (Chicago: University of Chicago Press, 1980), 106–9, 117–21, 124–30; Alfred H. Barr, Jr., *Picasso: Fifty Years of his Art* (New York: Arno Press, 1966), 94–96, 102–3, 106–7, 115–20, 124–30; and Jane Fluegel, *Pablo Picasso, A Retrospective* (New York: Museum of Modern Art, 1980), 196–99.

30. Stravinsky, *Correspondence*, 1: 160; Steegmuller, 147–48; and Apollinaire, 440. With characteristic opportunism, Cocteau reversed his comparison in *Le rappel l'ordre* (1926), after Picasso had issued a statement in 1923 asserting that it was utterly false to speak of "the spirit of research" in his work. See Barr, *Picasso*, 270. An early juxtaposition of the term neoclassicism with Picasso was made by Oskar Schürer, "Der Neoklassizismus in der jüngsten französischen Malerei," *Jahrbuch für Philosophie*, 1925: 427–43.

31. Soby, *De Chirico*, 162; James Thrall Soby and Alfred H. Barr, Jr., *Twentieth-Century Italian Art* (New York: Museum of Modern Art, 1949), 25; Leroy C. Breunig, *Guillaume Apollinaire* (New York Columbia University Press, 1969), 39–40; and William A. Canfield, *Francis Picabia: His Art, Life and Times* (Princeton: Princeton University Press, 1979), 188.

32. While it has often been observed that Picasso's overt uses of the past (and of Ingres in particular) were contemporary to those of Stravinsky around 1920, it has rarely been noticed that, in old age, both artists came to view their early work as part of that same historical tradition that they had drawn from around 1920, and that they both reinterpreted youthful compositions late in their careers. For example, Picasso treated the theme of Salome dancing before Herod in etchings from 1905 and 1971. Stravinsky drew the theme for *Canon on a Russian Popular Tune* (1965) from *Firebird* (1909–10).

33. Picasso might well have disagreed with Diaghilev's characterization. In his statement of 1923, he not only disavowed "the spirit of research," but also stated that "the several manners I have used in my art must not be considered as an evolution, or as steps toward an unknown ideal of painting. All I have ever made was made for the present and with the hope that it will always remain in the present." See Barr, *Picasso*, 271.

Chapter 4

1. Boris de Schloezer, "La musique," *Revue contemporaine*, 1 February 1923: 257. Another extract from this article, under the title "Le couple Schoenberg-Stravinsky," was reprinted in *La revue musicale*, 1 March 1923: 189.

2. For *Pulcinella*, see Roman Vlad, *Stravinsky*, trans. Frederick and Ann Fuller (London: Oxford University Press, 1960), 74; Otto Deri, *Exploring Twentieth-Century Music* (New York: Holt, Rinehart, and Winston, 1968), 189; Mosco Carner, "Music in the Mainland of Europe: 1918–1939," *The Modern Age: 1890–1960*, ed. Martin Cooper (London: Oxford University Press, 1974), 217; Jim Samson, *Music in Transition* (New York: Norton, 1977), 48; Richard Shead, *Music in the 1920s* (London: Duckworth, 1977), 21; and Arnold Whittal, *Music since the First World War* (New York: St. Martin's Press, 1977), 69. For the *Octet*, see Peter S. Hansen, *An Introduction to Twentieth-Century Music*, 4th ed. (Boston: Allyn and Bacon, 1978), 159; Eric Walter White, "Stravinsky," *Music in the Modern Age*, ed. F. W. Sternfeld (New York: Praeger, 1973), 79; and Craft in Stravinsky, *Pictures and Documents*, 217.

3. Stravinsky, *Pictures and Documents*, 217.

4. Carl Van Vechten, *Music after the Great War and Other Studies* (New York: Schirmer, 1915), 92–93.

5. See, for example, Schoenberg's letter to Kandinsky, January 24, 1911: "One must express *oneself*! Express oneself *directly*! Not one's taste, or one's upbringing, or one's intelligence, knowledge or skill. Not all these *acquired* characteristics, but that which is *inborn*, *instinctive*." Arnold Schoenberg and Wassily Kandinsky, *Letters, Pictures and Documents*, trans. John C. Crawford, ed. Jelena Hahl-Koch (London: Faber and Faber, 1984), 23.

6. William Rubin, "Modernist Primitivism: An Introduction," *"Primitivism" in 20th Century Art*, ed. William Rubin, 2 vols. (New York, Museum of Modern Art, 1984), 1: 75; and Stravinsky, *Correspondence*, 3: 61.

7. Igor Stravinsky and Robert Craft, *Expositions and Developments* (Garden City: Doubleday, 1962), 157. The composer claimed he met Satie at Debussy's shortly after the first performance of *Petrushka* in 1911. Satie's photograph of Stravinsky and Debussy, however, is normally dated 1910. See Stravinsky, *Pictures and Documents*, 62; and François Lesure, *Debussy. Iconographie musicale* (Geneva: Editions Minkoff, 1980), 134–35. Misia Sert took credit for prompting Stravinsky to support Satie in a letter to Cocteau in June 1916. See Arthur Gold and Robert Fizdale, *Misia* (New York: Knopf, 1980), 188.

8. Stravinsky, *Conversations*, 81–82. Hearing of Stravinsky's illness in 1913, Satie wrote on June 14 of his intention to visit and offer consolation. Stravinsky, *Correspondence*, 3: 10.

9. Igor Stravinsky and Robert Craft, *Dialogues and a Diary* (Garden City: Doubleday, 1963), 41.

10. Ravel prefaced his work with an excerpt from Henri de Regnier's novel, *Les rencontres de Monsieur de Bréot* (1904): "The delightful and novel pleasure of a useless occupation." Satie chose classical authors—La Bruyère, Cicero, Cato—to introduce his three waltzes. Satie's

post-war jibes at Ravel are notorious. (Cocteau quoted him in *Le coq*, May 1920: "Ravel refuses the Legion of Honor, but all his music accepts it.") Satie's bantering at Ravel's expense contrasts with the latter's organization of a concert of Satie's music at an SIM soirée in 1911. Ironically, at the premiere of Ravel's waltzes on May 9, 1911, the audience, requested to guess the identity of the composer, chose Satie in many cases.

11. Stravinsky, *Pictures and Documents*, 612; Stravinsky, *Correspondence*, 2: 31, 452; and Stravinsky, *Correspondence*, 1: 87.

12. In addition to *Valse des fleurs,* the Waltz from the *Three Easy Pieces*, and the three waltz sketches, one may add *Valse pour les enfants*, 1917, published in *Le Figaro*, May 21, 1921; the Waltz from *Histoire du soldat*, 1918; and the waltz variation from the *Octet*, sketched in 1919. See Stravinsky, *Correspondence*, 2: 411, where the sketches are reproduced. The dance between the ballerina and the Moor in *Petrushka*—the former represented by a quotation of Joseph Lanner's *Die Schonbrunner*, op. 200, in B major and the latter appearing in a modal G♯ in duple meter—was the last waltz Stravinsky wrote before he met Satie. From a narrative standpoint, this scene from *Petrushka* is similar to the waltz, "The Dialogue of Beauty and the Beast," from Ravel's *Ma mère l'oye* (completed in April 1910) especially at the "1er Mouvt" at m. 106 where the white-note modal melody in the treble is juxtaposed against the chromatic triplets in the bass. Ravel's theme, in turn, is clearly modeled after Satie's *Gymnopédies* (1888).

13. Letter to Valentine Hugo, January 6, 1917. See Nigel Wilkins, "Erik Satie's Letters to Milhaud and Others," *The Musical Quarterly*, 66.3 (1980): 404–28. Reviewing *Socrate*, Auric described its contents as "une fraîche clarté." See Georges Auric, "Une oeuvre nouvelle de théâtre," *Littérature*, March 1919: 24.

14. *L'opinion*, 29 April 1922: 449. Another possible target of the *Sonatine bureaucratique* is Debussy's "Doctor Gradus ad Parnassum" from *Children's Corner* (1906–8).

15. Paul Landormy, "Le déclin de impressionisme," *La revue musicale*, 1 February 1921: 109; Rollo Myers, *Modern Music* (New York: Dutton, 1923), 73; Charles Koechlin, "Erik Satie," *La revue musicale*, 1 March 1924, 206–7; and H. H. Stuckenschmidt, "Notizen für jüngsten französischen Musik," *Musikblätter des Anbruch*, December 1925: 54.

16. Jean Cocteau, "Fragments d'une conférence sur Erik Satie," *La revue musicale*, March 1924: 223 (originally given as a speech in 1920).

17. Robert Craft, *Igor and Vera Stravinsky, A Photograph Album, 1921 to 1971* (New York: Thames and Hudson, 1982), 73. This opinion is also apparent in *An Autobiography* (New York: Norton, 1936), 93: "*Parade* confirmed me still further in my conviction of Satie's merit in the part he had played in French music by opposing to the vagueness of a decrepit Impressionism a language precise and firm, stripped of all pictorial embellishments."

18. Stravinsky, *An Autobiography*, 64, says that *Five Easy Pieces* were designed "for amateurs little practiced in the use of the instrument." In *Dialogues*, 41, he states that they "were composed as music lessons for my children." See Igor Stravinsky and Robert Craft, *Themes and Episodes* (New York: Knopf, 1966), 30, where he supports the latter contention when refering to *The Five Fingers*: "Unlike the *Easy Pieces* for piano duet, these studies were intended not for my children but for any piano debutant."

19. Shattuck, *Banquet Years*, 31.

20. As examples, see J. S. Bach's *Clavierbüchlein*, C. P. E. Bach's *Sonaten für Liebhaber*, and the *Leichten Sonaten* of Haydn and Beethoven.

21. See, for example, Mendelssohn's *Kinderstücke*, op. 71 (1842); Schumann's *Kinderszenen*, op. 15 (1838), *Album für die Jugend*, op. 68 (1848), *Ballszenen* (originally *Kinderball*), op. 109 (1851), and *Kinderball*, op. 130 (1853); Tchaikovsky's *Album pour enfants*, op. 38 (1878); and Mussorgsky's *Ein Kinderscherz* (1859) and *From Memories of Childhood* (1865).

22. The list includes Bizet, *Jeux d'enfants* (1871); Lalo, *La mère et l'enfant* (ca. 1873); Gounod, *Trois petits morceaux faciles* (1879); Pierné, *Album pour mes petits amis*, op. 14 (1887); Fauré, *Dolly Suite* (1893–96); Claude Terrasse, *Petites scenes familières* (1893, published with twenty lithographs by Pierre Bonnard, his brother-in-law); Schmitt, *Sur cinq notes*, op. 34 (1907); Debussy, *Children's Corner* (1908–10); Ravel, *Ma mère l'oye* (1910); Séverac, *En vacances* (1910); Inghelbrecht, *La nursery* (1905–11); Satie, *Enfantines* (1913); d'Indy, *Douze et treize petites pièces faciles*, opp. 68 and 69 (1908–15) and *Pour les enfants de tous les ages*, op. 74 (1919); Koechlin, *Douze et dix petites pièces faciles*, opp. 61a and 61b (1919–20); and Casella, *Undice pezzi infantili* (1920). Alain-Fournier's novel, *Le grand meaulnes* (1913), and Valéry Larbaud's short stories, *Enfantines* (1907–14, published 1918), are two literary examples. See Christopher Robinson, *French Literature in the Twentieth Century* (Totowa, N.J.: Barnes & Noble, 1980), 85–93. In May 1910, the *Société nationale des beaux-arts* held a retrospective exhibition of children's portraits and toys. In June 1914, the Malpel Gallery ran an exhibit of paintings by children of famous artists.

23. Several of Stravinsky's early borrowings are well-known: Dukas's *Sorcerer's Apprentice* (1897) in the *Scherzo fantastique* and Debussy's *Nuages* (1900) from the *Trois nocturnes* at the beginning of *Le rossignol*, both of which Stravinsky had heard in St. Petersburg. The author agrees with Martin Cooper, *French Music. From the Death of Berlioz to the Death of Fauré* (London: Oxford University Press, 1961), 149–50, that the superficial dynamism of "Danse de l'effroi" from Schmitt's *La tragédie de Salomé* (1911) influenced *Le sacre du printemps*. The C–F♯ piano cascade in the second tableau of *Petrushka* may owe its model to the cadenza at bar 72 of Ravel's *Jeux d'eau* (1901), also a possible source for a similar gesture in Berg's "Warm die Lüfte," op. 2, no. 4 (1910). The author considers that the repetitive four-note figure of "The Magic Trick" in the first tableau of *Petrushka* may have been prompted by the *idée fixe* of Ravel's *Rapsodie espagnole* (1906). Of his early knowledge of Ravel's works in St. Petersburg, Stravinsky recalled: "The piano music of Ravel was better known [than that of Debussy], and not only the piano music. Most of the musicians of my generation regarded the *Rhapsodie* [*sic*] *espagnole*, also conducted by Siloti, as the *dernier cri* in harmonic subtlety and orchestral brilliance (incredible as this seems now)." See Stravinsky, *Expositions*, 85–86. After the composer attended a rehearsal in 1916 at which Debussy and Ravel conducted their music, however, he wrote to Diaghilev on November 21: "Except for one or two pieces, I do not care for *Saint Sébastien*, but I greatly admire Ravel's *Rapsodie*." See Stravinsky, *Pictures and Documents*, 66.

24. In addition to the mutual dedications by Satie and Stravinsky, in the *Trois poésies de la lyrique japonaise* (1912–13) the latter dedicated "Mazatsumi" to Schmitt and "Tsaraiuki" to Ravel, and *Zvezdoliki* (1911–12) was dedicated to Debussy. Reciprocal gestures were made by Debussy in the third piece of *En blanc et noir* (1915); by Ravel in "Soupir" from *Trois poèmes de Stéphane Mallarmé* (1913); and by Schmitt in *La tragédie de Salomé* (1911). In 1910 Stravinsky briefly joined a group called *Les apaches* whose members included Ravel, Schmitt, Delage, Caplet, and Inghelbrecht. See Jann Pasler, "Stravinsky and the Apaches," *Musical Times*, June 1982: 403–7.

25. Stravinsky, *Themes*, 30. The composer's use of the term "row" was a result of his familiarity with serial procedures in the 1950s. The five-note diatonic collection he in fact used in *The Five Fingers* is in no way treated with such methods.

26. The melodic contour, key, and rhythm of Schmitt's theme are also similar to the clarinet tune from the last movement of Milhaud's chamber symphony, *Le printemps* (1919), one of the first post-war works to be dubbed neoclassic.

27. Ernest Ansermet, "The Man and his Work—Igor Stravinsky—his first String Quartet," *Musical Courier*, 25 November 1915: 41. On Ansermet's early career, see Jacques Burdet, "Les débuts d'Ernest Ansermet," *Revue musicale de suisse romande*, 26.4, (1973): 2–4. Early performances of the *Three Pieces* in Paris occurred on May 19, 1915; in November 1916; and on July 18, 1917. None apparently were reviewed. Casella arranged the first performance, Poulenc attended the second, and Milhaud and Honegger played in the third. See Stravinsky *Pictures and Documents*, 126, 617. A letter from Cocteau to Stravinsky indicates that he, Gide, and Misia Sert heard this last performance. Cocteau praised it effusively but Misia's criticism of it provoked a heated response from the composer. See Stravinsky, *Correspondence*, 1: 86–87.

28. This announcement was excerpted in *The Musical Times*, 1 March 1919, p. 113.

29. Igor Stravinsky and Robert Craft, *Memories and Commentaries* (Garden City: Doubleday, 1960), 76. In 1928, the composer affixed titles to the orchestral version of the *Three Pieces* as follows: "Dance," "Eccentric," and "Canticle." That Ansermet had probably discussed the matter of extra-musical inspiration with Stravinsky can be discerned from this statement: "It is enough to say that the first embodies the spirit of the dance, the third the spirit of religious melody, while the second has been developed in the region of the musically fantastic and bizarre." See Ansermet, 41. This assertion occurs immediately before the claim that the work was "absolute music!"

30. Stravinsky, *Correspondence*, 1: 132.

31. Stravinsky, *Correspondence*, 1: 147. Ansermet apparently gave a lecture at this concert and Stravinsky requested several copies of it.

32. Ernest Ansermet, "Russische Musik," *Melos*, August, 1922: 226–27, and quoted by Robert Craft in a footnote in Stravinsky, *Correspondence*, 1: 156.

33. Ansermet, *Quartet*, 41; and François Lesure, ed., *Le sacre du printemps. Dossier de Presse* (Geneva: Editions Minkoff, 1980), 76. Ansermet had much the same thing to say in "Einführung in das Schaffen," *Musikblätter des Anbruch*, June, 1922: 170–71.

34. Leigh Henry, "Igor Stravinsky," *Musical Times*, 1 June 1919: 268. See also by the same author, "Contemporaries," *Musical Opinion*, 20 February 1920: 371; and "La musique—Les ballets de Stravinsky," *L'action*, February 1920: 20.

35. Eugene Goossens, *Modern Tendencies in Music* (London: Arts League of Service, 1919), 11. Such early estimations traveled quickly beyond Paris and London. See Paul Rosenfeld, "Stravinsky," *The New Republic*, 14 April 1920: 207–10, and reprinted in *Musikblätter des Anbruch*, June 1921: 191–95.

36. Leigh Henry, "Igor Stravinsky and the Objective Direction in contemporary music," *Chesterian*, 1.4 (1920): 97–102. The concert consisted of the *Three Pieces for String Quartet*, *Chansons plaisantes*, *Berceuses du chat*, *Three Pieces for Clarinet*, and excerpts from *Histoire du soldat*. See also Leigh Henry, "Stravinsky, The New Lyric Expression," *Daily Telegraph*, 17 July 1920: 4.

37. Ernest Newman, *The Sunday Times* (London), 25 July 1920: 6. See also Ernest Newman, "Extremists vs. the Rest," *Musical Times*, 1 November 1920: 729. Similar reactions were those of Phillip Heseltine, "Sound for Sound's Sake," *Sackbut*, August 1920: 153; and Alfred Kalisch, "London Concerts," *Musical Times*, 1 September 1920: 621.

38. Edwin Evans, "The Stravinsky Debate," *Music Student*, 13.3 (1920): 139–45. Additional responses to Newman by Evans and Henry appeared in *Musical Times*, 1 December 1920: 831–33.

39. Edwin Evans, "Igor Stravinsky, Contrapuntal Titan," *Musical America*, 21 February 1921: 9.

40. *The Observer*, 3 July 1921. See Lesure, *Le sacre Dossier*, 76. Stravinsky, when writing, placed single quotation marks around terms for emphasis. This style has been retained in his extracts in this book.

41. Stravinsky, *Correspondence*, 1: 160.

42. The concept of octatonic-diatonic linkage is based upon and indebted to the significant and highly estimable work of Pieter van den Toorn, *The Music of Igor Stravinsky* (New Haven: Yale University Press, 1983), 147–53. His interpretation of the work at hand, however, does not give sufficient importance to the sustained D in the viola, even to the extent that it does not appear in the reproduction of the score in his example 31a (which also leaves out the opening three measures of sustained C#–D in the same instrument). Too, his point of climax differs from that of the above analysis. He places it at measures 41–42, and concludes that "confinement to the octatonic collection is unmistakable." This hearing permits him to conclude that the harmonic structure is generated purely by octatonic considerations and that, as a result, the movement belongs squarely in the "Russian" period. "And exceptions to this hearing and understanding—exceptions like the interpenetrating C-scale-on-G (or G-major scale) reference here in No. 1 of *Three Pieces*—are just that: exceptions. Manifestly, No. 1 of *Three Pieces*, along with Nos. 2 and 3 as well (although not examined here), figure in the 'Russian' nutshell." It is precisely this "exception" of the conflation of octatonic and diatonic collections, however, that places this composition apart from the pre-war ballets.

43. Ansermet, *Quartet*, 41. In 1929, Boris Asaf'yev described the *Three Pieces* in a similar fashion: "Of course, the ear is immediately struck by devices now familiar to us: percussive intonations (the 'pizzicato' qualities of the sounds), the 'play of melodic elements' (variations and rhythmic alerations), the avoidance of metrical uniformity and monotony, the use of timbres for expressive purposes, the careful calculation of dynamic accent and nuance and the designation of it in the most precise terms, leaving no room for arbitrary emotionalism." See Boris Asaf'yev, *A Book about Stravinsky*, trans. Richard F. French (Ann Arbor: UMI Research Press, 1982), 99–100. Unlike Ansermet, Asaf'yev gave an analytical description of the first movement: "In order to augment the number of possible combinations and to avoid reappearances of the same particles on the same beats of the measure, Stravinsky changes the lengths of the measures and also, at unequal time intervals, breaks the basic diatonicism of the material by inserting a chromatic progression of eight notes."

44. Arthur Berger, "Problems of Pitch Organization in Stravinsky," and Edward T. Cone, "Stravinsky: The Progress of a Method," *Perspectives on Schoenberg and Stravinsky*, ed. Benjamin Boretz and Edward T. Cone (New York: Norton, 1972), 244–66, 161–63.

45. Hansen, 166, calls this sonority "Stravinsky's favorite chord," and cites the beginning of the second movement of the *Symphony in Three Movements*; the postlude to Tom's aria, "Vary the song," which opens Act II of *The Rake's Progress*; the "Danse du diable" from *Histoire du soldat*; and the "Rondoletto" from the *Serenade en la*. White, 557, gives an example from the *Symphonies of Wind Instruments*. The latter example, together with Hansen's first three citations, are also quoted by Berger, 244–66.

46. Van den Toorn, 261–62.

47. Apollinaire, *On Art*, 256, 263; and Guillaume Apollinaire, *Calligrammes*, trans. Anne Hyde Greet (Berkeley: University of California Press, 1980), 342.

48. Shattuck, *Banquet Years*, 344–49.

49. Apollinaire, *On Art*, 263; Paul Klee "Die Ausstellung des Modernen Bundes," *Die Alpen*, August, 1912: 696–704; and Ferdinand Léger, "Les révélations picturales actuelles," *Les soirées de Paris*, June 1914: 349–56.

50. Linda Williams, *Figures of Desire. A Theory and Analysis of Surrealist Film* (Urbana: University of Illinois Press, 1981), 8.

51. John Golding, *Cubism. A History and an Analysis. 1907–1914* (London: Faber and Faber, 1959), 38; Riccioto Canudo, "A propos du 'Rossignol' d'Igor Strawinsky," *Montjoie!*, April–May–June 1914: 6, 31; and Stravinsky, *Correspondence*, 2: 425. Canudo was the founder and editor of *Montjoie!*, in which numerous statements and reproductions of modern art and literature appeared. In the April–May–June issue (31), the journal announced it had hosted a Monday soirée in honor of the composer.

52. On the friendship between Cendrars and Stravinsky, and the position of the former in Parisian avant-garde circles, see Jay Bochner, *Blaise Cendrars: Discovery and Re-creation* (Toronto: University of Toronto Press, 1978), 51–54. An exchange of letters between the two in 1918–19, concerning the poet's efforts to publish the *Ragtime* with Picasso's cover drawing, appears in Stravinsky, *Correspondence*, 2: 184–88.

53. For Shattuck, the one essentially visual aspect of Stravinsky's music is "his tendency to compose without transitions, by abrupt juxtapositions and interruptions" which he finds to be comparable to tendencies in pre-war avant-garde art in Paris. Roger Shattuck, *The Innocent Eye* (New York: Farrar, Strauss, Giroux, 1984), 270–71.

54. Egon Wellesz, "Schoenberg and Beyond," *The Musical Quarterly*, 2.1 (1916): 76–95. The literature on the relationship between primitive cultures and modern art is vast. See, for example, Mona Hadler, "Jazz and the Visual Arts," *Arts Magazine*, June 1983: 91–101; Gail Levin, "'Primitivism' in American Art: Some Literary Parallels of the 1910s and 1920s," *Arts Magazine*, November 1984: 101–5; Katia Samaltanos, *Apollinaire, Catalyst for Primitivism, Picabia, and Duchamp* (Ann Arbor: UMI Research Press, 1984); and Rubin, *Primitivism*, 1: 1–84.

55. For the composer's relationship to neo-primitivist Russian artists, see Richard Taruskin, "Stravinsky and the Painters," *Confronting Stravinsky: Man, Musician, and Modernist*, ed. Jann Pasler (Berkeley: University of California Press, 1986), 16–38.

56. Camilla Gray, *The Great Experiment: Russian Art 1863–1922* (New York: Harry N. Abrams, 1962), 126. On Larionov and cubism, see J. Garrett Glover, *The Cubist Theatre* (Ann Arbor: UMI Research Press, 1983), 27–28.

57. Stravinsky, *Pictures*, 131.

58. Albert Gleizes and Jean Metzinger, *Cubism* (London: T. F. Unwin, 1913), 30–32, 43.

59. On Apollinaire's authorship of *l'esprit nouveau*, see Shattuck, *Banquet Years*, 295. The poet first employed the term in his program note to *Parade*, printed in *Excelsior*, 11 May 1917, shortly before the ballet's premiere.

60. André Rigaud, "M. Igor Stravinsky nous parle de la musique de 'Pulcinella'," *Comoedia*, 15 May 1920: 1.

61. In Delaunay's series of views of the Eiffel Tower, *Fenêtres*, his "colored volumes" are juxtaposed so that the viewer cannot tell which side of the window he or the object is on. Although undoubtedly coincidental, as an illustration of the similarity in intent among con-

temporary artists, compare Stravinsky's choice of colors for his descriptive analogy of *Pulcinella* with the opening line of Apollinaire's *Les fenêtres*, inspired by Delaunay's paintings and appearing in *Calligrammes* (1918): "Du rouge au vert tout le jaune se meurt."

62. To judge from Stravinsky's references to it, this passage may have been among his favorites: "How few listeners have remarked the real joke in the *Pulcinella* duet, which is that the trombone has a very loud voice and the string bass has almost no voice at all." Stravinsky, *Dialogues*, 34. The composer described the passage in the same way to an orchestra during a rehearsal: "Duetto between two Pulcinellas. One has a voice—trombone—the other has no voice—bass." See Igor Stravinsky, *The Recorded Legacy*, CBS Masterworks 74048, vol. I, side 1.

63. Roland-Manuel, "Le théâtre—A l'Opéra—*Pulcinella*, Ballet de Stravinsky-Pergolesi," *L'amour de l'art*, June 1920: 71. See also A. Mangeot, "Opéra—Pulcinella," *Le monde musical*, 15–20 May 1920: 152; Louis Laloy, "A l'Opéra," *Comoedia*, 17 May 1920: 1; Raoul Brunel, "A l'Opéra," *L'oeuvre*, 19 May 1920: 3; Louis Schneider, "Musique," *Le gaulois*, 17 May 1920: 3; Gustave Samazeuilh, "La musique," *La république française*, 18 May 1920: 2; and Adolphe Boschot, "La musique—à l'Opéra—PULCINELLA," *Echo de Paris*, 17 May 1920: 2. Positive responses by English critics one month later are: CRESCENDO, "Russian Ballet—Old Wine in New Bottles," *The Star*, 11 June 1920: 3; Percy Scholes, "Return of the Russian Ballet—Stravinsky and Pergolesi," *The Observer*, 13 June 1920: 7; and M.W.D., "New Masterpiece by Massine, Return of the Russian Ballet to Covent Garden," *The Evening Standard*, 11 July 1920: 10.

64. Charles Tenroc, "OPERA: Les ballets russes. Pulcinella (création)," *Le courrier musical*, 1 June 1920: 178; Antoine Banès, "Courrier des théâtres," *Le Figaro*, 17 May 1920: 3; Maurice Brillant, "Les oeuvres et les hommes," *Le correspondant*, 25 June 1920: 1120–37; Gaston Carraud, "La musique," *Liberté*, 17 May 1920; Paul Lombard, "Ballets russes," *L'homme libre*, 19 May 1920: 2; Paul Landormy, "Les premières—A l'Opéra: *Pulcinella*," *La victoire*, 20 May 1920: 2; and Adolphe Jullien, "Revue musicale," *Journal des debats*, 6 June 1920: 2. Similar reviews by English critics are: Herbert Farjeon, "Return of Diaghilev—Brilliant Russian Ballets," *Daily Herald*, 11 June 1920: 8; and Frederic Delius, "At the Crossroads," *Sackbut*, September 1920: 207–8.

65. Paul Souday, "La semaine théâtrale et musicale," *Paris-Midi*, 18 May 1920: 3 (also in *Le siècle* on May 19 and *L'action* on May 19). See also André Coueroy, "Musique—Les ballets russes à l'Opéra," *L'ère nouvelle*, 18 May 1920: 6. In a rare display of sympathy, Ernest Newman voiced qualified support: "Pergolesi and Stravinsky, of course, do not mix. Perhaps that is just the secret of the charm of this music." See Ernest Newman, *The Sunday Times* (London), 13 June 1920: 6, and 27 June 1920: 6.

66. Reynaldo Hahn, "Les théâtres—Les premières," *Excelsior*, 17 May 1920: 4.

67. Louis Laloy, "Le courier de Paris—*La musique*—Les ballets russes—Stravinsky," *L'europe nouvelle*, 23 May 1920: 679–80.

68. André Rigaud, "M. Igor Stravinsky nous parle du 'Chant du rossignol'," *Comoedia*, 31 January 1920: 1, quotes the composer: "[*Pulcinella*] is more than just an adaptation, it is a complete musical recomposition." Two examples of the composer's procedure were given in a paper by Marilyn Meeker, "Stravinsky's Approach to Recomposition in *Pulcinella*," American Musicological Society National Conference, Ann Arbor, 5 November 1982. For another excellent recent analysis of the composer's treatment of borrowed material in the ballet, see Joseph N. Straus, "Recompositions by Schoenberg, Stravinsky, and Webern," *The Musical Quarterly*, 72.3 (1986): 301–28.

69. Massine recalled seeing the open-air marionette theatre in Viareggio during August 1914. See Léonide Massine, *My Life in Ballet* (New York: St. Martin's, 1968), 66. Stravinsky remembered viewing a commedia dell'arte performance in Naples in April 1917, in Picasso's company. See Stravinsky, *Conversations*, 118–19, where the composer also related Diaghilev's surprise at not receiving "a strict mannered orchestration of something very sweet." The character of Pulcinella did not enjoy a popularity equal to that of either Pierrot or Harlequin. However, he was the buffoon of choice for the Italian painter Giandomenico Tiepolo in decorating the walls of a villa in 1793. See Adriano Mariuz, *Tiepolo* (Venice: Alfieri, 1971), plates 370–83. He surfaced occasionally in French literature during the nineteenth century as well. Nodier (1831), Banville (1868), and Mallarmé (1876) wrote poems inspired by him, the latter's quatrain written to accompany an etching by Manet engraved that year. The French comedian Max Linder appeared in *La vie de polichinelle*, an early silent film, in 1905. Polichinelle was one of several commedia dell'arte characters to appear in Debussy's *La boîte à joujoux*. Closer in time to the collaborators in the *Ballets russes* was a series of articles that appeared in Edward Gordon Craig's *The Mask*, a bi-monthly journal of the arts published in Florence. Stravinsky recalled the impression made upon him when Craig displayed his puppets for him in Rome in 1917. See Stravinsky, *Dialogues*, 24. Commedia dell'arte characters had appeared in Russian ballets as well, such as Drigo's *Harlequinade* (1901) and the *Ballets russes* productions of *Carnaval* (1910) and *Les papillons* (1914).

70. Massine, 66.

71. See also David C. Large and William Weber, *Wagnerism in European Culture and Politics* (Ithaca: Cornell University Press, 1984), 296: "One has the sense that by the eve of the war (not to mention during the 1920s) Wagner's legacy was no longer quite so important to the European avant-garde as it had been in the late nineteenth century." Cultural elitism cut both ways however. Schoenberg, with obvious knowledge of this legacy, stated in an essay entitled "National Music:" "Here is a remarkable fact, as yet unnoticed: Debussy's summons to the Latin and Slav peoples, to do battle against Wagner, was indeed successful. . . . Remarkably, nobody has yet appreciated that my music, produced on German soil, *without foreign influences*, is a living example of an art able most effectively to oppose Latin and Slav hopes of hegemony and derived through and through from traditions of German music." See Arnold Schoenberg, *Style and Idea*, trans. Leo Black, ed. Leonard Stein (New York: St. Martin's, 1975), 172–73.

72. Antoine Banès, "Courrier des théâtres," *Le Figaro*, 13 May 1920: 3.

73. Louis Handler, "'Pulcinella' à l'Opéra," *Comoedia*, 14 May 1920: 1.

74. Louis Laloy, "A l'Opéra," *Comoedia*, 17 May,1920: 1; and Adolphe Boschot, "La musique—A l'Opéra—PULCINELLA," *Echo de Paris*, 17 May 1920: 2. An equal number of critics, however, noted that the likely precedent lay in *Le rossignol*. See Raoul Brunel, "A l'Opéra," *L'oeuvre*, 19 May 1920: 3; and Roland-Manuel, "Le théâtre—A l'Opéra—*Pulcinella*, Ballet de Stravinsky-Pergolesi," *L'amour de l'art*, June 1920: 71.

75. Nesta Macdonald, *Diaghilev Observed by Critics in England and the United States, 1911–1929* (New York: Dance Horizons, 1975), 225.

76. Stravinsky, *Correspondence*, 1: 32; and Stravinsky, *Pictures and Documents*, 29, 94, 605.

77. Stravinsky, *Correspondence*, 2: 87; Stravinsky, *Correspondence*, 3: 8; and Michel Georges-Michel, *De Renoir à Picasso. Les peintres que j'ai connus* (Paris: A. Fayard, 1954), 94–95.

78. Craft, *Stravinsky Photograph Album*, 13.

79. Igor Stravinsky, "Les espagnoles aux ballets russes," *Comoedia*, 15 May 1921: 1.

80. In so emphasizing the Russian-Spanish connection, Stravinsky was echoing a lengthy association: Glinka, *Capriccio brillante on the jota aragonesa* (1845) and *Recuerdos de Castilla* (1848); Balakirev, *Overture on a Spanish March Theme* (1886); Rimsky-Korsakov, *Capriccio espagnole* (1887); and Glazunov, *Sérénade espagnole* (1887–88).

81. André Rigaud, "M. Igor Stravinsky nous parle du 'Chant du Rossignol,'" *Comoedia*, 31 January 1920: 1.

82. The original, typed in French, is in the Bibliothèque nationale, fonds Kochno, Pièce 96, L̇.A.S. (Lettres autographes signes), 52. In an English translation by Edwin Evans, it appeared in *The Times* (London), October 21. The entire document appears in White, 573–74. White mistakenly gives the date of the original as October 10.

83. Stravinsky, *Correspondence*, 3: 65.; Léon Bakst, "Tchaikowsky aux ballets russes," *Comoedia*, 9 October 1921: 1. Bakst contrasted Tchaikovsky's instinctive "melody" with the cerebral "thematicism" of Wagner. It was possibly with satisfying irony that Stravinsky described *Mavra* to Ramuz on August 21, 1921 as "all 'very melodious'—as Bakst said of the Good Friday music in *Parsifal*." Stravinsky, *Correspondence*, 3: 61.

84. Igor Stravinsky, "Une lettre de Stravinsky sur Tchaikovsky," *Le Figaro*, 18 May 1922: 1.

85. Darius Milhaud, *Notes Without Music*, trans. Donald Evans, ed. Rollo Myers (New York: Knopf, 1953), 131.

86. Emile Vuillermoz, "Mavra," *Excelsior*, 12 June 1922: 4–5. Other negative reviews were by Pierre Lalo, "La musique," *Le temps*, 30 June 1922: 3; and Boris de Schloezer, "La musique," *Nouvelle revue française*, 1 July 1922: 115–20. Schloezer wrote an apologetic letter to the composer on June 27 because the review had the following sentence deleted: "It is entirely possible that I *was* wrong in my evaluation of *Mavra*, but if, after a year, I see that I *was* wrong, I want to be the first to admit it and shall be very glad to say that I made a mistake, critics' mistakes (there have been so many) being much less significant than those of artists and authors." See Stravinsky, *Correspondence*, 1: 157–58; for the composer's tart response. Schloezer did amend his opinion the following year.

87. Ernest Ansermet, "Russische Musik," *Melos*, July–August 1922: 226–27. See also Erik Satie, "Propos à propos d'Igor Stravinsky," *Feuilles libres*, October-November 1922: 347–53; Francis Poulenc, "La musique. A propos de 'Mavra' de Igor Strawinsky," *Feuilles libres*, June–July 1922: 222–24; Georges Auric, "Du 'Sacre du printemps' à 'Mavra,'" *Les nouvelles littéraires*, 6 January 1923: 4; Louis Laloy, "Au théâtre de l'Opéra: 'Mavra,'" *Comoedia*, 5 June 1922: 1; and Maurice Brillant, "Les oeuvres et les hommes," *Le correspondant*, 25 July 1922: 366–68. Poulenc's article was retained by the composer, as a letter of August 5, 1922, attests. See Stravinsky, *Correspondence*, 1: 158, where a portion of the article also appears in translation.

88. G. Suarez, "Esthétique musicale—Igor Stravinsky n'est pas wagnérien," *Paris-Midi*, 13 January 1921: 1. Two years later, the composer was quoted as saying: "Wagner, like the whole German school, is music *fabricated* from *coups de thèmes* and leitmotives. Tchaikovsky by contrast is melody flowing from a spontaneous source, like the first Russians and Latins, including the Austrians; Mozart, Schubert, and even Johann Strauss." See George-Michel, *Ballets russes*, 8.

89. *The Observer*, 3 July 1921. See Lesure, *Le sacre Dossier*, 76.

90. George-Michel, *De Renoir à Picasso*, 95.

91. Stravinsky, *Correspondence*, 1: 160. Diaghilev was purported to have looked at Mozart's works for a suitable companion to be performed with *Sleeping Beauty*. See André Rigaud, "Les avant premières," *Comoedia*, 3 June 1922: 1. The Russians were surely acquainted with Tchaikovsky's immense admiration for Mozart and the part that the latter's music played in several of his works. The Suite No. 4, op. 61, (1887) consists of four movements, each based upon a composition by Mozart. In *Pikovaya Dama* (1890) the duet between Chloe and Daphnis (act 2, scene 1) appears to be modeled on "La ci darem la mano" from *Don Giovanni*. Other eighteenth-century allusions in the opera are the appearance of an air from Grétry's *Richard Coeur de Lion* (1784) in act II, scene 2; and Tomsky's aria in act III, scene 3, set to words by Derzhavin, an eighteenth-century poet. In Brussels on January 15, 1924, Stravinsky was quoted as saying: "Tchaikovsky, of course, adored Mozart, but he was an Austrian, which is very different from being a German." See Stravinsky, *Pictures and Documents*, 201.

92. Darius Milhaud, "The Evolution of Modern Music in Paris and in Vienna," *North American Review*, April 1923: 544–54. Sixty years later Aaron Copland recalled the era in similar terms: "There seemed a wealth of new voices from all parts of Europe, North and South America. Among them were two dominant musical personalities who would profoundly influence twentieth-century musical thinking: Stravinsky and Schoenberg, or, if you prefer, Schoenberg and Stravinsky. Each represented a distinct aesthetic, a different manner of composing, and a quite different way of thinking about the whole problem of the composer's art." Aaron Copland and Vivian Perlis, *Copland: 1900–1942* (New York: St. Martin's, 1984), 55–56.

93. Georges Auric, *Quand j'étais là* (Paris: B. Grasset, 1979), 57. In Poulenc's Trio for trumpet, horn, and trombone a satiric quote from the finale of Beethoven's Third Piano Concerto complements Stravinsky's anti-Beethoven posture at this time. Stravinsky expressed his fondness for Poulenc's Sonata for two clarinets in a letter of October 1, 1919. See Stravinsky, *Correspondence*, 3: 199.

94. "Une lettre inédite d'Ansermet à Stravinsky à propos du *Sacre du printemps*," *Revue musicale de suisse romande*, 33.5 (1980): 215. Salzburg refers to the first International Festival of Contemporary Music held there on August 7–10. Hindemith's score is not identified but, from the date of the letter, it may be *Kammermusik No. 1*. The composer does not reveal "les autres sous-Schoenberg" but a possible candidate is Webern. Several of his works were performed in Paris at this time. Although Stravinsky claimed late in life that he did not know Webern's music at this time, Craft considers it possible that he did hear the early string quartet and violin pieces. See Robert Craft, "Assisting Stravinsky," *The Atlantic Monthly*, December 1982: 74.

95. Stravinsky, *Correspondence*, 1: 171; and Stravinsky, *Correspondence*, 3: 76.

96. Early performances included *Pierrot lunaire* on March 10, 1922, at the Concerts Wiéner in the Salles des Agriculteurs, Darius Milhaud conducting, Marya Freund vocalist; *Herzgewächse* and the String Quartet No. 2 on March 30, 1922, at the Concerts Wiéner, Jean Wiéner conducting; *Five Pieces for Orchestra* in April 1922, at the Concerts Pasdeloup in the Opéra, André Caplet conducting; and *Kammersymphonie* on April 24, 1923, at the Concerts Straram, Walter Straram conducting.

97. Paul Le Flem, "La musique au concert," *Comoedia*, 13 March 1922: 4. See also Emile Vuillermoz, "L'édition musicale," *Le temps*, 27 January 1922: 4; and Robert Brussel, "Les concerts," *Le Figaro*, 24 April, 1922: 4, for similar responses. For negative reviews that emphasized Schoenberg's "disheveled romanticism" and "extremist expressionism" see Jean Poueigh, "Les grands concerts," *Comoedia*, 24 April 1922: 4; Jean Marnold, "Musique," *Mercure de France*, 1 July 1923: 198–203; and Boris de Schloezer, "La saison musicale," *Nouvelle revue française*, 1 August 1923: 238–48.

98. Paul Landormy, "Schönberg, Bartók, und die französische Musik," *Musikblätter des Anbruch,* May 1922: 142–43. See also H. H. Stuckenschmidt, "Ausblick in der Musik," *Das Kunstblatt* 5 (1921): 220.

99. Ernest Newman, "Extremists vs. the Rest," *Musical Times,* 1 November 1920: 729; and Edwin Evans, "The Stravinsky Debate," *Music Student,* 13.3 (1920): 139–45.

100. Emile Vuillermoz, "La musique," *Excelsior,* 1 May 1922: 4; and Ernest Ansermet, "Einführung in das Schaffen," *Musikblätter des Anbruch,* June 1922: 170–71.

101. Igor Stravinsky, "Stravinsky Brieffragment," *Musikblätter des Anbruch,* February 1920: 161.

Chapter 5

1. Boris de Schloezer, "La musique," *La revue contemporaine,* 1 February 1923: 245–48.

2. Schloezer's relationship with Stravinsky improved briefly after their first meeting in June 1923. Maurice Brillant reported in November that it was the critic who had shown him the manuscript of the Octet. See Maurice Brillant, "Les oeuvres et les hommes," *Le correspondant,* 25 November 1923: 753. Stravinsky later considered parts of Schloezer's 1929 biography to be pretentious nonsense.

3. André Coeuroy, "Les revues et la presse—Chroniques et notes," *La revue musicale,* 1 March 1923: 189.

4. Georges Auric, "M. Vuillermoz et la musique d'aujourd'hui," *Les nouvelles littéraires,* 10 March 1923: 4. Auric also chastised Vuillermoz for extolling *Pierrot lunaire* and criticizing *Mavra.*

5. Boris de Schloezer, "La saison musicale," *Nouvelle revue française,* 1 August 1923, 238–48.

6. See Ernest Marion, "La politique musicale," *Fortunio,* 1 November 1923: 145–49: "The young French school should know its limits and resist with all the force of our national genius the intrusion of foreign elements which are unable to coexist with it without constraining or deforming it. In a word, it would be regrettable if young French composers who still are finding their own voice would broach a school after Stravinsky or Schoenberg."

7. Boris de Schloezer, "Igor Stravinsky," *La revue musicale,* 1 December 1923: 97–141.

8. Roland-Manuel, "La quinzaine musicale—L'octuor d'Igor Stravinsky," *L'éclair,* 29 October 1923: 3. Stravinsky had met Roland-Manuel in 1911 and admired his *Isabelle et Pantalon* in 1923, possibly in part because its subject so clearly recalled *Pulcinella.*

9. Roland-Manuel, *L'éclair,* 3. Another reviewer of the Octet dubbed these superimpositions as "bifurcations." See Maurice Brillant, "Les oeuvres et les hommes," *Le correspondant,* 25 November 1923: 743–58.

10. Nadia Boulanger, "Concerts Koussevitsky," *Le monde musical,* November 1923: 365.

11. See Georges Auric, "La musique," *Les nouvelles littéraires,* 27 October 1923: 5; Darius Milhaud, "Concerts Koussevitsky," *Le courrier musical,* 1 November 1923: 340–41; Theodore Lindenlaub, "Les concerts de l'Opéra," *Le temps,* 27 October 1923: 4; and André Schaffner, "Concerts divers," *Le ménestrel,* 26 October 1923: 440–41. For pejorative comments, see Emile Vuillermoz, "La musique," *Excelsior,* 22 October 1923: 4; Camille Bellaigue, "Revue musicale," *Revue des deux mondes,* 1 December 1923: 698–708; Robert Dezarnaux, *La liberté;* and Robert Brussel, *Le Figaro;* the latter two reprinted in "Les oeuvres nouvelles et la critique," *Revue Pleyel,* 15 December 1923: 22.

12. Michel Georges-Michel, "Sur Stravinsky," *La revue musicale*, December, 1923: 145–47; *Le matin* (Antwerp), 10 January 1924, in Craft, *Stravinsky Photograph Album*, 14; and White, 574–77.

13. Writing to Stravinsky on July 7, Schloezer mentioned the "fond memories of the two hours I spent in your company." See Stravinsky, *Correspondence*, 2: 158.

14. Edwin Evans, "Igor Stravinsky: Contrapuntal Titan," *Musical America*, 12 February 1921: 9.

15. Lesure, *Le sacre Dossier*, 76 (in *The Observer*, 3 July 1921). Severing Bach from the lineage of nineteenth-century German music in this manner echoes Debussy before World War I: "It is difficult to measure precisely the influence of Goethe's *Faust* or of the Mass in B minor of Bach; these works will remain as monuments of beauty as unique as they are inimitable; they have an influence similar to that of the sea or the sky, that which is not essentially German but universal." See Morland, *Enquête*, 89.

16. See Lawrence Gilman, "From Stravinsky to Sibelius," *North American Review*, January 1922: 117–21: "Only the other day his chief apostle, the able if not wholly persuasive Edwin Evans, hailed him as in fact 'the Bach of today.'"

17. In contemporary reviews, references to Stravinsky's indebtedness to specific works by Bach are rare. Jean Marnold ("Musique," *Mercure de France*, 1 October 1925: 229), with malicious intent, claimed that the opening of the second movement of the Concerto was modeled on the slow movement from the Sonata in D minor. Stravinsky later stated that the *Two-Part Inventions* "were somewhere in the remote part" of mind when writing the final movement of the Sonata. Stravinsky, *Dialogues*, 71. Those works were at least *au courant* in Paris at the time. Landowska's essays on the interpretation of the *Inventions* had appeared in *Le monde musical* in July 1921, and September 1922.

18. Roland-Manuel, "Concerto pour le piano, de Stravinsky," *Revue Pleyel*, 15 July 1924: 27. The original review appeared in *L'éclair*. See also Roland-Manuel, "Stravinsky et la critique," *Revue Pleyel*, 15 June 1924: 17–18. Upset by Robert Kemp's review in *La liberté*, 4 June 1924, he wrote in part: "In an epoch where the romantic passion for originality takes on epidemic proportions, the classicism of Stravinsky seems to us essentially more French than the extravagance of entrepreneurs of nightmares and the sentimental chastity of the latest followers of Franckism."

19. André Schaffner, "Concerts divers," *Le ménestrel*, 30 May 1924: 248; and Jean-R. Bloch, "Une insurrection contre la sensibilité," *Le monde musical*, September 1924: 303–4.

20. Boris de Schloezer, "La musique—Chronique musicale," *Nouvelle revue française*, 1 July 1924: 112–14. For negative reviews of the Concerto, see G. Allix, "Concerts Koussevitsky," *Le monde musical*, 22 May 1924: 181; and Jean Marnold, "Musique," *Mercure de France*, 1 July 1924: 240. The latter wrote in part: "His return backward now to a verbose and austere pseudo-classicism attests to the artificiality of his evolution or, better, his non-existence."

21. Georges Auric, "La musique," *Les nouvelles littéraires*, 26 April 1924: 7. For a considerably less strident comparison, see Alfredo Casella, "Tone Problems of Today," *The Musical Quarterly*, 10.2 (1924): 159–71. Casella wrote in part: "To sum up: we have in the above recognized the perfect legitimacy of the two grand evolutionary phenomena at present controlling our art. We have established their deep-seated and essential divergence—a divergence, however, which does not at all exclude a frequent cooperation between the two systems for the creation of new forms of expression."

22. Ernest Ansermet, "Introduction à l'oeuvre d'Igor Stravinsky," *Revue Pleyel*, 15 March 1925: 15–20.

23. Stravinsky, *Correspondence*, 3: 83. Stravinsky was outlining the program of an upcoming performance in Lausanne, which was to include the Octet and the Concerto and works of Bach chosen by Ansermet.

24. Adolf Weissmann, "Strawinsky," *Musikblätter des Anbruch*, June–July, 1924: 230–34. See also by Weissmann, "Stravinsky spielt sein Klavierkonzert," *Muskblätter des Anbruch*, November–December, 1924: 407–9; "Musical Notes from Abroad," *Musical Times*, 1 January 1925: 73; and "Musik-1924-Berlin," *Musikblätter des Anbruch*, January 1925: 24–25. By the time of the last article, Weissmann appears to have modified the tone of his comparison of the two composers, suggesting that although "Schoenbergians declare themselves against Stravinsky, whose adherents however are more numerous . . . I don't see that both ways clash forcibly; even if slogans appear to point to it, they are seldom far from each other in method and in result."

25. Edward Burlinghame Hill, *Modern French Music* (Boston: Houghton Mifflin, 1924), 3–4.

26. Unsigned, *Kunstblatt*, 8 (1924), 31.

27. Boris de Schloezer, "Igor Stravinsky und Serge Prokofieff," *Melos*, May, 1925: 470–71.

28. Arthur Lourie, "La sonate pour piano de Strawinsky," *La revue musicale*, 1 August 1925: 100–104. See also Boris de Schloezer, "A propos de la sonate de Stravinsky," *Revue Pleyel*, 15 November 1925: 19–20.

29. Lourie, 101.

30. Charles Joseph, *Stravinsky and the Piano* (Ann Arbor: UMI Research Press, 1983), 167; and Alan Lessem, "Schoenberg, Stravinsky, and Neo-Classicism: The Issues Reexamined," *The Musical Quarterly*, 68.4 (1982): 541. For an argument that Beethoven's formal procedures influenced Stravinsky, see Ronald Chittum, "Compositional Similarities: Beethoven-Stravinsky, *Music Review*, 30.4 (1969): 285–90 (comparing the Ninth Symphony with *Symphony of Psalms*).

31. Richard Taruskin, "Chernomor to Kashchei: Harmonic Sorcery; or, Stravinsky's 'Angle,' " *Journal of the American Musicological Society*, 38.1 (1985): 72–142.

32. Stravinsky, *Pictures and Documents*, 250; and Igor Stravinsky, "Chronological progress in Musical Art," *Etude*, 44.8 (1926): 559–60. That the central section of the second movement of the Sonata appears to resemble the main theme from Liszt's *Festklänge* is probably a superficial coincidence. Yet at one point in the tone poem (mm. 345–49), Liszt repeats the theme at ascending intervals of a minor third, C–Eb–Gb, with corresponding major thirds, E–G–Bb, above them. Together they produce a portion of the octatonic collection, C–(Db)–Eb–E–Gb–G–(A)–Bb, used by Stravinsky in the melody of the second movement (mm. 13–16) which resembles Liszt's theme. Once again, however, such passages can be found in works by other composers. Chopin employs such a progression in the Mazurka, op. 50, no. 3. Stravinsky is likely to have known this work as any by Liszt insofar as it was orchestrated by Glazunov in 1907 for the Fokine ballet, *Les sylphides*. Stravinsky later orchestrated two other Chopin pieces for an updated version of the work.

33. One formal procedure that may link Beethoven and Liszt to Stravinsky's music of the 1920s is the reappearance of themes between movements of a work. Such cyclic allusions appear in both Concerto and Sonata. If this relationship is not coincidental, then the exclusion of *fin-de-siècle* composers from neoclassicism by critics of the 1920s was poorly argued: both Schoenberg (Serenade) and Ravel (*Duo*) were preoccupied with cyclic procedures as a means of formal coherence during the 1920s.

34. Walter Tschuppik, "Gespräch mit Strawinsky," *Der Auftakt*, 4.10 (1924): 280–81.

35. The reference comes from a statement dated 21 April 1923. A reproduction of the original typescript and a translation appear in Leonard Stein, "Schoenberg: Five Statements," *Perspectives of New Music*, 24.1 (1975): 161–73. The original typescript indicates that Schoenberg had first written *Atonalisten* and had then crossed it out and substituted Stravinsky's name. Confusion over the return of a copy of the *Three Pieces for String Quartet* in 1922, and which Stravinsky had sent to Schoenberg in 1919, may not have helped their relationship. See Stravinsky, *Pictures and Documents*, 637.

36. Moldenhauer, 229; and Alban Berg, *Letters to his Wife*, trans. and ed. Bernard Grun (New York: St. Martin's, 1971), 275. That Schoenberg did not approve music for the Society on the basis of his own taste is suggested by his attitude toward Milhaud. On October 26, 1922, he wrote to Alexander Zemlinsky: "Milhaud strikes me as the most important representative of the contemporary movement in all Latin countries: Polytonality. Whether I like him is not to the point. But I consider him very talented. But that is not a question for the Society, which sets out *only to inform.*" See Arnold Schoenberg, *Letters*, trans. Eithne Wilkins and Ernst Kaiser, ed. Erwin Stein (New York: St. Martin's, 1965), 80. See also Joan Allen Smith, *Schoenberg and his Circle* (New York: Schirmer, 1986), 88–90.

37. Weissmann, "Musical Notes," *Musical Times*, 73. See also Emerson Whitmore, "And after Stravinsky?," *Modern Music*, February 1924: 24: "In a period when a masterly technic is the common property of all forward-looking composers, the influence of an outstanding individuality such as Stravinsky is bound to manifest itself in diverse musical climes." The widespread performance in Germany of most of Stravinsky's scores dates from the Berlin premiere of *Le sacre du printemps* in November 1922. See Hans Curjel, "Strawinsky in Berlin," *Melos*, 39.3 (1972): 154–58.

38. See "The Young and I" (August 19–21, 1923); "My Blind Alley" (July 23, 1926); and "How one becomes lonely" (October 11, 1937), in Schoenberg, *Style and Idea*, 93–95.

39. For representative examples, see Adolf Diesterweg, "Berliner Musik," *Zeitschrift für Musik*, February and March 1924: 76, 131; Martin Friedland, "Konzertsaal oder psychiatrischer Hörsaal?," *Allgemeine Musik-Zeitung*, 10 October 1924: 741–42; Frank Wohlfart, "Arnold Schoenbergs Stellung innerhalb der heutigen Musik," *Die Musik*, September 1924: 889; and Emil Petschnig, "Arnold Schönberg, der Psychopath," *Allgemeine Musik-Zeitung*, 28 November 1924: 875–77.

40. Olin Downes, "Music from abroad," *The New York Times*, 17 August 1924, sec. 7: 5.

41. Adolf Diesterweg, "Berliner Musik," *Zeitschrift für Musik*, January 1925: 23. Even in conservative journals like *ZfM*, Stravinsky fared better than Schoenberg. See Joel Sachs, "Some Aspects of Musical Politics in Pre-Nazi Germany," *Perspectives of New Music*, Fall–Winter 1970: 74–95: "Stravinsky, however, was a problem for *ZfM*. His early music, particularly *Le sacre du printemps*, was amply obnoxious, but what was one to make of the newer, 'neo-classical' works? Although on one occasion—a performance of *Le baiser de la fée* in 1928—Stravinsky's combining the 'classical' and the new merely as an experiment was declared a manifestation of the decadence of music, his music of the 1920s seemed in general less offensive."

42. See, for example, Paul Pisk, "Arnold Schoenbergs Serenade," *Musikblätter des Anbruch*, May 1924: 201–2; Erwin Stein, "Neue Formprinzipien," *Musikblätter des Anbruch*, August/September 1924: 286; Hans Eisler, "Arnold Schoenberg der musikalische Reaktionar," *Musikblätter des Anbruch*, August/September 1924: 313; Erwin Stein, "Über

den Vortrag von Schoenbergs Musik," *Pult und Takstock*, September 1924: 73–76; and Felix Griessle, "Die Formalen Grundlagen des Bläserquintetts von Arnold Schoenberg," *Musikblätter des Anbruch*, February 1925: 67. *Musikblätter des Anbruch* was produced by Universal Edition, Schoenberg's publisher.

43.   Schoenberg, *Letters*, 86, 109–10; and Berg, *Letters*, 342.

44.   H. O. Osgood, "Stravinsky conducts an interview and a concert," *Musical Courier*, 15 January 1925: 7. The composer appeared six times in New York in the first two months of 1925. On January 8–10, he conducted the New York Philharmonic in concerts that included *Song of the Volga Boatmen*, *Fireworks*, *Scherzo fantastique*, *Chant du rossignol*, *Firebird*, *Petrushka*, and *Pulcinella*. On January 25, he conducted two songs from *Rossignol*, *Ragtime*, *Renard*, and the Octet. On February 5–6 he was the soloist in the Concerto with Mengelberg conducting. The composer also performed in Chicago, Boston, Detroit, Cleveland, Cincinnati, and Philadelphia.

45.   Henrietta Malkiel, "Modernists Have Ruined Modern Music, Stravinsky Says," *Musical America*, 10 January 1925: 9.

46.   Malkiel, 9. See also "Igor Stravinsky not a Modernist," *The New York Times*, 6 January 1925: 23. "Can you fancy the 'Matthäus Passion' as Bach made it for wind instruments, organ and *Männerchor*? We hear it today with the voices and orchestra of a Wagner, so to speak, all the harmonies softened and made agreeable to the ear of our own musical contemporaries."

47.   "Herr Stravelinski verabscheut die moderne Musik oder die enttäuschten Reporter," *Der Auftakt*, 5.2 (1925): 56–57. See also "Sharps and Flats," *Musical Times*, 1 February, 1925: 159–60; and Max Chop, "Strawinsky-Abend in der Staatsoper," *Signale für die musikalische Welt*, 17 June 1925: 1055–57. The latter quotes from a program note to a June 7 performance of Stravinsky's music: "Debussy's subjectivism has even laid the groundwork for atonality which, according to Stravinsky, must lead to the dissolution of all forms."

48.   Schoenberg, *Style and Idea*, 481–82. The copy is preserved in the Schoenberg Archives. A facsimile of it with a translation of both the article and Schoenberg's marginalia appear in Leonard Stein, "Schoenberg and 'Kleine Modernsky,'" *Confronting Stravinsky: Man, Musician, and Modernist*, ed. Jann Pasler (Berkeley: University of California Press, 1986), 319–24.

49.   Paul Rosenfeld, *Musical Impressions: Selections from Paul Rosenfeld's Criticism* (New York: Hill and Wang, 1969), 147.

50.   Edward Dent, then president of the I.S.C.M., recalled an exchange between himself and Schoenberg over rehearsal time. To Dent's reminder that "you are not the only composer at this festival, and I think you ought to show some consideration for your colleagues," Schoenberg purportedly replied: "I have always understood that at all musical festivals I am the only composer." Schoenberg was clearly upset by the circumstances. In 1932 he refused a request by Webern, the Austrian representative to the I.S.C.M. at the time, to contribute a work of his to the current festival because of Dent's treatment of him six years earlier. See Edward J. Dent, *Selected Essays*, ed. Hugh Taylor (Cambridge: Cambridge University Press, 1979), 288–90. A letter from Werner Reinhart to Stravinsky on July 29, 1925, has been cited as evidence to suggest that the latter may have been reluctant to participate in the festival because of Schoenberg's presence. See Stravinsky, *Pictures and Documents*, 259.

51.   Edwin Evans, "Venice Festival," *Musical Times*, 1 October 1925: 920; Evans, "International Festival at Venice," *Chesterian*, September–October 1925: 17–21; Yvonne Lefebure, "Le festival de la société internationale pour la musique contemporaine à Venise," *Revue Pleyel*,

15 September 1925: 16–17; Raymond Petit, "Notes et documents de musique," *Mercure de France*, 1 October 1925: 248; and Paul Stefan, "Donauschingen-Venedig," *Musikblätter des Anbruch*, October 1925: 449.

52. Stuckenschmidt, *Schoenberg*, 309.

53. Ernst Schön, "A Stravinsky Festival at Frankfurt-am-Main," *Chesterian*, January–February 1926: 127–28. See also Eric Doflein, "Über Strawinsky," *Melos*, January–February, 1926: 158.

54. Dates of completion for the three movements are: "Am Scheideweg," November 12; "Vielseitigkeit," December 31; and "Der Neue Klassizismus," December 22. The earliest sketches for the *Suite* date from 1924. The date of completion for the "Gigue" is May 1, 1926. See Joseph Rufer, *The Works of Arnold Schoenberg*, trans. Dika Newlin (London: Faber and Faber, 1962), 129–30.

55. Arnold Schoenberg, Foreword, *Drei Satiren* (Vienna: Universal Edition, 1926), 3–4.

56. One manuscript of "Am Scheideweg" bears the title of its first line, "Tonal oder atonal?" Schoenberg may have been led to these words by their frequent contemporary appearance. See Paul von Klenau, "Tonal—A-tonal," *Musikblätter des Anbruch*, August/September 1924, and later in *Prisma*, 5.21 (1924): 273–74. *Signale für die musikalische Welt* (8 April 1925: 4565) refers to an inauguration speech, "Tonalität und Atonalität," by Josef Marx, newly appointed rector of the Austrian *Hochschule für Musik*, and reprinted in the *Neue Freie Presse* in 1925. Schoenberg used the words "Tonal oder atonal" at the beginning of his essay "Gesinnung oder Erkenntnis," *Jahrbuch 1926 der Universal-Edition, 25 Jahre Neue Musik*; translated in Stein, 258–64, and reprinted as "Tonal ou atonal," *Le monde musical*, 31 December 1927. Regarding the title "Vielseitigkeit," one manuscript version has two other titles, "Vielseitig veranlagt" and "Vielseitige Anlage." Regarding the title, "Der Neue Klassizismus," Schoenberg knew the article by Egon Wellesz, "Probleme der modernen Musik," *Musikblätter des Anbruch*, October 1924: 392–402, which uses this term as a sectional heading. See also Egon Wellesz, "Problems of Modern Music," *The Musical Quarterly*, 10.1 (1924) 1–12 (trans. Theodore Baker). Schoenberg made annotations to his copy, but did not comment on the section about *neue Klassisizmus*.

57. The parenthetical reference to "one droll mediocrity" (medio*kre nek*ische [italicized by the author]) is an allusion to Ernst Krenek. Berg appreciated this jest, because on May 30, 1926, he wrote to Schoenberg: "Oh, how your 'Foreword' pleased me, dearest honored friend. With it you have critically dispatched Krenek and with him half—what am I saying?—9/10 of the U.S. catalog! And not only on account of Krenek's original ideal in the yearbook (How did you like my article in the yearbook? I would really like to know!) did it please me, but also, because I, in a change of direction—to become acquainted with modern operas at once—have examined Krenek's *Orpheus and Eurydike* rather closely, with the greatest conceivable lack of prejudice and was filled with tremendous doubt, whether that which this Ernst meant with this music is actually meant in earnest—in any case the least of all is to be taken seriously." Unpublished letter in the Library of Congress. The article by Krenek that Berg refers to is "Musik in der Gegenwart," *25 Jahre neue Musik*, ed. Hans Heinsheimer and Paul Stefan (Vienna: Universal Edition, 1926), 43–59. Krenek's opera, with a text by Kokoschka, premiered on November 27, 1926, in Cassel.

58. Ansermet, "Une lettre à propos du *Sacre du printemps*," 215.

59. In Schoenberg's case, his 1925 essay, "Tonality and Form," begins: "I read in a newspaper that a group of modern composers has decreed that tonality must be restored as, without it, form cannot exist." See Schoenberg, *Style and Idea*, 255–57. The article to which the

composer refers is Elsa Bienenfeld, "Die Musik der Fünf und der Sechs," *Neues Wiener Journal* (preserved in the Schoenberg Archives with no date other than 1925), which contrasts French and Russian composers against those in Germany, Schoenberg in particular.

60. Riemann, for example, believed Brahms and Bruckner were thesis and antithesis. Schoenberg's squib, "Source-Poisoner Riemann" (Rufer, II.D.11), is dated May 11, 1923.

61. Milton Babbitt, "Some Aspects of Twelve-Tone Composition," *The Score and IMA Magazine*, 12 (1955): 53–61: "It is of interest to note that Schoenberg employed set (5) [C–C#–E–F–G#–A–D–D#–F#–G–A#–B] in his *Suite*, op. 29, but only as if it were semi-combinatorial." The sketches for "Am Scheideweg" indicate that construction of a new work did not begin with the row itself, but rather with an idea. Only after the idea was arrived at would the working out of the row continue. In this case, the idea is the opening 8-note motive, C–E–G–C#–A–B–F–D#, whose symbolism is predicated on the satiric meaning of the syllables "to-o-nal o-der a-to-nal?" The first three syllables underlay a C-major triad. They are followed by four pitches which are almost an exact inversion of pitches 4–7 of the opening ostinato of *Pierrot lunaire*.

62. See "New Music" (September 29, 1923), "Tonality and Form," (1925), and "Opinion or Insight" (1926) in Schoenberg, *Style and Idea*, 137–39, 255–57, 258–64. See also two untitled essays (June 1 and April 21, 1923) in Stein, *Perspectives*, 165–67. Many still unpublished essays in the Schoenberg Archives only reinforce these points.

63. In the Schoenberg Archives. Rufer, II.D.5. Used by permission of Belmont Music Publishers.

64. Schoenberg Archives. Rufer, II.D.34. Used by permission of Belmont Music Publishers.

65. Schoenberg Archives. Rufer, II.C.100. The essay is undated, but it probably was written shortly after op. 28 was completed. Used by permission of Belmont Music Publishers.

66. Erwin Stein, "Schoenberg and the German Line," *Modern Music*, May–June 1926: 22–28; Egon Wellesz, "Arnold Schoenberg," *La revue musicale*, November 1926: 38–46; Erwin Stein, "Neue Chöre von Schoenberg," *Musikblätter des Anbruch*, December 1926: 421–23; Hans Redlich, Schönbergs Tonalität," *Pult und Taktstock*, March–April 1927: 22–24; and Erwin Stein, "Schönberg's Third String Quartet," *The Dominant*, March 1928: 14.

67. Hans Mersmann, Hans Schultze-Ritter, and Heinrich Strobel, "Arnold Schönberg: Drei Satiren, Op. 28," *Melos*, April 1929: 174–76. Inasmuch as this issue of *Melos* was a *Stravinsky-Heft*, devoting four articles to the composer, Stravinsky may have become aware of *Three Satires* through this article, which reproduced the text of "Vielseitigkeit."

68. Lotte Kallenbach-Greller, "Klanggestaltungswerte in der neueren französischen Musik," *Melos*, January/February 1926: 149: "Architectonic forms in the spirit of the old masters through a nonfunctional tonal organization became the French problem. So they were obliged to regard Schoenberg . . . as romantic and Stravinsky as classic. . . . On the other hand Schoenberg's responsibility became apparent to him as the destiny of German art in general, to search for a new form through a new organization of sounds." See also Alexander Landau, "Sociologische Perspektiven auf neue Musik," *Melos*, October 1926: 327–32.

69. J. Weterings, "Stravinsky," *La revue musicale belge*, 20 September 1927: 1–4. Stravinsky's essay, "Avertissement" ("A Warning"), is reproduced in English and French in White, 578. It appeared simultaneously in *The Dominant*, December 1927: 13–14, and in *Musique*, 15 December 1927: 106. Edwin Evans was the editor of the former.

70. Ironically this definition approximated Schoenberg's own at this time: form was "achieved because (1) a body exists, and because (2) the members exercise different functions and are created for these functions." Schoenberg, *Style and Idea*, 257. Dated by the composer on 29 July, 1925, the article first appeared in *The Christian Science Monitor*, 19 December 1925.

71. Karl Schönewolf, "Gespräch mit Strawinskii," *Die Musik*, April 1929: 499–503.

72. André Coeuroy, *Panorama*, (Paris: Kra, 1928), 129–33; Mario Castelnuovo-Tedesco; "Neoclassicismo musicale," *Pegaso*, February 1929: 197–204; Ernst Schön, "Uber Strawinskys Einfluss," *Melos*, April 1929: 162–66; Alfredo Casella, "Il neoclassicismo mio e altrui," *Pegaso*, May 1929: 576–83; and P. O. Ferroud, "The Role of the Abstract in Igor Strawinsky's Work," *Chesterian*, March 1930: 141–47.

73. Arthur Lourie, "Neogothic and Neoclassic," *Modern Music*, March 1928: 3–8. That Lourie's intimacy with Stravinsky did not make him any more adept at juggling contemporary terminology is suggested by contrasting the above with his review of *Apollo*: "The first work of Stravinsky which reveals tendencies alien to so-called 'pure' music. For my part I see in it a decline of the neo-classic current and an attempt to make room for the romantic tendency. For that matter the symptoms can already be noted in the musical atmosphere of the moment." See Arthur Lourie, "Stravinsky's 'Apollo,'" *The Gamut*, August–September 1928: 20–21.

74. Adolf Weissman, "The Influence of Schoenberg and Stravinsky in Germany," *The Music Bulletin*, February 1927: 45–51. See also Juan Thomas, "Un musicien méditerranéen," *Musique*, 15 September 1928: 485–87; Heinrich Strobel, "Strawinskys Weg," *Melos*, April 1929: 158–62; and Schönewolf, "Gespräch," *Die Musik*, 499–503.

Conclusion

1. This point has recently been made by Straus, "Recompositions," 302–3.

2. The French composer was taken aback by the reverence for Bach shown by Germans: "They believe in Bach, they worship him. It never for a moment occurs to them that his divinity could be questioned. A heretic would horrify them; the very idea is unthinkable." Hector Berlioz, *Memoirs*, trans. and ed. David Cairns (New York: Knopf, 1969), 333. It was with intentional romantic irony, rather than with solemn admiration for Bach's counterpoint, that Berlioz wrote an academically correct fugue exposition for the round dance of the final movement of the *Symphonie fantastique*.

3. Robert Craft, "My Life with Stravinsky," *The New York Review of Books*, 10 June 1982: 6–8. Several recent essays stress Stravinsky's cultural estrangement: Straus, 317; Lessem, 532–33; and Richard Taruskin, "Stravinsky and the Traditions: Why the Memory Hole?," *Opus*, June 1987: 10–17.

4. Heinrich Strobel, "Igor Strawinsky," *Melos*, 14.13 (1947): 379, quotes the composer: "I am not neo-classic; I have simply devoted mysef to a more austere form of construction, but I have remained a modern composer." Robert Craft, "'Dear Bob(sky)' (Stravinsky's Letters to Robert Craft, 1944–1949), *The Musical Quarterly*, 65.3 (1979): 424, quotes an interview between the composer and Hubert Roussel from the Houston Post on January 26, 1949: "'Neo-classicism?' he scoffed. 'A label that means nothing whatever. I will show you where you should put it.'—and he gave his derriere a firm pat." On his father's attitude toward the term, Soulima Stravinsky reported: "I know he didn't like it. But he had nothing to substitute for it." Ben Johnston, "Interview with Soulima Stravinsky," *Perspectives of New Music*, 9.2 and 10.1 (1971): 23.

5. As an example of this position, see Milton Babbitt, *Perspectives of New Music*, 9.2 and 10.1 (1971): 106–7: "For, to Stravinsky, 'back to Bach,' was just that, an alliteratively catchy slogan, which had no pertinence to professional activity or professional discourse. It was there, permitted to be concocted, like 'neoclassicism,' to be talked about by those who could not and should not talk about the music, who didn't even bother to hear the music, but who, when they bandied about the catch words, were 'talking about Stravinsky.'"

6. Schoenberg, *Style and Idea*, 173–74.

7. *Roger Sessions on Music*, ed. Edward T. Cone (Princeton: Princeton University Press, 1979), 35–36.

8. Rosen, *Schoenberg*, 72.

9. Rosen, *Schoenberg*, 73. For similar statements, see Leo Schrade, "Strawinsky—Synthese einer Epoche," *Universitas*, 17.4 (1962): 385–92; William Austin, Kurt von Fischer, and Halsey Stevens, "Critical Years in European Musical History, 1915–1925," *Report of the Tenth IMS Congress* (Kassel: Bärenreiter, 1970), 228–30; Pierre Boulez, "Stravinsky and the Century: Style or Idea?," *Saturday Review*, 29 May 1971: 39–59; and Donald Harris, "Stravinsky and Schoenberg: A Retrospective Review," *Perspectives of New Music*, 9.2 and 10.1 (1971): 108–23.

Bibliography

Aber, Adolf. "Wohin des Wegs." *Melos*, 16 October 1920: 378–84.

Apollinaire, Guillaume. *Apollinaire on Art: Essays and Reviews 1902–1918*. Trans. Susan Suleiman. Ed. Leroy C. Breunig. New York: Viking Press, 1972.

————. *Oeuvres complètes*. Ed. Michel Décaudin. 4 vols. Paris: Balland and Lecat, 1965–66.

Ansermet, Ernest. "Einführung in des Schaffen." *Musikblätter des Anbruch*, June 1922: 169–72.

————. "Introduction à l'oeuvre d'Igor Stravinsky." *Revue Pleyel*, 15 March 1925: 19–20.

————. "The Man and his Work—Igor Stravinsky—his first String Quartet." *Musical Courier*, 25 November 1915: 41.

————. "Russische Musik." *Melos*, August 1922: 225–27.

————. "Une lettre inédite d'Ansermet à Stravinsky à propos du *Sacre du printemps*." *Revue musicale de suisse romande*, 33.5 (1980): 215.

Asaf'yev, Boris. *A Book about Stravinsky*. Trans. Richard F. French. Ann Arbor: UMI Research Press, 1982.

Auric, Georges. "Du 'Sacre du printemps' à 'Mavra'." *Les nouvelles littéraires*, 6 January 1923: 4.

————. "M. Vuillermoz et la musique d'aujourd'hui." *Les nouvelles littéraires*, 10 March 1923: 4.

————. "La musique." *Les nouvelles littéraires*, 26 April 1924: 7.

————. "La musique: quelques maîtres contemporains." *Les écrits nouveaux*, March 1922: 70–78.

————. "Une oeuvre nouvelle de théâtre." *Littérature*, March 1919: 24.

————. *Quand j'étais là*. Paris: B. Grasset, 1979.

Austin, William. *Music in the 20th Century*. New York: Norton, 1966.

Austin, William, Kurt von Fischer, and Halsey Stevens. "Critical Years in European Musical History." In *Report of the Tenth IMS Congress*. Kassel: Bärenreiter, 1970.

Babbitt, Milton. "Some Aspects of Twelve-Tone Composition." *The Score and IMA Magazine*, 12 (1955): 53–61.

Banès, Antoine. "Courrier des théâtres." *Le Figaro*, 13 May 1920: 3.

Barnes, Albert C., and Violette de Mazia. *The Art of Renoir*. New York: Minton, Blach & Co., 1935.

Barnes, Harry Elmer. *A History of Historical Writing*. 2nd ed. New York: Dover, 1962.

Barr, Alfred H., Jr. *Picasso: Fifty Years of his Art*. New York: Arno Press, 1966.

Barton, Brigid S. *Otto Dix and Die neue Sachlichkeit, 1918–1925*. Ann Arbor: UMI Research Press, 1981.

Baudelaire, Charles. *Baudelaire as a Literary Critic*. Trans. and ed. Lois Boe Hyslop and Francis E. Hyslop. University Park: Pennsylvania State University Press, 1964.

Beaumont, Antony. *Busoni the Composer*. Bloomington: Indiana University Press, 1985.

Bekker, Paul. *Neue Musik*. Berlin: E. Reiss, 1920.

Benois, Alexandre. *Reminiscences of the Russian Ballet*. Trans. Mary Britnieva. New York: Da Capo Press, 1977.

Berg, Alban. *Letters to his Wife*. Trans. and ed. Bernard Grun. New York: St. Martin's, 1971.

―――― . "Die musikalische Impotenz." *Musikblätter des Anbruch*. June 1920: 399–408.

Berlioz, Hector. *Memoirs*. Trans. and ed. David Cairns. New York: Knopf, 1969.

Bernard, Emile. "Sur la méthode picturale." *La rénovation esthétique*, May–September 1905: 191–92.

Bertrand, Louis. *La fin du classicisme et le retour à l'antiquité*. Paris, 1897.

―――― . Preface to *Les chants séculaires,* by Joachim Gasquet. Paris: P. Ollendorff, 1903.

Billy, André. *L'époque contemporain*. Paris: Tallandier, 1956.

Bloch, Jean-R.. "Une insurrection contre la sensibilité." *Le monde musical*, September 1924: 303–4.

Bochner, Jay. *Blaise Cendrars: Discovery and Re-creation*. Toronto: University of Toronto Press, 1978.

Bordes, Charles. "Credo d'art." *La tribune de Saint Gervais*, September 1903: 307.

Boretz, Benjamin, and Edward T. Cone, eds. *Perspectives on Schoenberg and Stravinsky*. New York: Norton, 1972.

Boulanger, Nadia. "Concerts Koussevitsky." *Le monde musical*, November 1923: 365.

Boulez, Pierre. "Stravinsky and the Century: Style or Idea?." *Saturday Review*, 29 May 1971: 39–59.

Bourgault-Ducoudray, Louis. "Discours à l'overture du congrès." *Congrès international d'histoire de la musique, memoires et voeux*. Ed. Jules Combarieu. Solesmes: Imprimerie Saint-Pierre, 1901.

Boutarel, Amadée, and Louis Schneider. "Nouvelles diverses—concerts et soirées. Deux soirées de musique ancienne et moderne." *Le ménestrel*, 27 January and 3 February 1889: 31, 39.

Boutari, Amadée. "Revue des grand concerts." *Le ménestrel*, 23 April 1910: 133.

Brettell, Richard R., and Suzanne Folds McCullagh. *Degas in the Art Institute of Chicago*. Chicago: Art Institute of Chicago, 1984.

Brillant, Maurice. "Les oeuvres et les hommes." *Le correspondant*, 25 February 1921: 742–56.

―――― . "Les oeuvres et les hommes." *Le correspondant*, 25 November 1923: 743–58.

Brion-Guerry, Liliane, ed. *L'année 1913. Les formes estéthiques de l'oeuvre d'art à la veille de la première guerre mondiale*. Paris: Klincksieck, 1971.

Briscoe, James. "The Compositions of Claude Debussy's Formative Years." Diss. University of North Carolina, 1979.

Brussel, Robert. "Les concerts." *Le Figaro*, 10 April 1922: 4.

Buckle, Richard. *Diaghilev*. New York: Atheneum, 1979.

Burdet, Jacques. "Les débuts d'Ernest Ansermet." *Revue musicale de suisse romande*, 26.4 (1973): 2–4.

Bürgin, Hans, and Hans-Otto Mayer. *Thomas Mann, a Chronicle of his Life*. Trans. Eugene Dobson. University of Alabama Press, 1969.

Busoni, Ferruccio. *Busoni: Letters to his Wife*. London: E. Arnold, 1938.

―――― . *Essence of Music and Other Essays*. Trans. Rosamond Ley. London: Rockliff, 1957.

―――― . *Fünfundzwanzig Busoni-Briefe*. Vienna: H. Reichner, 1937.

―――― . "Gedanken zu einer 'Neuen Klassizität'." *Musica Viva*, October 1936: 27–28.

―――― . "'Neue Klassizität'?." *Frankfurter Zeitung*, 1st morning ed., 9 February 1920: 1.

―――― . *Sketch of a New Esthetic of Music*. Trans. Theodore Baker. New York: Schirmer, 1911.

―――― . *Von der Einheit der Musik, Verstreute Aufzeichnungen* Berlin: M. Hesse, 1922.

Canfield, William A. *Francis Picabia: His Art, Life and Times*. Princeton: Princeton University Press, 1979.

Canudo, Riccioto. "A propos du 'Rossignol' d' Igor Strawinsky." *Montjoie!*, April–May–June 1914: 6.

Casella, Alfredo. "Il neoclassicismo mio e altrui." *Pegaso*, May 1929: 576–83.

―――― . "Tone Problems of Today." *The Musical Quarterly*, 10.2 (1924): 159–71.

Castelnuovo-Tedesco, Mario. "Neoclassicismo musicale." *Pegaso*, February 1929: 197–204.

Cézanne, Paul. *Letters*. Trans. Marguerite Kay. Ed. John Rewald. Oxford: B. Cassirer, 1976.

Chalupt, René. *Ravel au miroir de ses lettres.* Paris: R. Laffont, 1956.

―――. "Ravel." *Les écrits nouveaux*, December 1918: 312–19.

Cherney, Robert. "The Bekker:Pfitzner Controversy (1919–1920), its significance for German Music Criticism during the Weimar Reupblic." Diss. University of Toronto, 1974.

Chirico, Giorgio de. "Une lettre de Chirico." *Littérature*, 1 March 1922: 11–3.

Chittum, Ronald. "Compositional Similarities: Beethoven–Stravinsky." *Music Review*, 30.4 (1969): 285–90.

Chop, Max. "Strawinsky-Abend in der Staatsoper." *Signale für die musikalische Welt*, 17 June 1925: 1055–57.

Clouard, Henri. *Les disciplines. Nécessité littéraire et sociale d'une renaissance classique.* Paris: M. Rivière, 1913.

Cocteau, Jean. *Cocteau's World.* Trans. and ed. Margaret Crosland. New York: Dodd, Mead, 1972.

―――. "Fragments d'une conférence sur Erik Satie." *La revue musicale*, 1 March 1924: 217–23.

―――. "Nous voudrions vous dire un mot." *Le mot*, 27 February 1915: 1.

―――. *Oeuvres complètes de Jean Cocteau.* 11 vols. Geneva: Marguerat, 1950.

Coeuroy, André. *Panorama de la musique contemporaine.* Paris: Kra, 1928.

―――. "Les revues et la presses—Chroniques et notes." *La revue musicale*, 1 March 1923: 187–90.

Combarieu, Jules. "Camille Saint-Saëns et l'opinion musicale de l'étranger." *La revue musicale*, October 1901: 355–63.

Cooper, Jeffrey. *The Rise of Instrumental Music and Concert Series in Paris, 1828–1871.* Ann Arbor: UMI Research Press, 1983.

Cooper, Martin. *French Music. From the Death of Berlioz to the Death of Fauré.* London: Oxford University Press, 1961.

―――. ed. *The Modern Age: 1890–1960.* London: Oxford University Press, 1974.

Copland, Aaron, and Vivian Perlis. *Copland: 1900–1942.* New York: St. Martin's, 1984.

Craft, Robert. "Assisting Stravinsky." *The Atlantic Monthly*, December 1982: 68–74.

―――. "'Dear Bob(sky)' (Stravinsky's Letters to Robert Craft, 1944–1949)." *The Musical Quarterly*, 65.3 (1979): 424.

―――. *Igor and Catherine Stravinsky, A Photograph Album, 1921 to 1971.* New York: Thames and Hudson, 1982.

―――. "My Life with Stravinsky." *The New York Review of Books*, 10 June 1982: 6–8.

―――. *Stravinsky, Chronicle of a Friendship, 1948–1971.* New York: Vintage Books, 1973.

Curjel, Hans. "Strawinsky in Berlin." *Melos*, May-June 1972: 154–58.

Dale, Peter Allan. *The Victorian Critic and the Idea of History.* Cambridge: Harvard University Press, 1977.

Daniel, Keith W. *Francis Poulenc: His Artistic Development and Musical Style.* Ann Arbor: UMI Research Press, 1982.

Daulte, Francis. "Renoir's 'Ingres' Crisis." In *Paintings by Renoir.* Chicago: Art Institute of Chicago, 1973.

Debusmann, Emil. *Ferruccio Busoni.* Wiesbaden: Brucknerverlag, 1949.

Debussy, Claude. *Correspondence de Claude Debussy et P.-J. Toulet.* Paris: Le Divan, 1929.

―――. *Debussy on Music.* Trans. and ed. Richard Langham Smith. Intro. and Coll. François Lesure. New York: Knopf, 1977.

―――. *Lettres de Claude Debussy à son editeur.* Paris: Durand, 1927.

―――. *Lettres inédites à André Caplet.* Paris: Editions du Rocher, 1957.

De La Grange, Henri-Louis. *Mahler.* Garden City: Doubleday, 1973.

Deldevez, E. -M. E. *La société des concerts, 1860 à 1885.* Paris, 1887.

Demuth, Norman. *Ravel.* London: Dent, 1947.

Denis, Maurice. "Cézanne." *L'occident*, September 1907: 118–33.

―――. "La peinture." *L'ermitage*, 15 May 1905: 310–20.

Dent, Edward. "Italian Neo-Classicists." *The Nation and the Athenaeum*, 3 September 1921: 807.

————. *Selected Essays*. Ed. Hugh Taylor. Cambridge: Cambridge University Press, 1979.

Deri, Otto. *Exploring Twentieth-Century Music*. New York: Holt, Rinehart and Winston, 1968.

Diesterweg, Adolf. "Berliner Musik." *Zeitschrift für Musik*. February and March 1924: 75–77, 131–34.

————. "Berliner Musik." *Zeitschrift für Musik*, January 1925: 22–24.

Digeon, Claude. *La crise allemande de la pensée française*. Paris: Presses universitaires de France, 1959.

Dujardin, Edouard. "Chronique: fin de saison; M. Lamoureux; M. d'Indy et Chabrier." *Revue wagnérienne*, 8 April 1886: 97–99.

————. "Chronique (Les wagnéristes)." *Revue wagnérienne*, 8 April 1885: 57–8.

————. *Mallarmé par un des siens*. Paris: A. Messein, 1936.

Dukas, Paul. "A propos César Franck." *La chronique des arts*, 33 (1904): 273.

————. *Chroniques musicales sur deux siècles, 1892–1932*. Paris: Stock, 1980.

————. "Le nouveau lyricisme." *La revue musicale, Paul Dukas*. numéro spécial, May–June 1936, 8–17.

Eckart-Bäcker, Ursula. *Franckreichs Musik zwischen Romantik und Moderne*. Regensburg: Bosse, 1965.

Eisler, Hans. "Arnold Schoenberg der musikalische Reaktionar." *Musikblätter des Anbruch*, August/September 1924: 312–13.

Evans, Edwin. "The Foundations of twentieth-century Music." *Musical Times*, 1 August 1917: 347.

————. "Igor Stravinsky, Contrapuntal Titan." *Musical America*, 21 February 1921: 9.

————. "International Festival at Venice." *Chesterian*, September-October 1925: 17–21.

————. "The Stravinsky Debate." *Music Student*, 13.3 (1920): 139–45.

————. "Venice Festival." *Musical Times*, 1 October 1925: 920.

Expert, Henri, ed. *Les maîtres-musiciens de la renaissance française*. 23 vols. Paris, 1894.

Ferroud, P. O. "The Role of the Abstract in Igor Strawinsky's Work." *Chesterian*, March 1930, 141–47.

Fluegel, Jane. *Pablo Picasso, A Retrospective*. New York: Museum of Modern Art, 1980.

Fontane, André. *Les doctrines d'art et la renaissance de l'antiquité*. Paris: H. Laurens, 1909.

Francke, Kuno. *A History of German Literature as determined by Social Forces*. New York: Holt, 1901.

Friedland, Martin. "Konzertsaal oder psychiatrischer Hörsaal?." *Allgemeiner Musik-Zeitung*, 10 October 1924: 741–42.

Gay, Peter. *The Bourgeois Experience, Victoria to Freud*. New York: Oxford University Press, 1984.

Gedo, Mary Mathews. *Picasso: Art as Autobiography*. Chicago: University of Chicago Press, 1980.

Georges-Michel, Michel. *Ballets russes. Histoire anecdotique*. Paris: Aux éditions du monde nouveau, 1923.

————. *Les peintres que j'ai connus*. Paris: A. Fayard, 1954.

————. "Sur Stravinsky." *La revue musicale*, 1 December 1923: 145–47.

Gilman, Lawrence. "From Stravinsky to Sibelius." *North American Review*, January 1922: 117–21.

Gleizes, Albert, and Jean Metzinger. *Cubism*. London: T. F. Unwin, 1913.

Glover, J. Garrett. *The Cubist Theatre*. Ann Arbor: UMI Research Press, 1983.

Goethe, Johann Wolfgang. *Goethes Gespräche*. 5 vols. Leipzig: F. W. v. Biedermann, 1910

————. *Goethes Werke*. 36 vols. Stuttgart: J. G. Cotta, 1866.

Gold, Arthur, and Robert Fizdale. *Misia*. New York: Knopf, 1980.

Golding, Jon. *Cubism. A History and an Analysis. 1907–1914*. London: Faber and Faber, 1959.

Goossens, Eugene. *Modern Tendencies in Music*. London: Arts league of service, 1919.

Gray, Camilla. *The Great Experiment: Russian Art 1863–1922*. New York: Harry N. Abrams, 1962.

Griessle, Felix. "Die Formalen Grundlagen des Bläserquintetts von Arnold Schoenberg." *Musikblatter des Anbruch*, February 1925: 63–68.

Hadler, Mona. "Jazz and the Visual Arts." *Arts Magazine*, June 1983: 91–101.

Haftmann, Werner. *The Mind and Work of Paul Klee*. New York: A. Praeger, 1967.

Hahn, Reynaldo. "Les théâtres—Les premières." *Excelsior*, 17 May 1920: 1.

Handler, Louis. "'Pulcinella' à l'Opera." *Comoedia*, 14 May 1920: 1.

Hansen, Peter S. *An Introduction to Twentieth-Century Music*. 4th ed. Boston: Allyn and Bacon, 1978.

Hanslick, Edouard. *Als neuer und neuester Zeit. Der modernen Oper*. Berlin: Allgemeiner Verein für deutsche Literatur, 1900.

————. *The Beautiful in Music*. Trans. Gustave Cohen. Indianapolis: Bobbs-Merrill, 1957.

Harding, James. *Artistes Pompiers, French Academic Art in the 19th Century*. New York: Rizzoli, 1979.

Harris, Donald. "Stravinsky and Schoenberg: A Retrospective Review." *Perspectives of New Music*, 9.2 and 10.1 (1971): 108–23.

Hautecoeur, Louis. *Rome et la renaissance de l'antiquité à la fin du xviie siècle*. Paris: Fontemoing et Cie., 1912.

Heinsheimer, Hans, and Paul Stefan, eds. *Jahrbuch 1926 der Universal-Edition, 25 Jahre Neue Musik*. Vienna: Universal Edition, 1926.

Henry, Leigh. "Contemporaries." *Musical Opinion*, 20 February 1920: 371.

————. "Igor Stravinsky." *Musical Times*, 1 June 1919: 268.

————. "Igor Stravinsky and the Objective Direction in Contemporary Music." *Chesterian*, 1.4 (1920): 97–102.

————. "London Letter." *Chesterian*, January 1921: 371.

————. "La musique—Les ballets de Stravinsky." *L'action*, February 1920: 20.

————. "Stravinsky, The New Lyric Expression." *Daily Telegraph*, 17 July 1920: 4.

"Herr Stravelinski verabscheut die moderne Musik oder die enttäuschten Reporter." *Der Auftakt*, 5.2 (1925): 56–57.

Hettner, Hermann. *Literaturgeschichte des achzehnten Jahrhunderts*. 4 vols. Brauenschweig, 1879.

Hill, Edward Burlinghame. *Modern French Music*. Boston: Houghton Mifflin, 1924.

Holloway, Robin. *Debussy and Wagner*. London: Eulenburg, 1979.

Honour, Hugh. "Neo-classicism." In *The Age of Neo-classicism*. London: Arts Council of Great Britain, 1972.

Huré, Jean. "The Immediate Future of French Music." *The Musical Quarterly*, 4.1 (1918): 74–77.

Huysmans, Joris-Karl. *Oeuvres complètes*. 18 vols. Paris: G. Crès et Cie., 1926.

Imbert, Hughes. "Johannes Brahms." *La revue bleue*, 17 January 1903: 79–84.

d'Indy, Vincent. *César Franck*. Paris: F. Alcan, 1906.

————. *Cours de composition musicale*. 3 vols. Paris: Durand, 1902.

————. "De la sophistication de l'oeuvre d'art par l'édition." *Dritter Kongress der Internationalen Musikgesellschaft. Bericht*. Vienna, 1909.

————. "Jeunes musiques." *La tribune de Saint Gervais*, January 1901: 16.

————. "Une école d'art repondant aux besoins modernes." *La tribune de Saint Gervais*, November 1900: 305.

————, et al. *La Schola Cantorum en 1925*. Paris: Bloud & Gay, 1927.

Jarnach, Philipp. "Das Romanische in der Musik." *Melos*, November 1924: 191–95.

————. "Das stilistische Problem in der neuen Klassizität in Busonis Werk." *Musikblätter des Anbruch*, January 1921: 16–19.

Jean-Aubry, Georges. "Claude Debussy." *The Musical Quarterly*, 4.4 (1918): 542–54.

————. *French Music of Today*. Trans. Edwin Evans. London: K. Paul, Trench, Trubner & Co., 1919.

Johnston, Ben. "Interview with Soulima Stravinsky." *Perspectives of New Music*, 9.2 and 10.1 (1971): 23.

Joseph, Charles. *Stravinsky and the Piano*. Ann Arbor: UMI Research Press, 1983.

Kallenbach-Greller, Lotte. "Klanggestaltungswerte in der neueren französischen Musik." *Melos*, January–February 1926: 144–52.

Kerman, Joseph. "Theories of Late Eighteenth-Century Music." In *Studies in Eighteenth-Century British Art and Aesthetics*, ed. Ralph Cohen. Berkeley: University of California Press, 1985.

Kern, Stephen. *The Culture of Time and Space (1880–1918)*. Cambridge: Harvard University Press, 1983.

Klee, Paul. "Die Ausstellung des Modernen Bundes." *Die Alpen*, August 1912: 696–704.

———. *Watercolors, Drawings, Writings*. New York: H. Abrams, 1969.

Koch, Max. *Geschichte der Deutschen Literatur von dem ältesten Zeiten*. Leipzig, Bibliographischen Instituts, 1914.

Koechlin, Charles. "Erik Satie." *La revue musicale*, 1 March 1924: 193–207.

Kostlin, Heinrich Adolf. *Geschichte der Musik im Umriss*. Berlin, 1899.

Krummacher, Friedrich. "Klassizismus als musikgeschichtliches Problem." *International Musicological Society Report*, 2 (1972): 518.

Kunstblatt, 8 (1924), 31.

Laforgue, Jules. *Selected Writings of Jules Laforgue*. Trans. and ed. William Jay Smith. Westport, Conn.: Greenwood Press, 1956.

Lalo, Charles. *Esquisse d'une esthétique musicale scientifique*. Paris: F. Alcan, 1908.

Laloy, Louis. "Le courrier de Paris—*La musique*—Les ballets russes." *L'Europe nouvelle*, 23 May 1920: 679–80.

———. "Wagner et nos musiciens." *La grande revue*, 10 April and 10 May 1909: 558–66 and 160–64.

Landau, Alexander. "Sociologische Perspektiven auf neue Musik." *Melos*, October 1926: 327–32.

Landormy, Paul. "Le déclin de l'impressionisme." *La revue musicale*, 1 February 1921: 97–113.

———. "L'état actuel de la musique française." *La revue bleue*, 26 March and 2 April 1904: 394–97 and 421–26.

———. "Johannes Brahms et le goût français." *La revue bleue*, 7 January 1905: 30–32.

———. "Schönberg, Bartók und die französische Musik." *Musikblätter des Anbruch*, May 1922: 142–43.

Landowska, Wanda. "Bach et ses interprètes. Sur l'interprétation des oeuvres de clavecin de J.-S. Bach." *Mercure de France*, 15 November 1905: 214–30.

———. *Landowska on Music*. Trans. and ed. Denise Restout and Robert Hawkins. New York: Stein and Day, 1964.

Large, David C., and William Weber, eds. *Wagnerism in European Culture and Politics*. Ithaca: Cornell University Press, 1984.

Lavignac, Albert. *Le voyage artistique à Bayreuth*. Paris, 1898.

Lefebure, Yvonne. "Le festival de la société internationale pour la musique contemporaine à Venise." *Revue Pleyel*, 15 September 1925: 16–17.

Le Flem, Paul. "La musique au concert." *Comoedia*, 13 March 1922: 4.

Léger, Ferdinand. "Les révélations picturales actuelles." *Les soirées de Paris*, June 1914: 349–56.

Leichtentritt, Hugo. "German Music of the Last Decade." *The Musical Quarterly*, 10.2 (1924): 193–218.

Lendvai, Edwin. "Spaziergang am Diesterweg." *Melos*, 1 November 1920: 421–23.

Lessem, Alan. "Schoenberg, Stravinsky, and Neo-Classicism: The Issues Reexamined." *The Musical Quarterly*, 68.4 (1982): 541.

Lesure, François. "Claude Debussy after his Centenary." *The Musical Quarterly*. 49.3 (1963), 268.

———. "Debussy et le xvie siècle." In *Hans Albrecht in Memoriam*. Ed. W. Prennecke and H. Hasse. Kassel: Bärenreiter, 1962.

———. *Debussy. Iconographie musicale*. Geneva: Editions Minkoff, 1980.

———. *Igor Stravinsky. Le sacre du printemps. Dossiers de presse*. Geneva: Editions Minkoff, 1981.

Levin, Gail. "'Primitivism' in American Art: Some Literary Parallels of the 1910s and 1920s." *Arts Magazine*, November 1984: 101–5.

Little, Roger. *Guillaume Apollinaire*. London: Athlone Press, 1976.

Lockspeiser, Edward. *Debussy, his Life and Mind*. 2 vols. London: Cassell, 1965.

――――. "The Renoir portraits of Wagner." *Music and Letters*, 28.3 (1937): 18.

Locquin, Jean. *La peinture d'histoire en France de 1747 à 1785*. Paris: H. Laurens, 1912.

Lourie, Arthur. "La sonate pour piano de Strawinsky." *La revue musicale*, 1 August 1925: 100–104.

――――. "Neogothic and Neoclassic." *Modern Music*, March 1928: 3–8.

――――. "Stravinsky's 'Apollo'." *The Gamut*, August–September 1928: 20–21.

Macdonald, Nesta. *Diaghilev Observed by Critics in England and the United States, 1911–1929*. New York: Dance Horizons, 1975.

McLain, William H. "Wagnerian overtones in *Der Tod in Venedig*." *Modern Language Notes*, 79 (1964): 481–95.

Mahar, W. J. "Neo-classicism in the Twentieth Century: A Study of the Idea and its Relationship to Selected Works of Stravinsky and Picasso." Diss. Syracuse University, 1972.

Mahler, Alma. *And the Bridge is Love*. In collaboration with E. B. Ashton. New York: Harcourt, Brace, 1958.

――――. *Gustav Mahler, Memories and Letters*. New York: Viking, 1969.

Mahler, Gustav. *Selected Letters of Gustav Mahler*. Trans. Eithne Wilkins, Ernst Kaiser, and Bill Hopkins. Ed. Knud Martner. New York: Farrar, Strauss, Giroux, 1979.

Malkiel, Henrietta. "Modernists Have Ruined Modern Music, Stravinsky Says." *Musical America*, 10 January 1925: 9.

Mallarmé, Stephane. *Stephane Mallarmé: Selected Prose, Poems, Essays and Letters*. Trans. and ed. Bradford Cook. Baltimore: Johns Hopkins Press, 1956.

Mann, Thomas. "Auseinandersetzung mit Richard Wagner." *Der Merker*, 2.9 (1911): 21–23.

――――. *Die Briefe Thomas Manns, Regesten und Register*. Ed. Yvonne Schmidlin, Hans Bürgin, and Hans-Otto Mayer. 3 vols. Frankfurt-am-Main: S. Fischer, 1976.

――――. *Stories of Three Decades*. Trans. H. T. Lowe-Porter. New York: Knopf, 1936.

Mann, William. *Richard Strauss: A Critical Study of the Operas*. 2 vols. Philadelphia: Chilton, 1962.

Marion, Ernest. "La politique musicale." *Fortunio*, 1 November 1923: 145–49.

Marnold, Jean. "Musique." *Mercure de France*, 1 July 1924: 235–40.

――――. "Musique." *Mercure de France*, 1 October 1925: 226–33.

Massine, Léonide. *My Life in Ballet*. New York: St. Martin's Press, 1968.

Mauclair, Camille. *L'art indépendant français*. Paris: La Renaissance du livre, 1919.

――――. "Le classicisme et l'académisme." *La revue bleue*, 14 March 1903: 335–40.

――――. "La fin de l'impressionisme." *La revue bleue*, 14 January 1905: 5–53.

――――. *La religion de la musique*. Paris: Fischbacher, 1909.

Maurras, Charles. "Barbares et romanes." *La plume*, 1 July 1891: 229–30.

Mendès, Catulle. "Le jeune prix de Rome et le vieux wagnériste." *Revue wagnérienne*. 8 June 1885: 131–35.

Mersmann, Hans, Hans Schultze-Ritter, and Heinrich Strobel. "Arnold Schönberg: Drei Satiren, op. 28." *Melos*, April 1929: 174–76.

Milhaud, Darius. "Concerts Koussevitsky." *Le courrier musical*, 1 November 1923: 340–41.

――――. "The Evolution of Modern Music in Paris and in Vienna." *North American Review*, April 1923: 544–54.

――――. *Notes Without Music*. Trans. Donald Evans. Ed. Rollo Myers. New York: Knopf, 1953.

Miltitz, C. B. von. "Was heisst klassisch in der Musik?." *Allgemeine Musikalische Zeitung*. December 1835: 838–43.

Mitchell, Allan. *The German Influence in France after 1870. The Formation of the Third Republic*. Chapel Hill: University of North Carolina Press, 1979.

Mitchell, Donald. *Gustav Mahler, the Wunderhorn Years*. London: Faber and Faber, 1975.
———. *The Language of Modern Music*. New York: St. Martin's Press, 1963.
Mithouard, Adrien. "Le classique de demain." *L'occident*, April 1902: 289–300.
———. "Le classique occidental." *L'occident*, March 1902: 179–87.
Moldenhauer, Hans and Rosaleen. *Anton von Webern: A Chronicle of his Life and Work*. New York: Knopf, 1979.
Moréas, Jean. *Cent soixante-treize lettres de Jean Moréas à Raymond de la Tailhede et à divers correspondants*. Ed. Robert A. Jouanny. Paris: Lettres modernes, 1968.
———. *Jean Moréas, ecrivain français*. Ed. Robert A. Jouanny. Paris: Lettres modernes, 1969.
———. *Les syrtes*. Paris, 1892.
Morland, Jacques. "Enquête sur l'influence allemande: VI. Musique." *Mercure de France*, January 1903: 89–110.
Morton, Frederic. *A Nervous Splendor*. Boston: Little, Brown, 1979.
Myers, Rollo. *Modern Music*. New York: Dutton, 1923.
———. *Ravel, Life and Works*. New York: Yoseloff, 1960.
Le néoclassicisme dans l'art contemporain. Rome: Editions de "valori plastici," 1923.
Neumeyer, David. *The Music of Paul Hindemith*. New Haven: Yale University Press, 1986.
Newman, Ernest. "Extremists vs. the Rest." *Musical Times*, 1 November 1920: 729.
———. "The New French Recipe." *Musical Times*, 1 October 1917: 441.
———. "The Present Trend." *Musical Times*, 1 June 1917: 249.
Nichols, Roger. *Ravel*. London: Dent, 1977.
Northcote-Bade, James. "The Background to the 'Liebestod' Plot Pattern in the Works of Thomas Mann." *The Germanic Review*, 59.1 (1984): 11–18.
Orenstein, Arbie. *Ravel. Man and Musician*. New York: Columbia University Press, 1975.
Osgood, H. O. "Stravinsky conducts an interview and a concert." *Musical Courier*, 15 January 1925: 7.
Pasler, Jann, ed. *Confronting Stravinsky: Man, Musician, and Modernist*. Berkeley: University of California Press, 1986.
———. "Stravinsky and the Apaches." *Musical Times*, 1 June 1982: 403–7.
Perloff, Nancy. "Klee and Webern: Speculations on Modernist Theories." *The Musical Quarterly*, 69.2 (1983): 180–208.
Petit, Raymond. "Notes et documents de musique." *Mercure de France*, 1 November 1924: 816–20.
———. "Notes et documents de musique." *Mercure de France*, 1 October 1925: 246–51.
Petschnig, Emil. "Arnold Schönberg, der Psychopath." *Allgemeine Musik-Zeitung*, 28 November 1924: 875–77.
Peyser, Joan. *The New Music*. New York: Delacorte, 1971.
Pisk, Paul. "Arnold Schoenbergs Serenade." *Musikblätter des Anbruch*, May 1924: 201–3.
Pougin, Arthur. "Nouvelles diverses—Paris et départements." *Le ménestrel*, 5 May 1895: 143.
Poulain de Corion, E. "Séances de musique de chambre à l'exposition universelle de 1889." *Le guide musicale*, 9 June 1889: 5.
Poulenc, Francis. "La musique. A propos de 'Mavra' de Igor Strawinsky." *Les nouvelles littéraires*, June–July 1922: 222–4.
Ravel, Maurice. "Esquisses autobiographiques." *La revue musicale*, 1 December 1938: 17–23.
———. "Les nouveaux spectacles de la saison russe—*Le rossignol*." *Comoedia illustré*, 5 June 1914: 811–14.
Raynaud, Ernest. "L'école romane française." *Mercure de France*, May 1895: 131–45.
Redlich, Hans. "Schoenbergs Tonalität." *Pult und Taktstock*, March–April 1927: 22–24.
Reich, Willi. "Hermann Scherchen und *Melos*." *Melos*, June–July 1951: 188–89.
Rewald, John. *Post-Impressionism from Van Gogh to Gaugin*. New York: Museum of Modern Art, 1978.

Reyval. "Chronique de la semaine." *Le guide musicale*, 12 May 1895: 448.

Riemann, Hugo. *Geschichte der Musik seit Beethoven*. Berlin and Stuttgart, W. Spemann, 1901.

————. *Musik-Lexikon*. Trans. J. S. Shedlock, 10th ed. London: Augener, 1922.

Rigaud, André. "M. Igor Stravinsky nous parle du 'Chant du rossignol'." *Comoedia*, 31 January 1920: 1.

————. "M. Igor Stravinsky nous parle de la musique de 'Pulcinella'." *Comoedia*, 15 May 1920: 1.

Ritchie, J. M., ed. *Periods in German Literature*. London: Wolff, 1966.

Robinson, Christopher. *French Literature in the Twentieth Century*. Totowa: Barnes & Noble, 1980.

Roh, Franz. *Nach-Expressionismus: Magischer Realismus*. Leipzig: Klinhardt & Biermann, 1925.

Roland, Michel. *Autour du néo-classicisme*. Paris: Galerie Cailleux, 1973.

Roland-Manuel. "Concerto pour le piano, de Stravinsky." *Revue Pleyel*, 15 July 1924: 27.

————. "La quinzaine musicale—L'octuor d'Igor Stravinsky." *L'éclair*, 29 October 1923: 3.

————. "Maurice Ravel." *La revue musicale*, 1 April 1921: 1–21.

————. *Ravel*. Trans. Cynthia Jolly. London: B. Dobson, 1947.

————. "Stravinsky et la critique." *Revue Pleyel*, 15 June 1924: 17–18.

————. "Le théâtre—A l'Opéra—*Pulcinella*, ballet de Stravinsky-Pergolesi." *L'amour de l'art*, June 1920: 7.

Rolland, Romain. "Les concerts." *La revue musicale*, November 1902: 480–83.

————. *Musicians of Today*. Trans. Mary Blaiklock. New York: H. Holt and Company, 1915.

————, and Richard Strauss. *Richard Strauss and Romain Rolland Correspondence*. Ed. Rollo Myers. Berkeley: University of California Press, 1968.

Rosen, Charles. *Arnold Schoenberg*. New York: Viking Press, 1975.

Rosenblum, Robert. *Modern Painting and the Northern Romantic Tradition*. New York: Harper & Row, 1975.

Rosenfeld, Paul. *Musical Impressions: Selections from Paul Rosenfeld's Criticism*. New York: Hill and Wang, 1969.

————. "Stravinsky." *The New Republic*, 14 April 1920: 207–10.

Rubin, William. Introduction. *"Primitivism" in 20th Century Art*. Ed. William Rubin. 2 vols. New York: Museum of Modern Art, 1984.

————, Elaine L. Johnson, and Riva Castleman.. *Picasso in the Collection of the Museum of Modern Art*. New York: Museum of Modern Art, 1972.

Rudorff, Raymond. *The Belle Epoque, Paris in the Nineties*. London: Hamilton, 1972.

Rufer, Joseph. *The Works of Arnold Schoenberg*. Trans. Dika Newlin. London: Faber and Faber, 1962.

S. [pseud.] "Concerts Colonne: La 'deuxième symphonie,' de M. Gustav Mahler." *La revue musicale*. 1 May 1910: 226–30.

Sachs, Joel. "Some Aspects of Musical Politics in Pre-Nazi Germany." *Perspectives of New Music*, Fall–Winter 1970: 74–90.

Saint-Saëns, Camille. *Harmonie et mélodie*. Paris, 1885.

Salzman, Eric. *Twentieth-Century Music: An Introduction*. 2nd ed. Englewood Cliffs: Prentice-Hall, 1974.

Samaltanos, Katia. *Apollinaire, Catalyst for Primitivism, Picabia, and Duchamp*. Ann Arbor: UMI Research Press, 1984.

Samson, Jim. *Music in Transition*. New York: Norton, 1977.

Satie, Erik. *Ecrits*. Ed. Ornella Volta. Paris: Editions champ libre, 1977.

————. "Propos à propos d'Igor Stravinsky." *Feuilles libres*, October–November 1922: 347–53.

Schaffner, André. "Concerts divers." *Le ménestrel*, 30 May 1924: 248.

Schenker, Heinrich. *Free Composition*. Trans. and ed. Ernst Oster. New York: Longman, 1979.

Scherchen, Hermann. *Alles hörbar machen. Briefes eines Dirigenten*. Berlin: Henschel, 1976.

————. "Neue Klassizität." *Melos*, 16 July 1920: 242–43.

_____. "Zu Hans Pfitzner's Aesthetik der musikalischen Impotenz." *Melos*, 1 February 1920: 20.

Scherer, Paul, and Hans Wysling. *Quellenkritische Studien zum Werk Thomas Manns*. Bern: Francke, 1967.

Schilling, Gustav. *Encyclopädie der gesammten musikalischen Wissenschaften, oder Universal-Lexikon der Tonkunst*. 2nd ed. 8 vols. Stuttgart, 1841.

Schloezer, Boris de. "A propos de la sonate de Stravinsky." *Revue Pleyel*, 15 November 1925: 19–20.

_____. "Igor Stravinsky." *La revue musicale*, 1 December 1923: 97–141.

_____. "Igor Stravinsky und Serge Prokofieff." *Melos*, May 1925: 469–81.

_____. "La musique—Chronique musicale." *Nouvelle revue française*, 1 July 1924: 112–22.

_____. "La musique." *Nouvelle revue française*, 1 July 1922: 115–20.

_____. "La musique." *Revue contemporaine*, 1 February 1923: 257.

_____. "La saison musicale." *Nouvelle revue française*, 1 August 1923: 238–48.

Schneider, Herbert. "Die Parodieverfahren Igor Strawinskys." *Acta Musicologica*, 54 (1982): 286–99.

Schön, Ernst. "A Stravinsky Festival at Frankfurt-am-Main." *Chesterian*, January–February 1926: 127–28.

_____. "Über Strawinskys Einfluss." *Melos*, April 1929: 162–66.

Schoenberg, Arnold. "Foreword." *Three Satires*. by Schoenberg. Vienna: Universal Edition, 1926.

_____. *Letters*. Trans. Eithne Wilkins and Ernst Kaiser. Ed. Erwin Stein. New York: St. Martin's, 1965.

_____, and Wassily Kandinsky. *Letters, Pictures and Documents*. London: Faber and Faber, 1984.

_____. *Style and Idea*. Trans. Leo Black. Ed. Leonard Stein. New York: St. Martin's Press, 1975.

Schönberger, Elmer, and Louis Andriessen. "The Apollonian Clockwork." *Tempo*, 141 (1982): 3–21.

Schönewolf, Karl. "Gespräch mit Strawinskii." *Die Musik*, April, 1929: 499–503.

Schopenhauer, Arthur. *Das Welt als Wille und Vorstellung*. 2 vols. Leipzig, 1891.

Schorske, Carl. *Fin-de-siècle Vienna*. New York: Knopf, 1980.

Schrade, Leo. "Strawinsky—Synthese einer Epoche." *Universitas*, 17.4 (1962): 385–92.

Schürer, Oskar. "Der Neoklassizismus in der jüngsten französischen Malerei." *Jahrbuch für Philosophie*, 1925: 427–43.

Schweitzer, Albert. *J. S. Bach*. Trans. Charles Marie Widor. Leipzig: Breitkopf & Härtel, 1908.

Scott, Cyril. "The Genius of French Music." *The Musical Times*. 1 October 1917: 447.

Selden-Goth, Gisella. *Ferruccio Busoni*. Leipzig: E. P. Tal & Co., 1922.

Sessions, Roger. *Roger Sessions on Music*. Ed. Edward T. Cone. Princeton: Princeton University Press, 1979).

Severini, Gino. *Du cubisme au classicisme*. Paris: Povolovsky, 1921.

Shattuck, Roger. *The Banquet Years*. New York: Vintage Books, 1968.

_____. *The Innocent Eye*. New York: Farrar, Strauss, Giroux, 1984.

Shead, Richard. *Music in the 1920s*. London: Duckworth, 1976.

Sitsky, Larry. *Busoni and the Piano*. New York: Greenwood Press, 1986.

Smith, Joan Allen. *Schoenberg and his Circle*. New York: Schirmer, 1986.

Soby, James Thrall. *Giorgio de Chirico*. New York: Arno Press, 1966.

_____, and Alfred H. Barr, Jr. *Twentieth-century Italian Art*. New York: Museum of Modern Art, 1949.

Souday, Paul. "La semaine théâtrale et musicale." *Paris-Midi*, 18 May 1920: 3.

Steegmuller, Francis. *Cocteau*. New York: Macmillan, 1970.

_____. "New York Celebrates the Genius of Jean Cocteau." *The New York Times*, 14 May 1984.

Stefan, Paul." Donaueschingen-Venedig." *Musikblätter des Anbruch*, October 1925: 442–50.

Stein, Erwin. "Neue Chöre von Schoenberg." *Musikblätter des Anbruch*, December 1926: 421–23.
———. "Neue Formprinzipien." *Musikblätter des Anbruch*, August/September 1924: 286–303.
———. "Schoenberg and the German Line." *Modern Music*, May–June, 1926: 22–28.
———. "Über den Vortrag von Schoenbergs Musik." *Pult und Taktstock*, September 1924: 73–76.
Stein, Leonard. "Schoenberg: Five Statements." *Perspectives of New Music*, Fall–Winter 1975: 161–73.
Sternfeld, F. W., ed. *Music in the Modern Age*. New York: Praeger, 1973.
Stevenson, Ronald. "Busoni and Mozart." *The Score*, September 1955: 25–28.
Straus, Joseph N. "Recompositions by Schoenberg, Stravinsky, and Webern." *The Musical Quarterly*, 72.3 (1986): 301–28.
Strauss, Richard. *Instrumentationslehre von Hector Berlioz*. 2 vols. Leipzig: Peters, 1905.
Stravinsky, Igor. *An Autobiography*. New York: Norton, 1962.
———. "Chronological Progress in Musical Art." *Etude*, 44.8 (1926): 559–60.
———. "Les espagnoles aux ballets russes." *Comoedia*, 15 May 1921: 1.
———. *The Recorded Legacy*. CBS Masterworks 74048.
———. *Selected Correspondence*. Ed. Robert Craft. 3 vols. New York: Knopf, 1982–85.
———. "Stravinsky Brieffragment." *Musikblätter des Anbruch*, February 1920: 161.
———. "Une lettre de Stravinsky sur Tchaikovsky." *Le Figaro*, 18 May 1922: 1.
———, and Robert Craft. *Conversations*. Garden City: Doubleday, 1959.
———, and Robert Craft. *Dialogues and a Diary*. Garden City: Doubleday, 1963.
———, and Robert Craft. *Expositions and Developments*. Garden City: Doubleday, 1962.
———, and Robert Craft. *Memories and Commentaries*. Garden City: Doubleday, 1960.
———, and Robert Craft. *Themes and Episodes*. New York: Knopf, 1966.
Stravinsky, Vera, and Robert Craft. *Stravinsky in Pictures and Documents*. New York: Simon and Schuster, 1976.
Strobel, Heinrich. "Strawinskys Weg." *Melos*, April 1929: 158–62.
Stuckenschmidt, H. H. *Arnold Schoenberg, his Life, World and Work*. Trans. Humphrey Searle. New York: Schirmer, 1977.
———. "Ausblick in der Musik." *Kunstblatt*, 5 (1921): 220.
———. *Maurice Ravel*. Trans. Samuel R. Rosenbaum. Philadelphia: Chilton, 1968.
———. "Notizen für jüngsten französischen Musik." *Musikblätter des Anbruch*, December 1925: 538–43.
Suarez, G. "Esthétique musicale—Igor Stravinsky n'est pas wagnérien." *Paris-Midi*, 13 January 1921: 1.
Sutton, Denys. *André Derain*. London: Phaidon Press, 1959.
Swart, Koenraad W.. *The Sense of Decadence in Nineteenth-century France*. The Hague: M. Nijhoff, 1964
Taruskin, Richard. "Chernomor to Kashchei: Harmonic Sorcery; or, Stravinsky's 'Angle.'" *Journal of the American Musicological Society*, 38.1 (1985): 72–142.
———. "Stravinsky and the Traditions: Why the Memory Hole?." *Opus*, June 1987: 10–17.
Thomas, Juan. "Un musicien méditerranéen." *Musique*, 15 September 1928: 485–87.
Thomas, R. Hinton. *German Perspectives: Essays on German Literature*. Cambridge: W. Heffer, 1946.
———. *Thomas Mann, the Meditation of Art*. Oxford: Clarendon Press, 1956.
Tienot, Yvonne. *Chabrier par lui-même et par ses intimes*. Paris: H. Lemoine, 1965.
Tiersot, Julien. "Promenades musicales à l'exposition." *Le ménestrel*, 9 June 1889: 180.
———. "Promenades musicales à l'exposition." *Le ménestrel*, 23 June 1889: 196.
Tschuppik, Walter. "Gespräch mit Strawinsky." *Der Auftakt*, 4.10 (1924): 280–81.
Tuchman, Barbara. *The Proud Tower*. New York: Macmillan, 1966.

Vallas, Léon. *Claude Debussy, his Life and Works*. London: Oxford University Press, 1933.
———. *Vincent d'Indy*. 2 vols. Paris: A. Michel, 1946.
Van Gogh, Vincent. *The Complete Letters of Vincent van Gogh*. 3 vols. London: Thames and Hudson, 1958.
Van den Toorn, Pieter. *The Music of Igor Stravinsky*. New Haven: Yale University Press, 1983.
Van Vechten, Carl. *Music after the Great War and Other Studies*. New York: Schirmer, 1915.
Varèse, Louise. *Varèse, A Looking-Glass Diary*. New York: Norton, 1972.
Vlad, Roman. *Stravinsky*. Trans. Frederick and Ann Fuller. London: Oxford University Press, 1960.
Vogel, Vladimir. *Schriften und Aufzeichnungen*. Zurich: Atlantis-Verlag, 1977.
Vollard, Ambroise. *Renoir, an intimate Record*. Trans. Harold L. van Doren and Randolph T. Weaver. New York: Knopf, 1925.
Vuillermoz, Emile. "Mavra." *Excelsior*, 12 June 1922: 4–5.
———. "La musique." *Excelsior*, 1 May 1922: 4.
Wagner, Richard. *Gesammelte Schriften und Dichtungen*. 3rd. ed. 10 vols. Leipzig, 1897.
Webern, Anton von. *Letters to Hildegarde Jone and Josef Humplik*. Bryn Mawr: T. Presser, 1967.
———. *The Path to the New Music*. Trans. Leo Black. Ed. Willi Reich. Bryn Mawr: T. Presser, 1963.
———. *Sketches: 1926–1945*. New York: C. Fischer, 1968.
Weissmann, Adolf. "Musik–1924–Berlin." *Musikblätter des Anbruch*, January 1925: 20–26.
———. "The Influence of Schoenberg and Stravinsky in Germany." *The Music Bulletin*, February 1927: 45–51.
———. "Musical Notes from Abroad." *Musical Times*, 1 January 1925: 73.
———. "Stravinsky spielt sein Klavierkonzert." *Musikblätter des Anbruch*, November–December 1924: 407–9.
———. "Strawinsky." *Musikblätter des Anbruch*, June–July 1924: 228–34.
Wellek, René. *Discriminations: Further Concepts of Criticism*. New Haven: Yale University Press, 1970.
———. *A History of Modern Criticism*. 5 vols. New Haven: Yale University Press, 1955.
Wellesz, Egon. "Arnold Schoenberg." *La revue musicale*, 1 November 1926: 38–46.
———. "Die jüngste Entwicklung der neufranzösische Musik." *Der Merker*, 2.16 (1911): 665.
———. "Die letzten Werke Claude Debussys." *Melos*, 16 May 1920: 166–68.
———. "Maurice Ravel." *Musikblätter des Anbruch*, October 1920: 544–46.
———. "Schoenberg and Beyond." *The Musical Quarterly*, 2.1 (1916): 76–95.
Weterings, J.. "Stravinsky." *La revue musicale belge*, 20 September 1927: 1–4.
Whaples, Miriam K. "Mahler and Schubert's A Minor Sonata D. 784." *Music and Letters*. 65.3 (1984): 255–62.
White, Eric Walter. *Stravinsky, the Composer and his Works*. 2nd ed. Berkeley: University of California Press, 1979.
Whitmore, Emerson. "And after Stravinsky?." *Modern Music*, February 1924: 24.
Wilkins, Nigel. "Erik Satie's Letters to Milhaud and Others." *The Musical Quarterly*, 66.3 (1980): 404–28.
Williams, Linda. *Figures of Desire. A Theory and Analysis of Surrealist Film*. Urbana: University of Illinois Press, 1981.
Wohlfart, Frank. "Arnold Schoenbergs Stellung innerhalb der heutigen Musik." *Die Musik*, September 1924: 889.
Wolf, Hugo. *The Music Criticism of Hugo Wolf*. Trans. and ed. Henry Pleasants. New York: Holmes & Meier, 1978.
Wyzewa, Téodore de. "La musique descriptive." *Revue wagnérienne*. 8 April 1885: 75–76.
———. "Pierre-Auguste Renoir." *L'art dans les deux mondes*. 6 December 1890: 27–28.
Zeldin, Theodore. *France, 1848–1945*. 2 vols. Oxford: Clarendon Press, 1973.
Zuckerman, Elliot. *The First Hundred Years of Wagner's "Tristan."* New York: Columbia University Press, 1964.

Index